Crimes
of the
Century

Crimes of the Century

From Leopold and Loeb
to O. J. Simpson

GILBERT GEIS
AND LEIGH B. BIENEN

Northeastern University Press
Boston

Northeastern University Press

Copyright 1998 by Gilbert Geis and Leigh B. Bienen

Library of Congress Cataloging-in-Publication Data
Geis, Gilbert.
Crimes of the century : from Leopold & Loeb to O. J. Simpson /
Gilbert Geis and Leigh B. Bienen.
p.   cm.
Includes bibliographical references and index.
ISBN 1-55553-360-4 (cloth : alk. paper)
ISBN 1-55553-427-9 (pbk. : alk. paper)
1. Trials—United States.   I. Bienen, Leigh B.   II. Title.
KF220.G45   1998
345.73'07—dc21   98-23180

Designed by Diane F. Levy

Composed in Baskerville by Wellington Graphics, Boston, Massachusetts.
Printed and bound by Thomson-Shore, Inc., Dexter, Michigan.
The paper is Glatfelter Supple Opaque, an acid-free sheet.

MANUFACTURED IN THE UNITED STATES OF AMERICA
02 01 00   5 4 3

To Dolores, and in memory of Robley Geis

To Henry and all of our wonderful family

Let the young take note:
Three short generations span the century. Our parents were contemporaries of
Lindbergh and Hiss, our grandparents followed the cases of Leopold and Loeb
and Scottsboro, and we all lived through Simpson together.

Contents

Illustrations

Crimes
of the
Century

Chapter One

Introduction

What is it that catapults a crime—or, at times, an event that allegedly is criminal—into a realm where it remains deeply embedded in our collective imagination many decades later? Precise details may fade from memory, and people who were born after the case first dazzled the media and the public may be aware of only a few shreds of information vaguely connected with what went on. But they sense that the case stood for something important, not only representing the facts about the crime itself, but also offering a commentary on the condition of the time. Such criminal cases find their way into history books and become the stuff that endlessly feeds into television docudramas and other media reference points. Near the end of 1997, to take but one example, a play, *Never the Sinner*, opened in New York on an off-Broadway stage. Its theme revolves around the killing of Bobby Franks by Nathan Leopold and Richard Loeb, the first of the five cases that we consider in this book. The Leopold-Loeb killing took place seventy-three years before its current presentation in drama form.

A review of the play in the *New York Times* tells us some of the reasons why the Leopold-Loeb case continues to serve as the backdrop for a fascinating examination of human nature. The reviewer declared that the drama "has emotional and intellectual force." The play rejects the wild emotionalism of the case itself, it is noted, but it portrays the public mood that surrounded the crime: the blaring headlines, "the almost erotic public revulsion," the national newspaper-sponsored contest for women that offered as the prize a date with Dickie Loeb. This stage version of the case, we are told, "concentrates on the personalities of the men and on the moral environment they lived in, with the result that the world is uglier and colder and more sinister than ever."

The criminal justice landscape has been so altered since the earlier epic cases that some of the conditions they reflect seem outdated, hardly creditable.

But the cases themselves will not be forgotten. Depending on the criminal sensation of the moment, they will be disinterred to provide object lessons about how much has changed and, yet, how very much human behavior and elements of criminal adjudication remain unaltered. Only recently, for instance, the inability of the Boulder, Colorado, police to solve the case of the Christmas Day 1996 garroting of JonBenet Ramsey, a six-year-old beauty contest winner, led a curator of the Colorado Historical Society to say that "JonBenet is our generation's Lindbergh baby." The Denver newspaper felt compelled to explain to a newer generation that the curator was referring to "the 1932 kidnapping and murder of the infant son of Charles and Anne Lindbergh."

The cases we review here rescue the American criminal justice system from abstraction. For each of them we have paid particular attention not only to the intricacies of the events but also to their relationship to important issues in criminology and in the administration of criminal justice. Three of the five cases that we examine came to be known in their time as the "crime of the century"—in reverse chronological order these are the alleged murder of Nicole Simpson and her ill-starred friend, Ron Goldman, by O. J. Simpson (1994), the kidnapping and death of Charles Lindbergh's infant son (1932), and the killing of Bobby Franks by Richard Loeb and Nathan Leopold (1924).

The label "crime of the century," it is worth noting, was not a new coinage. In 1898, Henry Hunt wrote *The Crime of the Century: Or the Assassination of Dr. Patrick Henry Cronin*. Hunt could at least review what had gone on for almost the entire nineteenth century before offering his judgment that this was its most significant criminal episode. The case Hunt examined involves the hacking to death of Patrick Cronin, a Chicago physician, by members of an Irish secret society. Cronin had accused the group's leaders of embezzling organization funds. Of the five persons tried for the murder, two received life sentences. The driver of the buggy that had decoyed Cronin to the scene of his death received a three-year prison term for manslaughter, while the head of the clan that condemned the doctor was found not guilty. The case has long since sunk into obscurity, a very unlikely fate for those we will scrutinize in the following pages.

The pair of cases we examine that did not earn crime-of-the-century distinction also are central to an understanding of the relationship between sensational criminal trials and the operation of the criminal justice system. They tell us a great deal about the social messages that such crimes convey and the manner in which they can cause a more critical and constructive appraisal of criminal justice administration in the United States. One is the Scottsboro case (1931), involving a charge of forcible rape of two white women by nine young black men, allegedly while they hoboed their way on a freight train from Tennessee to Alabama. The other is the perjury trial of Alger Hiss (1949), an object lesson in the interconnection among the temper of the time, political considerations, and the operation of the criminal justice process. There are those who maintain that these cases should not have been exempted from the already overcrowded crime-of-the-century designation. Whittaker Chambers, the chief prosecution witness in the Hiss case, for instance, rather immodestly (though perhaps accurately) told a Rotary Club audience that the Hiss trial was "the most important case of the first half of the twentieth century."

The most obvious way to determine ingredients that elevate the ordinary in crime to the extraordinary is to examine the major aspects of these five cases to determine if any particular pattern emerges. Categories that seem relevant are geographic setting, the nature of the offenders and the victims, and the details of the offense.

The locations are rather what might be expected. One occurred in each of the three largest cities in the country: New York (Hiss), Los Angeles (Simpson), and Chicago (Leopold-Loeb). The fourth case (Lindbergh) was tried close to New York City and drew massive metropolitan and world press coverage. But the fifth set of trials took place in Scottsboro and Decatur, Alabama, far from any hive of activity or media center. Location probably feeds into the question of whether a case will rise above the ordinary, but it is obviously not a necessary consideration.

The crimes all are offenses that most people would regard as outrageous, moving downward on that scale from the seemingly senseless murder of fourteen-year-old Bobby Franks by Leopold and Loeb, to the slaughter of Nicole Simpson and Ron Goldman, to the kidnap-murder of a twenty-month-old child, to the alleged forcible rape by nine black men of two white women. Precisely where Alger Hiss's trial for perjury might rank on such a scale is not immediately obvious because the crux of the matter, despite the criminal charge, involved peacetime espionage by a government employee for a foreign country regarded as a threatening enemy. What we can conclude, again, is that the offense is not in itself determinant of the judgment on the case's prominence, though it is necessary that it be something consequential—or perhaps the better phrase would be something sensational. Three of the cases involved the death penalty. But it remains difficult to untangle the question of whether public clamor represents a response to the media's judgment about the event or whether the media are responding to the public's concern and, at times, its frenzied outrage.

How important are the victims? In Scottsboro, the accusers were two disreputable young women; in the case of Leopold and Loeb, a fourteen-year-old boy, chosen for death apparently for no particular reason related to him; in the Lindbergh kidnapping, a twenty-month-old infant; in the Hiss case, a rising star in the political world, with outstanding professional credentials; and in the O. J. Simpson case, the beautiful thirtyish ex-wife and a male friend who was part of the crowd around her. In the Lindbergh case, the victim, a helpless child, triggered some of the notoriety that the case received, but it was not the victim himself but his father, Charles Lindbergh, a national hero, who elevated the case to the crime-of-the-century category.

In terms of offenders, the O. J. Simpson case clearly hogged the spotlight because of the celebrity of the accused perpetrator, a former football hero. But it is questionable that the case would have gained the attention that it did had the victim been a black woman, though the interracial elements of the murder, if Simpson had committed the crime, were too delicate a matter to give rise to much overt discussion in a country where people now are sensitive to public manifestations that might earn the epithet "racist."

In the other three cases it was elements of the situation, combined with "suitable" (that is, suitable for the circumstances of the case) protagonists that rendered the episodes famous—or, if you will, infamous. The Scottsboro case clearly was transformed from a routine matter because the persons accused, nine young black men, were seen by outsiders hostile to southern racial etiquette as innocent sacrifices in an effort by bigoted Alabamans to maintain indecent rules that dictated the "proper place" and behavior for blacks. The case also gained the limelight because of the obvious innocence of at least some of the accused and very likely all of them. As we point out in our consideration of the trial, had the accusing women named but one or two men as their assailants, the case probably would have had a short life—as would the black men singled out as rapists.

The circumstances of the times played an important part in escalating these five cases to a plane well above the ordinary. A newspaperman, Ralph Frammolino, notes that "a crime truly becomes historic when, like an eclipse, its timing brings into alignment many profound and often troubling questions about society. Acting as a prism the macabre crime has the power to show the spectrum of various ongoing struggles in the culture."

In the Scottsboro case, the events fed directly into the interest of the American Communist Party in forming a strong base among blacks, who it believed would be particularly discontented with their lot and sympathetic to Soviet pledges about racial justice. The Alger Hiss case was played out against a backdrop of deep concern in the United States with the threat of Soviet Communism and the fear that traitors in our midst were jeopardizing national security. Whittaker Chambers, the man who accused Hiss, would write that the events were bigger than either man. The case, Chambers proclaimed, "was an epitomizing drama" in which he and Hiss were "archetypes," that is, standard-bearing representatives of opposing ideological and philosophical positions. That was what, in Chambers's words, "gave the peculiar intensity to the struggle." Diana Trilling, a social commentator, made the same point, noting that controversial and well-publicized cases such as that involving Chambers and Hiss "provoke within their society a basic confrontation between opposing social principles." The Lindbergh case brought to the surface fears of parents throughout the country about the vulnerability of their children to kidnapping, to their being wrenched away from their hearth by monstrously evil people. That an illegal immigrant from Germany was accused of the crime fed into the growing American hatred of the country he had come from and of the Hitler regime that was posing a threat to world peace.

The Simpson case, for its part, told a tale of a kind of racial revolution. The Scottsboro defendants had been poor black men railroaded by powerful whites. Simpson was a very rich black man being judged by a jury made up predominantly of black citizens. Simpson had been accused, as had the Scottsboro defendants, of a crime against a white woman. The dramaturgy of the Simpson trial itself and the not-guilty verdict told a very different story about race relations and criminal justice in America from the one that had unfolded more than half a century earlier in Scottsboro.

The cases also served to showcase the politically ambitious and to bring to them that most important of assets, name recognition. At Scottsboro, Thomas Knight took over from the local district attorney and relentlessly prosecuted the case at succeeding trials, even when he was lieutenant governor of the state, in considerable part because his eyes were fixed on becoming governor. David Wilentz, the New Jersey attorney general, also usurped the local prosecutor and with the Hauptmann case launched a political career that lasted forty years. Richard Nixon, then a first-term congressman, leaned on the Hiss case as a strong force in his successful run for the Senate, the vice presidency, and the presidency. But for Nixon the matter was double-edged: he made implacable enemies for his handling of the Hiss case and also developed a cynicism about political realities and the manipulation of public opinion and public power that, in Greek tragedy fashion, contributed to his unprecedented fall from power, with his humiliating resignation heading off a likely impeachment and a possible prison sentence.

Most of all, though, what characterizes the "crimes of the century" and the other memorable cases here is something not usually noted—their mystery, the ambiguity of the evidence paraded in the courtroom, often combined with the intransigent denials of guilt by the accused.

Uncertainty is the awful nemesis in a criminal trial. The English courts at one time solemnly tried cases involving charges of witchcraft against women (for it almost always was women) and after a formal hearing judges and juries determined that they were guilty of entering into a compact with the devil and should forfeit their lives. Today, the evidence that led to the hanging of the accused witches can be seen as self-evidently nonsensical, the sacrifice of lives due to the superstitions, fears, and anger of the prosecutors. Among the cases we discuss, the Scottsboro trials were in many respects a playing out of similar vengeful impulses. The Hauptmann trial and the trial of Alger Hiss, however correct or unsatisfactory the verdicts may have been, were permeated by a moral outrage that may have wrapped the blindfold on Justice much too tightly.

In earlier times, determination of criminal guilt involved tactics such as trial by ordeal, in which the accused and accuser fought each other to determine which one God would allow to triumph, which party was the righteous one. The Catholic Church's Fourth Lateran Council in 1215 outlawed such practices, declaring them blasphemous, and the justice system was compelled to invent new methods to assure that the guilty were adequately differentiated from the innocent. Now there was a need for standards of certain proof—proof so high, as John Langbein notes, "that no one would be concerned that God was no longer being asked to resolve the doubts."

In continental cases, proof of guilt could come only from the victim. The Inquisition, with its rituals of savage torture, sought to do defendants a favor and to relieve the uneasiness of those who were terrified of divine judgment if they were complicit in the execution of an innocent person. If those accused confessed, they were told they could go to their deaths with clear consciences and were more likely to be admitted to paradise. Besides, if the sentence was death by burning, those who confessed usually would be strangled before the fire was lighted.

England, and later the United States, hit upon a different approach—a jury system. The jury substituted for God and, as Langbein observes, "because criminals could not be punished on evidence short of full proof, confessions were no longer essential." But several of our cases illustrate that in the absence of a confession and with the presence of rebuttable evidence, matters can become sticky and satisfactory closure unattainable. This remains one of the inducements to eliminate capital punishment, an irrevocable act. But in some trials, such as that of Hauptmann, the desire for blood, for revenge, was too pronounced to spare a life until a much greater degree of certainty could be achieved. That case also might be taken as illustrative of one of the dangers of posting high rewards for information: the lure of money can make people invent and stubbornly stick to fictive stories so that they can qualify for part of the bounty.

Of the five cases we consider, only in the Leopold-Loeb case were the facts clear-cut and uncontroverted. The mystery there—the one that still haunts those who examine the case—remains the question of motive, the seemingly inexplicable issue of why the two young men murdered a fourteen-year-old selected casually—indifferently—from the streets.

In the other four cases, those accused steadfastly maintained their innocence, perplexing onlookers who wanted certainty. Their adamant denials of guilt and their continuous challenge to the allegations pose conundrums that engage those who review the evidence.

The Scottsboro defendants proclaimed their innocence because they were, almost certainly, truly innocent. In the Hiss case, there was a hung jury at the end of the first trial and a defendant whose impeccable personal credentials contrasted profoundly with the endless lies and admitted traitorous activities that marked the life of his accuser. Hauptmann went to his execution stoutly proclaiming his innocence, and several comprehensive recent examinations of the case insist that he was a man executed on grounds that failed to come close to the standards required for a criminal conviction. The mystery surrounding the case is melodramatically caught in the reflections of a person involved in investigating the Lindbergh kidnapping: "Hauptmann told his story and left much in doubt. Perhaps this doubt will remain until someone on his deathbed comes up with the truth. The secrets of the Lindbergh case still challenge the world." So too with Hiss, who died recently at the age of ninety-two, still maintaining that he had been unjustly charged and convicted and that some day, to use a word he greatly favored, he would be "vindicated."

O. J. Simpson never wavered from his official protestations that he was not responsible for the murders with which he was charged, though, as in the Hiss case, there was an array of evidence that argued otherwise. But there also were things about the Simpson case, most particularly the inept performance of the police and the prosecutors, that easily could lead an unbiased observer to conclude that reasonable doubt existed regarding Simpson's culpability. Many people remain perplexed by a nagging question: How could a human being have possibly done so terrible a thing—the savage slaughter of the mother of his children, a woman he undoubtedly had once loved—and yet maintain a posture of innocence, even self-pity, regarding what was being done to him? Others cynically observe that it probably makes little difference, except to those close to the victims, whether Simpson was convicted, even if he was guilty. His example is hardly going to encourage other men to kill their wives, nor is Simpson himself very likely to commit another murder, given (again, *if* he was guilty) the years that it took him to build up the ferocious anger that drove him to virtually decapitate his former wife.

The mystery and the uncertainty in each of the five cases and the public battleground on which they sought resolution cannot explain totally our interest in the cases. Any one of them under slightly different circumstances might have been no more than a footnote in the recorded parade of crime. Scottsboro, as we said, would have remained localized if the accusation had not been so obviously fraudulent; and Leopold and Loeb probably would have pled guilty to murder if they had been guaranteed a life sentence. It took more than two years to locate Hauptmann, and the case never would have been "solved" had he not been caught spending some of the ransom money. The Hiss case likely would have evaporated if Richard Nixon had not, with extraordinary insight, recognized the potential it had to advance his political career and had he not also developed a strong personal dislike of Alger Hiss. O. J. Simpson apparently came very close to killing himself during his run on southern California freeways; had he done so, the case would have been wrapped up rather quickly and with little fanfare.

Studies of specific criminal cases provide a rich source of information through which to examine how the criminal justice system operates and how crime is handled. It can be argued, with truth, that celebrated cases by definition are unusual and unrepresentative and therefore distort the processes of criminal law. After all, about 90 percent of all criminal charges are resolved by plea bargaining, not by the kinds of emotion-laden public trials examined in the following pages. But such a position appears to us to miss the central point: it is the dramatic, well-publicized, highly controversial trials that disclose the tensions, the inadequacies, and the underlying elements of criminal justice adjudication.

The Simpson case, for example, let the public learn in dramatic fashion how judges have become careless in regard to requirements for search warrants, how they routinely accept police testimony that they are perfectly aware is untrue because they themselves typically come to the bench from positions as prosecutors and because they perceive that the system would be seriously hampered if the letter of the law was strictly followed. Sloppy practices go unchallenged until a defendant can pay for the legal talent and investigative resources that confront the routine but inadequate procedures that pass muster in more ordinary kinds of situations. A particularly pertinent observation to preface this volume is that of the novelist E. L. Doctorow in *The Book of Daniel*, a fictionalized account of the consequences for their children of the execution for espionage of Julius and Ethel Rosenberg. "If justice cannot be made to operate under the worst possible conditions of social hysteria," Doctorow writes, "what does it matter how it operates at other times?"

Chapter Two

Leopold and Loeb (1924) and the Cause of Crime

A fourteen-year-old boy, Bobby Franks, was cold-bloodedly clubbed to death with a chisel after being picked up during the late afternoon of May 21, 1924, in Chicago by two young men driving a rented Willys-Knight automobile. The killers came from very wealthy families and had remarkable academic records. Richard A. Loeb, eighteen years old, committed the murder, while Nathan F. Leopold, Jr., who was nineteen, drove the car. The victim had been selected virtually at random—by "pure accident" was how his killers put it—while he was walking home from a schoolyard where he had been playing. Erle Stanley Gardner, a well-known mystery writer, would note that Bobby Franks merely was "the most likely-looking subject who became available."

Another boy, initially picked for this death-dealing enterprise, had been spared because he could not be located. Seventy-two years later, Armand Deutsch, the eleven-year-old boy who had been slated for death, would look back on what he sardonically called "my murder," and remember that he had been saved only because he had been picked up from school that day by the family chauffeur who took him to a dental appointment. Deutsch was the grandson of Julius Rosenwald, probably the richest man in Chicago. In his later life, Deutsch would reflect whimsically on the vagaries of fate as they bear upon human life—and death:

> When one measures the number of my dental appointments against the number of days in the school year, the odds against me were so formidable that no self-respecting Las Vegas gambler would have made book on it. While not partial to dentists, since then I have always viewed the breed with an understandable tolerance.

Deutsch went on to work as a motion picture producer with Metro-Goldwyn-Mayer and Warner Brothers, and wrote a book describing his very close friendships with Frank Sinatra, Nancy and Ronald Reagan, the comedian Jack Benny, the multimillionaire Walter Annenberg, and the publisher Bennett Cerf.

Leopold and Loeb's lawyer would say that his clients killed Bobby Franks "not for money, not for spite, not for hate. They killed as they might kill a spider or a fly, for the experience."

After the murder, Leopold and Loeb wrapped the body in a blanket and placed it on the floor in front of the back seat of the car. They then drove to the Dew Drop Inn, a restaurant in Hammond, Indiana, where they had a hot dog and beer. After that, they rode about aimlessly until it got dark. Finally, they carried the body some two hundred feet and placed it face down and head forward into a waterlogged culvert under a railroad embankment in Wolf Lake, an out-of-the-way marshy area twenty miles south of Chicago. They presumed the body would not be found in this remote spot and that in time it would decompose from the water running over it. They had stripped Bobby Franks naked. To make identification difficult they used hydrochloric acid to burn his face, his circumcised penis, and a scar on his body. Earlier Leopold and Loeb had argued about whether it was better to use hydrochloric or sulfuric acid for the job.

The murderers had composed a ransom note addressed to "Dear Sir," since when they wrote it they did not know who their victim would be. The letter, typed on good quality linen paper, was signed "George Johnson" and self-evidently had been written by someone quite literate. It emphasized the "futility" of calling the police, threatened death to Bobby for the slightest "infraction" of the instructions, and talked about the "execution" of the planned ransom exchange.

Leopold and Loeb had concocted what they believed was a foolproof method to obtain money from the Franks family. A few hours after they had murdered his son, they called Jacob Franks, a multimillionaire real estate dealer, and told him that the boy was safe, but that he would be killed if the police were informed that he was missing. The next morning, a special delivery letter to Franks demanded a cash ransom of ten thousand dollars in old twenty- and fifty-dollar bills. Further instructions were relayed by telephone that evening: the father was told that a taxi would be sent to his home to take him to a pay phone located in a nearby pharmacy. The kidnappers planned to call there and to order Franks to board a specified train heading to Michigan City, Indiana. He would have been directed to look for a message stored in the box in the last train car, a box that was used for the deposit of communications that were later to be telegraphed. The message would direct Franks to throw the ransom from the rear platform of the train while facing east. He was to count to three after the train passed a red building with a black water tower that had the word CHAMPION (for the Champion Manufacturing Company) in white letters on its side. The boys anticipated being at the site to retrieve the package after it was tossed from the train.

Bobby Franks's father had gathered together the ransom money, but the scheme collapsed when Bobby's body was discovered by a work crew member who saw the feet sticking out beyond the funnel-shaped culvert opening. The father, having just heard from the kidnappers, was certain that the body was not that of his son. An uncle was dispatched to the morgue. Just before the father was to leave to hand over the ransom money, the uncle telephoned to tell him that it was his son's body in the morgue.

A number of teachers at the private school attended by Bobby Franks were early suspects. One later won a claim against the city of Chicago on the charge that his fingers had been crushed in a doorway as part of the interrogation process. In one of the more bizarre aspects of the case, Loeb voluntarily assisted the detectives trying to track the killers, and several times supplied leads for them to follow.

A pair of horn-rimmed glasses had been found next to Bobby Franks's body. The frame spring on the glasses had been patented recently and it was sold by just one Chicago outlet, Almer and Coe, a fashionable optical company. Only three people had purchased glasses with this kind of frame. One was Leopold, who had bought the eyeglasses to try to relieve headaches but had stopped wearing them three months before. Psychiatrists, amateur and professional, later would claim that the dropped glasses were a giveaway sign of Leopold's desire to be caught.

Leopold had taken off his jacket when he was disposing of Bobby Franks's body and the glasses had fallen from a pocket when Loeb was handing the garment back to him. Those less disposed to psychiatric explanation would charge the dropped glasses to bad luck, compounded perhaps by anxiety associated with what was going on. That poor luck was multiplied manyfold by the fact that the glasses, with a prescription that fit thousands of Chicago residents, happened to have the most unusual frame.

When the police questioned Leopold, he insisted that he had probably dropped the glasses when he was shepherding one of the numerous bird-watching groups he worked with: Leopold was an expert ornithologist and had published papers on the subject. He said that he had spent the day of the murder with Loeb and two young women they had picked up; he knew only the first names of the women. When Loeb was taken to the police station, he soon told the police all about the killing, though he maintained that he had driven the car and that it was Leopold who had killed Bobby Franks. Loeb said that their original plan had been to knock Bobby unconscious and then to strangle him with each of them pulling on different ends of the rope in order to share the guilt equally.

The best understanding today is that Leopold and Loeb killed Bobby Franks purely for the excitement, a monstrously daring adventure made more exhilarating by the necessity to avoid being caught. Six months earlier, the two boys had begun their adventures by robbing Loeb's fraternity house at three o'clock in the morning. They wore masks and carried two loaded revolvers and a rope for tying anyone who might interrupt them. They also had a chisel wrapped in tape, to knock persons they might encounter unconscious. They stole several watches, a typewriter, and about seventy-five dollars in cash. This business apparently was too tame; murder was more challenging.

The absence of a sensible motive for the killing of Bobby Franks, the stunning intellectual abilities of the killers, the great wealth and high social standing of their families, and their "different" (that is, Jewish) cultural heritage contributed to the most intense public attention ever to be focused on a murder in the United States. In the Jewish community it was regarded as fortunate, in a terrible kind of way, that the boys had chosen a Jewish victim. Otherwise, as one writer noted, "righteous public indignation, combined with Ku Klux Klan leadership, might have resulted in race riots." Newspaper reporters dubbed the killing the "Crime of the Century," presumably confident that in the seventy-six years that remained in the twentieth century nothing so sensational possibly could occur.

Loeb had graduated from the University of Michigan at seventeen; no one younger had ever received a degree from that institution. Leopold, who obtained his bachelor's degree from the University of Chicago when he was eighteen, was attending law school at Chicago and anticipated transferring to Harvard Law School the following fall. Of the two, Leopold was the smarter, with an IQ so far above the regular scale that it was impossible to attach a precise figure to it. Estimates are that he scored between 210 and 220 on the Binet scale. Loeb had an IQ of 160. Leopold also had been a precocious child. It is said that he had taken his first step at two months and was talking clearly when he was four months old.

Leopold, though brighter, was relatively unattractive, awkward, and socially ill at ease. William Byron, a longtime professor of sociology at Northwestern University, an elite school in the Chicago suburbs, later would befriend Loeb and Leopold: Leopold would dedicate his prison autobiography to Byron. When Byron taught at Pomona College in California after his retirement, he would tell a visitor that among the thousands of highly intelligent college students with whom he had associated, he would rate Dickie Loeb as possessing the most winning personality. Leopold described Loeb similarly: "His charm was magnetic—maybe mesmeric is the better word. He could charm anybody he had a mind to. He seemed to have an inborn knack of making friends, of winning everyone's affection."

The families of the accused boys hired Clarence Darrow to defend their sons. Darrow was then sixty-seven years old and the most famous criminal lawyer of the time. The newspapers called it the "million-dollar defense." Darrow, lumbering about, his hands buried in old galluses, his hair unkempt, his briefcase a battered relic, and his wrinkled clothes looking as if he had slept in them for days on end, gave the impression of a country hayseed on a jaunt away from the family farm. But Darrow had a razor-sharp mind, and his bumpkin ways often endeared him to the common folk who made up the juries with which he dealt.

In a surprise legal maneuver, Darrow elected to have Leopold and Loeb plead guilty to the two offenses they were charged with—first-degree murder and kidnapping for ransom—either of which could be punished by death. The latter had only recently been made a capital offense in Illinois over the objection of people who sensibly pointed out that since kidnapping and murder carried the same penalty, kidnappers now were more likely to kill their victims to prevent identification.

Instead of a jury, which Darrow believed would be irretrievably hostile to the defendants, he chose to argue his case in a mitigation or aggravation hearing that would deal with the sentence the judge would impose. During the hearing, which took three months, Darrow sought to persuade the judge that there were sufficient circumstances favoring life imprisonment instead of the death penalty. The judge, sixty-four-year-old John R. Caverly, had been born in England and was a devout Catholic who had paid for his legal education by carrying water in steel mills for eighty-seven cents a day. As Chicago's city attorney, he had broken up a ring of personal-injury lawyers who had swindled the city out of millions of dollars. He was rewarded with a municipal court judgeship and later promoted to the trial court.

An array of psychiatric talent testified on Leopold and Loeb's behalf, seeking to persuade the judge that the killers were strange, different, and immature, though these expert witnesses had to maneuver delicately to avoid claiming that Leopold and Loeb were not legally responsible because of their mental condition. That would have demanded a plea of "not guilty by reason of insanity" and a mandatory jury trial. So intense was the public interest in the mental processes of the killers that publisher William Randolph Hearst, searching for a scoop, offered to pay Sigmund Freud half a million dollars plus his transportation costs from Europe to examine the accused killers. Freud backed off, saying that he was too ill to travel.

The major defense psychiatrists—dubbed the "Three Wise Men from the East" by the prosecutor and the press—were William Alanson White, director of St. Elizabeth's Hospital for the Insane in Washington, D.C.; William Healy, onetime director of the psychopathic clinic in Chicago, who in collaboration with Augusta F. Bronner, his wife, had done pioneering work on the causes of juvenile delinquency; and Bernard Glueck, formerly the alienist (as forensic psychiatrists were then called) at Sing Sing Prison in New York, and in 1924 a staff member at Columbia University College of Physicians and Surgeons. There were lesser lights on the defense psychiatric team as well, including James Whitney Hall, who made the uncommon professional gaffe of putting on record a prediction that was categoric—and, as it turned out, quite inaccurate. "Within five years Leopold will go crazy," Hall insisted. "Loeb will follow, though his lack of reaction will buoy him up for a while." Despite the pressures of the prison environment, both killers remained satisfactorily sane for the remainder of their lives.

Though Darrow was willing to stipulate to the truth of the case, the prosecution insisted on parading 102 witnesses to the stand, only two of whom Darrow elected to cross-examine. In his summation, Darrow, who had considerable experience as a stump speaker and often had debated in opposition to capital punishment, talked for twelve hours over two days, presenting his plea for mercy in a courtroom where the temperature reached ninety-seven degrees. "I had exhausted all the strength I could summon," Darrow would say later. His address often has been reproduced as a masterpiece of courtroom eloquence. Analyzing Darrow's speech, Alan Dershowitz of the Harvard Law School thinks that "its brilliance lies in the obviousness of his arguments. He makes it easy for the listener to agree with him. He appeals to common sense, to every experience and to moral consensus. As you read his words, you begin to nod your head in agreement with his premises. Before long, he has you agreeing with his conclusions."

Darrow called attention to the violence that he said had been magnified in the United States by the First World War, then only six years behind the country. But the shrewdest segments of Darrow's speech were his appeals to Caverly's humane impulses. First there was this observation:

> *I am aware that a court has more experience, more judgment, and more kindliness than a jury. And then, your honor, it may not be hardly fair to the court, because I am aware that I have helped to place a serious burden upon your shoulders. And at that I have always meant to be your friend. But this was not an act of friendship. . . . If these boys hang, you must do it. There can be no division of responsibility here. You must do it. You can never explain that the rest overwhelmed you. It must be your deliberate, cool, premeditated act.*

Then Darrow stated his view regarding the archaic and ugly nature of capital punishment:

> *Your Honor stands between the past and the future. You may hang these boys; you may hang them by the neck until they are dead. But in doing so you will turn your face toward the past. . . . I am pleading for the future; I am pleading for a time when hatred and cruelty will not control the hearts of men, when we can learn by reason and judgment and understanding and faith that all life is worth saving, and that mercy is the highest attribute of man.*

Darrow pointed out that during the previous ten years 450 persons had pled guilty to murder in Illinois and only one had been hanged, and that person was forty years old. The judge who had ordered hanging in that case was Robert E. Crowe, the present prosecutor.

Crowe, visualizing the Leopold-Loeb case as the key to his aspiration for higher political office, in a pique of temper said that Darrow had sought a "friendly judge" who would buy into his shabby arguments. Caverly took strong exception to this remark. For the first time during the trial, one reporter wrote, the judge "showed a flash of passion," and called the comment "a cowardly and dastardly attack on the integrity of this court," one intending to "intimidate" him. Crowe apologized hastily, but his innuendo may well have harmed his case. The judge also probably was less than pleased with Crowe's indelicate observation that "if a jury . . . returned a verdict without death punishment, every person in the community . . . would feel that the verdict was founded on corruption."

Darrow also focused on an item that more than any other would dictate the judge's decision. "Is youth a mitigating circumstance?" he asked rhetorically, then answered his own question:

We have all been young, and we know that fantasies and vagaries haunt the daily life of a child. . . . Here are two boys who are minors. The law would forbid them making contracts, forbid them marrying without the consent of their parents, would not permit them to vote. Why? Because they haven't that judgment which only comes with years, because they are not fully responsible.

The strong effect of Darrow's appeal was obvious. On its conclusion, a newspaper correspondent wrote: "There was scarcely any telling where his voice had finished and where silence had begun. Silence lasted a minute, two minutes. His own eyes, dimmed by years of serving the accused, the oppressed, the weak, were not the only ones that held tears." Several newspaper stories said that the judge himself was crying by the time Darrow had finished his speech.

Caverly's decision, announced two weeks after the end of the hearing, wrote off the voluminous psychiatric testimony as beside the point. The judge echoed Darrow's emphasis on the burden he had been made to bear; then he offered his reason for choosing life imprisonment instead of death by hanging for the killers of Bobby Franks:

It would have been the path of least resistance to impose the extreme penalty of the law. In choosing imprisonment instead of death, the Court is moved chiefly by the consideration of the age of the defendants, boys of eighteen and nineteen years. . . . [T]he court thinks it is within his province to decline to impose the sentence of death on persons who are not of full age.

This determination appears to be in accordance with the progress of criminal law all over the world and with the dictates of enlightened humanity. More than that, it seems to be in accordance with the precedents hitherto observed in this state.

Caverly noted that "the records of Illinois show but two cases of minors put to death by legal process—to which number the court does not feel inclined to make an addition."

One wonders how Caverly would have ruled had the age of minority been defined then, as it is today, as under eighteen.

Caverly gave Leopold and Loeb penitentiary sentences of life plus ninety-nine years. Leopold, who has left a record of his time in prison, adjusted quite well, though he had some grievous times in solitary confinement, particularly after Loeb's death.

Loeb was killed in a shower-room brawl on January 28, 1936, stabbed fifty-two times by James Day, another inmate. A clever *Chicago Daily News* reporter wrote one of the meaner lines in the annals of journalism: "Richard Loeb, who graduated with honors from college at the age of fifteen," the story read (chopping two years off the actual figure), "and who was a master of the English language, today ended his sentence with a proposition." *Time* joined in the journalistic orgy. "Prison," it reported, "only exaggerated Loeb's unnatural appetites." The magazine also maintained that "non-partisan citizens," in the wake of Loeb's death, were concerned that "prisons pamper wealthy prisoners" and "place perverts in positions of authority." This about a man who originally had been portrayed as a threat to young womanhood, with bevies of respectable ladies drawn like moths to the menacing glow of his radiant good looks. Loeb's death also played into the 1936 primary race for Illinois governor, as the Kelly-Nash machine smeared Henry Horner, the German-Jewish incumbent, for allowing "two degenerates to have private baths, conduct a school, and play poker for $1,500."

Records show a totally clean sexual slate for both Leopold and Loeb in prison. The best interpretation of Loeb's stabbing is that he was killed because he withdrew the financial help he had been giving Day, his onetime cellmate, after the warden cut the size of allowances prisoners could receive from their families. Day had been handed a straight razor by another inmate as a group of prisoners of which he was part marched by the room where Loeb was showering. Day slipped away from the pack and confronted Loeb. The incident obviously had been planned and obviously was retaliatory or designed to gain an advantage.

After Loeb's death, Leopold organized the prison library, contributing many of the books himself, inaugurated a pioneering and very successful correspondence school for prisoners, and taught himself braille so that he could train a blind inmate to read. Leopold also took a leading role in work to predict parole success inaugurated by Ernest W. Burgess, a preeminent University of Chicago sociologist. "Parole Prediction as a Science," written by Leopold under the pseudonym William F. Lanne to avoid calling public attention to himself, was published in the *Journal of Criminal Law* in 1935. Nonetheless, the *Chicago Tribune* learned of the actual author, and when it published the story, Leopold was transferred from the parole prediction office, though he later was permitted to resume his research work. Seventeen years later, with Lloyd Ohlin as the first author, Leopold would publish "A Comparison of Alternative Methods of Parole Prediction" in the *American Sociological Review*. This time he wrote under the name Richard A. Lawrence. The initials of the pseudonym are those of Loeb.

Leopold also worked for three and a half years during the Second World War as a volunteer for the Federal Coordinating Board for Malarial Studies on a project that involved testing the toxicity on human subjects of a band of new drugs that the government wanted to develop in seeking a cure for malaria. This was, Leopold noted, "probably the most stirring and exciting event of my life." He grants that one of his motives for taking part in the project was the hope of accruing points toward release. Over the protests of some of the doctors that he was more valuable as a laboratory assistant, Leopold insisted that he be included in the group of volunteers infected by malaria-carrying mosquitoes. Leopold also published a scientific paper based on the malaria experiments.

In time, inmates who participated in the malaria experiments were given some consideration toward release by the Illinois governor, but political issues constantly inhibited parole boards from freeing Leopold. One board chaired by Joseph Lohman, a former Cook County (Chicago) sheriff who later served as dean of the School of Criminology at the University of California, Berkeley, seemed on the verge of releasing Leopold after a number of impressive witnesses testified on his behalf. But that board was fired, and a different one appointed within hours after a new governor was sworn in on January 1, 1953. It would be another five years before Leopold was released. That release was helped greatly by the appearance before the parole board, speaking for Leopold, of the eminent poet Carl Sandburg and Father Eligius Weir, the Catholic chaplain when Leopold was admitted to Joliet and his friend thereafter.

Others supporting Leopold included Hans Mattick, who had worked closely with Leopold when Mattick served in the prison as sociologist-actuary, offering predictions on the likelihood of the success of individual inmates if they were to be paroled. In a previously unpublished letter, Mattick, who later ran the jail in Chicago and then joined the law faculty at the University of Chicago, offered his view about what had gone wrong in Leopold's case:

There was a certain ascetic strain in Leopold's upbringing, as if certain Protestant elements had joined into, and had a moderating effect on the already subdued American- ized Jewish tradition in which he was brought up. This expressed itself not only in the father's relative lack of approving response to Leopold's early achievements, but also had the effect of training him not to make a public display of his emotions. The criticism of lack of remorse for the crime is often imputed to Leopold, but this early training in emotional restraint is a more likely explanation for the lack of tears, breast-beating, and open effusions of verbal expression.

"I knew Leopold well" (his emphasis), Mattick pointed out to the parole board, adding that as part of his job he had interviewed thousands of prisoners with a critical mind, and had a large sample against which to evaluate Leopold. "On the basis of that experience, I do not hesitate to say that Leopold is one of the best candidates for parole that can be encountered."

Mattick ended his six-page, single-spaced communication with a plea:

> *Finally, gentlemen of the Parole Board, may I pray that God give you wisdom and strength to judge what passes for "public opinion" when you are obliged to act. . . . Partisan voices always seem disproportionately strong because the great majority of people remain silent and neutral while those with convictions make themselves heard. There will always be a small minority, vocal and strident, whose main talent lies in their ability to give the semblance of organized expression to emotional hysteria. . . . I urge you to note the qualifications of both those who speak for and those who speak against Leopold's parole. . . . For the sake of Leopold, for the sake of modern penology, and for the sake of Christian virtues we all hold dear, I pray you grant Leopold parole.*

With this kind of support, after thirty-three years, six months, and two days of incarceration Leopold was given his freedom on March 13, 1958. By this time he was in poor health, suffering from rheumatism, diabetes, kidney trouble, and a heart ailment. Mercilessly hounded by the press (he had been forbidden as a condition of parole to deal with the media), Leopold vomited incessantly as he was driven away from the prison toward Chicago. A newspaper reporter, following Leopold's vehicle, laconically wrote: "Nathan Leopold walked out of Stateville Prison Thursday into the wonderful world of free men. He promptly got sick."

Leopold moved almost immediately to Castañer, a remote Puerto Rican village high in the mountains. There he went to work for the Church of the Brethren as an X-ray technician, a trade he had learned in prison. Later he obtained a master's degree in social medicine at the University of Puerto Rico, where he finished first in his class and was elected president of the student body. He thought passingly of going for a medical degree or a doctorate in sociology or parasitology, but decided he was too old to set out on so long an educational haul. Leopold also taught mathematics at the university, lecturing in Spanish, one of the many languages he commanded (as a young man he had taken Greek in college and pursued correspondence courses in French, Latin, Sanskrit, Umbrian, Russian, and Oscan). Leopold also published a book on ornithology and studied leprosy on the island. In 1961, he married Trudi Feldman Garcia Quevado, a woman he met at a Passover seder shortly after arriving in Puerto Rico.

Following completion of his time on parole, Leopold became a compulsive world traveler, trying during the thirteen and a half years before his death to see things he had missed while in prison. It was at the end of his first European tour that Leopold would write a friend that he felt the balance had finally tipped, that he now was glad that he had not committed suicide when he first was taken to the Illinois penitentiary. He died in San Juan of a heart ailment at the age of sixty-six on August 29, 1971. He had donated his body to the university's school of medicine and his eyes to the school's eyebank.

Why Did It Happen?

The killers of Bobby Franks defy standard theories of crime causation that pretend to offer thoroughly comprehensive explanations about why people commit illegal acts in general and why they commit specific offenses such as murder. At best, proponents of most such theories may shrug their shoulders and say that theory can explain only so much crime, not all of it.

Leopold himself deemed that trying to understand his own behavior was a hopeless endeavor. "How can anyone hope to enumerate the components of

At left, Richard Loeb and Nathan Leopold at the time of their trial in 1924; at right, a 1963 picture of Leopold in Puerto Rico, after his release from prison. AP/Wide World Photos

human motivation in real life? Isn't it only in fiction that jealousy, or revenge, or hatred, or greed is found, simple and unadulterated, as the wellspring of human action?"

Popular Culture and the Leopold-Loeb Case

The media, primarily newspapers and radio, engaged in a feeding frenzy from the moment the body of Bobby Franks was discovered. So intense did the media focus remain that Leopold and Loeb often suffered deprivations in prison because wardens sought to avoid any press report that they had been accorded favors, even though they might reasonably have been entitled to them.

Leopold was removed from a teaching position early in his stay at Joliet because of a newspaper comment that he was not a fit person to exercise influence over the minds of his fellow inmates. He undoubtedly would have been released earlier had not the authorities been wary of adverse political consequences. By 1958, Leopold had been imprisoned longer than all but three inmates at either Joliet or Stateville: many murderers with similar sentences and equally or more brutal offenses and much worse crime records had long since been back on the streets.

The explanations of the killing offered by the media changed dramatically as time passed. Paula Fass offers a meticulous analysis of what she labels these "reimaginings." At first, Leopold and Loeb were portrayed as monsters, bold and self-sufficient savages who thought they were supermen, not answerable to the rules that apply to ordinary mortals. In large measure, this caricature derived from their interest in the writings of Friedrich Nietzsche.

This initial analysis was abetted by reference to the "science" of constitutional research, popularized in the United States by the translation into English of the writings of Cesare Lombroso, an Italian medical doctor who maintained that atavism—that is, the possession of human bodily anomalies characteristic of lower forms of life—was responsible for criminal behavior. The testimony of one of the prosecutor's psychiatrists is vintage Lombroso: Dr. Harold S. Hulbert told the court that his examination of Leopold had located "considerable pathology." According to Dr. Hulbert, "The hair development is pronounced. His eyes are somewhat prominent. One eyelid is lower than the other. His face is not the same on two sides, there being asymmetry." The *Chicago Tribune*, following this line of reasoning, ran a sketch of the heads of Leopold and Loeb and noted that one or the other of them was marked by things such as "sensuous lips," "excessive vanity," "love of excitement," a lack of "reason," and an absence of "moral and benevolent power."

There were stray hints of sexual "irregularities" between Leopold and Loeb in the psychiatrists' reports, but the newspapers would not publish such material, regarding it as unfit for family consumption. A 1924 book on the case by Maureen McKernan, a Chicago reporter, after obliquely referring to the sexual information and innuendos, characterized them as "unprintable."

A few years later, the newspapers had turned to what they depicted as Leopold and Loeb's faulty upbringing. These stories were intended to convey moral lessons, warnings to parents of the dangers they faced if they failed to raise their children satisfactorily. The parents of Leopold and Loeb were too rich and too respectable for direct reproach. Instead, the newspapers reported that Leopold, whose mother had died when he was sixteen, had been scarred by feelings of physical inferiority and, at the age of fourteen, sexual abuse by a German-speaking governess—a women nicknamed "Sweetie" who was described by the psychiatrists as "homely, suspicious, irritable, not tactful, oversexed in unusual ways, scheming, and very immature in her judgment." Her seduction of Leopold was a matter that was discussed privately in the judge's chambers rather than in open court. Loeb, too, was portrayed as overindulged by the family's hired female help. Both boys now were depicted in the media as fragile, flawed, and lonely creatures rather than as brutal monsters.

After the Second World War, when public discussion of sex became more acceptable—even mandatory for newspapers seeking large circulations—the previous public image of Leopold and Loeb yielded to one focusing on what were said to be their sexual perversions. This lifting of taboos fueled portraits of Loeb as a master criminal, with Leopold his subordinate and willing sexual slave. The script now being sold was that Loeb would allow Leopold sexual access to him if Leopold, for his part, agreed to engage in whatever "adventure" Loeb conceived. Leopold was openly depicted as wildly in love with Loeb. Two motion pictures, *Compulsion* (1959) and *Swoon* (1992), would highlight erotic homosexual tension between Leopold and Loeb as the explanation for the plot that ended in the death of Bobby Franks.

For his part, Leopold would attempt to nudge public opinion toward still another perception of the murder of Bobby Franks. Eager to win the favor of the parole board, he diligently sought to distance himself from the now-dead Loeb. Paula Fass notes how a former university classmate of Leopold's pressed this new theme during a 1957 parole hearing:

In the minds of a good many people [Leopold and Loeb] have been thought of as one individual. This is not true. They were totally different as youngsters. Their life patterns have been totally different. Loeb was a leader, aggressive, crafty, smart. Leopold was definitely a follower. Loeb induced Leopold to make the tragic mistake of his life.

Though it sometimes can be risky to blame the dead for behavior in which the living also have been culpably involved, the tactic possesses the distinct advantage of not being directly rebuttable. Nonetheless, parole boards almost invariably are unrelenting in their demand for unqualified admissions of guilt and expressions of remorse if they are to permit an inmate to be released. Leopold artfully sought to place the blame for the planning of the murder and the actual death-dealing blows on Loeb, but he also invariably granted his own awful guilt. Nor did his affection for Loeb seem to diminish significantly after the murder. At first they were housed in separate penitentiaries, but later they were reunited and collaborated on a number of prison projects. When he was free and living outside the United States, Leopold hung on the wall of his house a few pictures of persons to whom he felt especially close. Loeb's was prominent among them.

Leopold on Leopold

Having spent a third of a century in close contact with convicts who had committed serious criminal offenses, Nathan Leopold developed his own ideas about what leads to law breaking, though he thought his own behavior pretty much inexplicable. Leopold had echoed Clarence Darrow, who described his crime as "a senseless, useless, purposeless, motiveless act of two boys." "Why did they kill little Bobby Franks?" Darrow had asked rhetorically during his summation at the sentencing hearing, and then sought to provide an answer:

Not for money, not for spite, not for hate. They killed him as they might kill a spider or a fly, for the experience. They killed him because they were made that way. Because somewhere in the infinite processes that go to the making up of the boy or the man something slipped, and those unfortunate lads sit here hated, despised, outcasts, with the community shouting for their blood.

Are they to blame for it? There is no man on earth who can mention any purpose for it all or any reason for it all. It is one of those things that happened; and it calls not for hate but for kindness, for charity, for consideration.

Thirty years later, a parole board member would ask Leopold why he had participated in the killing of Bobby Franks. "I had no answer that I could give," Leopold remembered of that hearing, "no reason that made sense even to me." Turned down by the board, Leopold knew that he had to offer some explanation when he had a rehearing. This is what he said then:

> *I have been trying desperately to fathom the situation. I will never quit trying. I admired Richard Loeb extravagantly, beyond all bounds. I literally lived and died on his approval and disapproval. I would have done anything he asked, even when I knew he was wrong, even when I was revolted by what he suggested. And he wanted to do this terrible thing. Why, I cannot be sure. Certainly it was mad, irrational. Maybe there was some kind of juvenile protest, an overwhelming desire to show that he could do it and get away with it.*

Leopold added: "The only thing that comes out of my thinking that even bears on it is that at nineteen my growth and development were unnatural; my thinking was of a grown person, but I had the feelings of an undeveloped infant."

"I was," he said, "like an intelligent savage."

More than three decades earlier, during the psychiatric examinations before his sentencing hearing, Leopold had supplied an inkling of another explanation in answer to a leading question by one of the examining doctors. Leopold recalled:

> *"Wait a minute, Nate," said Dr. Adler. "You and Dick set out to commit a crime that would startle the world, didn't you?"*
> *"Yes," I had to answer.*
> *"Well, you did!"*

Many who seek to understand the Leopold-Loeb case believe that the synergy, the coming together of these two very unusual boys, was essential for the murder to have taken place: neither youth would have done it alone, and it is unlikely that either might have located someone else who would have been able to play the part laid out for him in that lethal drama.

Criminal Justice and Leopold-Loeb

The sensational ingredients of the cold-blooded and seemingly senseless slaying of fourteen-year-old Bobby Franks thrust the Leopold-Loeb case into national prominence. Most murders go largely unattended, even in the city in which they occur, especially if it is a metropolitan area. It takes something very special to create intense national interest: how the killing was done (Lizzie

Borden took an axe and gave her mother forty whacks) or the uncommon nature of the victim or the perpetrator. The ancient Greeks appreciated that particularly powerful tragedy has to involve people on high who are doomed to meet a terrible destiny because of their personal failings.

These were the kinds of ingredients that made up the Leopold-Loeb case. Leopold and Loeb were very unlikely killers and they came from prominent families. There was an innocent youthful victim, an opportunity for some to feed their latent or overt anti-Semitism, and a colorful and extraordinarily articulate attorney. Neither radio broadcasts nor newspaper stories had the vivid immediacy that later would be conveyed by television, but at the same time there was a good deal less competition for citizens' attention. The lengthy hearing to determine whether Leopold and Loeb would live or die was a media sensation, heralded, as we have noted, as the "trial of the century."

What took place, though, was not a trial: the guilty plea eliminated that and probably explains why the Leopold-Loeb case had little if any impact on how criminal justice was then or would later be administered either in Chicago or nationally. But the case raised several issues that would be reprised in later criminal trials. The most important concerned the relationship between the wealth of the defendants and the search for an ideal form of criminal justice.

Darrow's striking talents had been purchased in large part because Leopold's and Loeb's parents could afford him, and probably in part because of the notoriety that followed the crime. If the defendants had been slum kids and the victim a member of a rival gang, the Leopold-Loeb case very likely would have been treated as a run-of-the-mill occurrence, worth a back-page newspaper item if it received any media attention at all. Paradoxically, though, the sentence might well have been much the same: the defendants likely would have been allowed to plead guilty to some degree of homicide in exchange for a life term or perhaps even more lenient treatment. In that sense, the wealth and social position of Leopold and Loeb may have not only endangered them more than otherwise, but also allowed them to employ a high-powered attorney able to convince the judge to spare their lives.

Without Darrow and with an attorney of the caliber usually available for murder defendants, Leopold and Loeb also possibly would have been hanged by the neck until dead. That they were not may have had a minor and temporary impact on the tendency of judges to spare the lives of killers under the age of twenty-one. While the case added nothing directly identifiable regarding issues of insanity, it demonstrated how a shrewd defense strategy could focus on irrationality without crossing the line into a plea of mental incompetence. Such defenses have recently come into play increasingly in the administration of criminal justice, involving such matters as victim trauma syndromes and prior wife-battering, tactics that may foreshadow successful pleas based on childhood sexual or physical abuse or on an upbringing in areas where few are able to avoid neighborhood brutishness.

Leopold and Loeb were spared from the gallows because, at eighteen and nineteen, they were considered too young for the judge's conscience to allow him to sentence them to hang. Today, of course, both young men would be treated as adults, with their age much less likely to have any influence on their fate.

Surprisingly, the issue of executing young persons has moved in a direction quite contrary to that advocated and presumed by Clarence Darrow. In the centuries before their time, the sentiments that saved Leopold and Loeb were much less pronounced; as late as 1833, a boy of nine had been hanged in England for stealing. But Darrow had correctly sensed the mood of his times. Capital punishment was declining throughout the world and seemed to be well on its way to removal from the roster of acceptable punishments for crime.

The resurgent "get tough" mood in the United States, however, has not only dramatically increased the imposition of the death penalty, but also elicited calls for the execution of juvenile murderers. Of the thirty-seven states now permitting capital punishment, fourteen set the lowest age for the penalty at eighteen, with sixteen establishing it at between fourteen and seventeen, and seven having no set minimum age for execution. In California, in 1997, the governor expressed his willingness to consider executing thirteen-year-olds.

About 300 persons under the age of eighteen have been executed in American history, with 125 of them under sixteen. Amnesty International reports that since 1979, thirteen youths under eighteen have been executed worldwide, nine in the United States, the remainder in Pakistan, Rwanda, Bangladesh, and Barbados. All of these other countries have since outlawed juvenile executions. As one commentator notes, "U.S. politicians vow to string up eighth-graders too young to smoke a last cigarette." All told, the story of capital punishment since Leopold and Loeb were spared its reach in 1924 indicates that today, all other things being equal, they would have been much more likely to have gone to the gallows.

The proper role of expert witnesses in criminal cases also came in for momentary attention in regard to the Leopold-Loeb case. John Wigmore, a giant figure in the field of criminal law, was appalled by the partisan roles played by the two sets of psychiatrists at the hearing. Wigmore pointed out that the defense psychiatrists always talked of Loeb as "Dickie or Dick," and spoke of Leopold by his nickname, "Babe," using, in Wigmore's words, these "endearing, youthful innocent epithets" in order to convey a certain image of the defendants to the judge. Wigmore thought that expert witnesses ought to be hired by the court and be responsible to the court, not to one or the other side. Almost seventy-five years later this issue remains unresolved.

Leopold on Crime Causation

Trying to understand the criminal behavior of his fellow inmates, Leopold indicated that existing explanations did not do a particularly good job. "I've read a good many different theories of crime," Leopold wrote in 1958, when there were many fewer such theories than there are today. "I must confess," he added, "that none of them satisfies me completely." Then he explained why he had come to that conclusion:

> *Each of them contains some element of truth, but where they fall down, it seems to me, is that they try to explain too much, to cover too much territory. Each takes one particular viewpoint, explains one facet of the problem, and then claims to cover the whole field.*

This is a notably intelligent observation, very much on the mark. Leopold goes on to point out that the category "criminal" embraces a very wide spread of offenses, including spitting on the sidewalk, parking near a fire hydrant, and failing to throw back a fish under the legal limit. Most everybody commits some of these offenses, so that any attempt at a general explanation of all crime degenerates into an attempt to interpret not crime but human behavior itself.

The most serious offenders, the felons who end up in the penitentiary, Leopold noted, seem to form "a class apart." Members of that criminal class appear to outsiders to be more or less homogenous, each like the other, because "their behavior is so foreign to the ordinary non-criminal norm." But to regard felons as similar, Leopold maintains, "is as grave an error as to believe that the stars that form the Great Dipper must be close together because we see that they are all so far from Earth."

The only characteristic that felons share, Leopold says, is that they've been convicted of a felony:

> *Any theory that tries to embrace all the individuals in prison is doomed to failure just because they have so little in common. The man guilty of manslaughter through negligence, the murderer who kills the man he finds with his wife, the pyromaniac who*

receives sexual stimulation from setting fires, the embezzling bank president, and the professional stick-up man are all as different from each other as they are from the normal, law-abiding citizen. No one causal explanation will cover all the cases.

Leopold recommends that for purposes of explanation, felons should be grouped into smaller units. For him, one large and important group comes close to what the average person means by "a criminal." That group consists of predatory offenders: murderers, burglars, automobile thieves, and rapists from the high-delinquency slum areas of the big cities. Members of this group, Leopold maintains, "are distinguished by a common social history, by a common world outlook." Looking for an interpretative rope that will bind together members of this group, Leopold first discounts heredity, then concentrates on their family and neighborhood environments. His explanation, Leopold says, is "sociological, not biological." Leopold labels the key factor "hereditary environment" and explains himself in the following manner:

> *The neighborhood play group is the child's primary group; it is here that he becomes a social being. What he has been taught about right and wrong at home and at Sunday School has made an impression . . . , but that all has been told him by grownups, those inexplicable and often arbitrary creatures from another world, whose dicta about things like how many pieces of candy you eat or how late you can stay up at night simply don't coincide with what you want to do. These kids in the gang are his own age, they see things as he does. He's got to go along and do what they do—or else. Or else he'll be considered a sissy, a scaredy-cat and—horrible thought—perhaps be excluded from the group entirely.*
> *With pressure like that, it takes extraordinary strength to hold out, to be different. . . . This is all social, environmental. But the kid didn't pick his own playfellows. That choice was determined for him by where he lived, where he went to school. And that, in turn, was determined largely by the socioeconomic status of his parents.*

These paragraphs contain a good number of tantalizing thoughts. Readers may note that while the final lines of the second paragraph refer to ghetto and slum conditions, the remainder of the quoted material is eerily apropos of Leopold and Loeb to a much greater extent than it is to the street-hardened felons among whom they found themselves in the Illinois penitentiary. What slum kid grows up in a home where the questions of how many pieces of candy he might eat and how late he can stay up at night are matters of deep import?

The follow-up to the paragraph about the terrible pressures of the peer group tells precisely the tale that analysts of the case thought applicable to Leopold's relationship to Loeb: his inability "to hold out, to be different" when faced with the pressure to "go along" or else be regarded as a "sissy" and be excluded. Leopold probably is revealing a good deal more about himself than he is telling us about the best way to understand the roots of the kinds of felonies that were so heavily represented in the prison population of which he was for so long a member.

Criminological Theory and the Leopold-Loeb Case

The killing of Bobby Franks by Nathan Leopold and Richard Loeb also stands as a challenge to the major interpretative and predictive powers of theories and ideas about crime. "Crime has its cause," Clarence Darrow proclaimed before Judge Caverly. For his part, Darrow gave a passing nod to biological explanations, noting rather ominously and perplexingly that at least one of his clients may have been corrupted by "the seed" of "remote ancestors." More than seventy years later, an attorney in a Georgia murder case would echo Darrow's theme when he sought to overturn a death sentence by claiming that his client's killing of a store manager was the result of the absence of free will, shown by the fact that vicious crimes had marked the lives of his aunts, uncles, and cousins. Therefore, the attorney argued, the tendency to murder was genetically programmed into the man who had been sentenced to die. The appeal was not successful, but similar kinds of claims surely will proliferate as scientific breakthroughs pinpoint biological roots of behavioral predispositions.

Darrow also told the Illinois court that "perhaps all crimes do not have the same cause, but they all have some cause. And people today are seeking to find that cause."

Where has this trail, this search for an understanding of the roots of crime, taken us during the past seven decades? What are the current prevailing explanations of criminal behavior offered by sociologists, psychologists, and others? And what can we learn by determining the fit between these formulations and the facts of the Leopold-Loeb case?

Academic criminologists have devoted a great deal of time, energy, and imagination to the search for a single cause of all crime and for particular causes of particular kinds of crimes. It is possible, of course, to deal with a condition without knowing its origin—note, in this regard, the use of quinine to control malaria before we became aware of the role of the anopheles mosquito in the genesis of the illness. But cures and control are much more likely to be effective if we understand what led to the situation we want to cure. And the desire to "cure" crime, or at least to bring it under more effective control, has become a paramount social and political issue of our time.

The pursuit of an explanation for crime both gains and suffers from the fact that most everybody is certain that they know what leads others to violate the law. Oldsters are more inclined than younger persons to mention drugs. The explanations also vary by gender, with women more likely than men to focus on dysfunctional families as the root of crime. Such commonsense wisdom, often apparently on target, or at least somewhere near the target, nonetheless has the tendency to fall short when studies seek to confirm or repudiate it. Poverty—another presumed cause—may feed into crime but, as we see in the case of Leopold and Loeb, the inevitable association of the two is far from certain. Oversimplified explanations constantly falter in the face of such "model" youngsters as Leopold and Loeb when they commit awful crimes. At the same time, the more sophisticated and sometimes convoluted explanations of crime by experts often suffer a similar fate. The biggest problem that these

Renowned attorney Clarence Darrow defends Nathan Leopold and Richard Loeb before Judge John R. Caverly. AP/Wide World Photos

grand theories have, Thomas Huxley once wisely pointed out, is that they often are put to shame by little facts.

How do the little facts of the crime of Leopold and Loeb contribute to or contradict the postulates of leading ideas about the causes of crime?

PSYCHIATRIC THEMES

The psychiatrists in the Leopold-Loeb case promoted the standard insights that their trade offered, views that unconscious conflicts from childhood traumas prompted the killings. Their report on Leopold illustrates the common tendency of psychiatrists to locate pathology after the fact by references to traits that never would have been taken to indicate such abnormality before the fact:

> *Leopold represents a picture of a special abnormal type, the paranoid psychopathic personality. His ability as a conversationalist and as a student has led to his being unrecognized for what he really is, and the delusional conceptions about himself have therefore not been taken seriously. His very manic (over-excitable and over-energetic) tendencies have been misinterpreted as evidence of cleverness. The fact that he has been able to carry himself along in the world without being recognized as abnormal is in itself typical of individuals who belong to this special group of mental disorders.*

There is a great deal of double-talk in this portrait. It was not Leopold's "over-excited and over-energetic" behavior that was "misinterpreted as cleverness," but rather an extraordinarily superior intelligence test score and an outstanding academic record. Nor was Leopold much of a conversationalist, then or later. And what is one to make of the proclamation that an ability to appear sane is a characteristic of a mental disorder? Yet, as we shall subsequently see, the marking of Leopold as psychopathic, entering him onto the rolls of a very controversial diagnostic category, at least offers more of an explanation than the other standard interpretations of the pair's murderous act.

WHAT SAY THE CRIMINOLOGISTS?

The Leopold-Loeb murder is a case study that demonstrates the inadequacy of every major social science theory that has been put forward to account for the genesis of actual criminal acts, a matter said by Robert Merton, a guru in the field of sociology, to reflect a prevailing separation of theory from empirical fact.

The grandfather of criminological theory—called "differential association"—was proposed by Edwin H. Sutherland who, as a faculty member at the University of Chicago, often visited Leopold in Stateville Prison in connection with the correspondence school for inmates that Leopold and Loeb operated. Sutherland was one of five persons on the advisory council for the correspondence school, and one of a dozen or so individuals Leopold would honor with the mock-serious award of a diploma written in formal Latin and conferring the degree of *Ovum Bonum*—Good Egg.

Leopold particularly remembered Sutherland's interest in the "glim box," a homemade device for lighting cigarettes that was put together because inmates were forbidden to possess matches. A glim box usually was built into an empty snuff can. Charred material from tobacco sacks that had been set afire earlier was placed in the box to provide tinder, which was lighted by blowing on a spark produced by whirling a metal shirt button rapidly on a piece of thread or string. Leopold constructed a glim box for Sutherland, who, he said, "was proud as a peacock when he learned to operate it."

Sutherland's differential association theory lists a conglomeration of principles of learning by means of which a person is said to come to engage in criminal behavior. In essence, the theory argues that those who commit crime learn to do so from association in intimate groups with others who transmit attitudes about lawbreaking. At best, such ideas provide only slight insight into the roots of Leopold and Loeb's murderous behavior. Except for each other, Leopold and Loeb were overwhelmingly in contact with persons who were upright and notably law-abiding. Loeb's enchantment with detective stories could be said to have played a part in generating the crime, but it is more likely that this reading reflected rather than impelled his drive to kill, if it had any effect at all.

It is interesting that Leopold persistently claimed afterward that he had never believed that he and Loeb actually would do what they talked about; for him, he would say, it was all words, until he found himself driving the rented car with the dead body of Bobby Franks in the back seat. Clearly, Leopold had not been able to pull back from the scheme. If his self-statement is accurate, his participation could be regarded (somewhat) more as a sin of omission than one of commission. But theories of human behavior tend to be deficient when it comes to providing insight into the roots of acts of omission. It is much easier to locate more or less persuasive reasons why somebody did something than to understand why he did not do something when he might reasonably have done it.

Another prominent interpretation of crime today is that it results from a failure in "social bonding," that is, from the weakness of a person's ties to legitimate society. Significant ties include those to parents, teachers, and peers. A person's belief in the legitimacy of conventional values and awareness of the costs involved in lawbreaking, such as its threat to aspirations for a college education and a high-status job, are also said to be related to criminal behavior. Finally, the theory maintains that time spent on "constructive" activities—that is, activities that relate to legitimate objectives—will reduce the likelihood of criminal activity.

Social bonding theory is no more persuasive than differential association for explaining the actions of Leopold and Loeb. The ties between the two young killers and their families were close, and Leopold constantly expressed deep and obviously sincere remorse about the shame that he had brought on his family. Members of that family visited him in prison regularly until their deaths, particularly his father, his aunt, and his older brother (who, as did another brother, changed his name to Lebold after the murder). The commitment of both boys to achievement by means of educational success was extraordinary and the jeopardy that the murder posed to their lifestyles, both present and future, would have been more than adequate if social bonding theory were relevant to their behavior. Leopold's family already had purchased tickets that would take him on a summer trip to Europe, and both boys enjoyed very generous allowances. Indeed, it is difficult to imagine two young men with rosier futures.

Failure in social bonding as the explanation of crime has been upstaged in recent years by the idea that all crime can be interpreted in terms of the absence of a single crucial factor—self-control. This theory is said to explain not only all illegal acts, but also some things not in violation of the law, such as alcoholism and smoking. Poor family upbringing is said to be the root cause of inadequate self-control, which is marked by (a) a failure to defer gratification; (b) an absence of diligence and tenacity; (c) a preference for adventure instead of caution; (d) a leaning toward physical activity rather than cognitive behavior; (e) self-centeredness and indifference to the suffering of others; and (f) minimal tolerance of frustration.

As a portrait of either Leopold or Loeb this list seems woefully off the mark. Some of the items may fit somewhat (as some undoubtedly would for most human beings), but others are very farfetched.

Other major attempts to explain the roots of criminal acts are no more helpful in analyzing what Leopold and Loeb did. Psychologists note that frustration can produce aggression, but the two Chicago killers seemed to suffer much less frustration than most of us. The widely-acclaimed thesis of Charles Murray and Richard Herrnstein that intelligence, genetically determined, is highly correlated with crime looks ludicrous in the face of the Leopold-Loeb facts. Nor were the two young men victims of slum conditions. The attempt by one commentator to locate the act of Leopold and Loeb in the temper of the times hardly helps us to understand why they killed Bobby Franks.

> *This was . . . a peculiar period in our history—a time of speakeasies, of devil-may-care attitudes, of lawbreakers who were not only accepted but even lionized. Al Capone gave lavish parties at his fabulous home in Florida. Pious churchgoers were known to accept invitations to them. Random killings were rife. It is conceivable that two adolescents, in the spirit of the age, may have contrived the slaying of Bobby Franks with careless gaiety.*

"Conceivable" most certainly, but our understanding is hardly advanced very significantly by such ideas. It does not tell us why these particular boys, rather than millions of others, might have succumbed to the atmosphere of the times.

Other concepts carry us no farther. Labeling theory suggests that responsibility for crime results from thrusting offenders out of the mainstream of society once they have been trapped in the jaws of the criminal justice system. "So they think I am bad," says the labeled transgressor. "I'll show them what bad really is." But there was no labeling imposed on Leopold or Loeb. Nor did the inordinate American stress on material achievement—the key explanatory theme of what is called strain theory—appear to play much of a role in Bobby Franks's murder. Rational choice theory assumes that offenders calculate the benefits and costs of breaking the law and then act in terms of that inventory. This idea is self-evident, but it has great difficulty saying, at least beforehand, how different people will regard what stands to be gained and what stands to be lost (for instance, the excitement of a random killing against being hanged, whatever the odds on the latter might be).

Ideas looking only at murder have focused on the fact that homicide offenders tend to be part of a "subculture of violence." Others have focused on the idea that murder is a form of "self-help" because it resolves what the killer sees as a moral imbalance created by acts of his victim. Since Bobby Franks merely happened to be a convenient target, such ideas could be supported only if his death had some deeper symbolic meaning, a conclusion that would have to be based much more on imagination than apparent fact.

Finally, critical or Marxist theories do not offer much help in comprehending what circumstances led to the murder of Bobby Franks. The killers were hardly hapless victims of capitalist exploitation.

Albert Einstein pointed out that "the supreme goal of all theory is to make the irreducible basic elements as simple and as few as possible without having to surrender the adequate representation of a single datum of experience." By that standard, none of the contemporary theories of criminal behavior approaches the kind of elegance that marks a satisfactory explanation. The reason is probably quite simple: that it is a feckless endeavor to look for explanations that adequately comprehend the roots of all crime. The well-known sociologist Anthony Giddens was right on target when he wrote:

> *The wish to establish a natural science of society, which would possess the same sort of logical structure and pursue the same achievements as the science of nature probably remains, in the English-speaking world at least, the dominant standpoint today. . . . But those who still wait for a [social science] Newton are not only waiting for a train that won't arrive, they're in the wrong station altogether.*

Also on target was the eighteenth-century satirist Jonathan Swift when he depicted the mythical Brobdingagian's employing a tactic used by today's criminological theorists to try to explain away the cases that fail to dovetail with their interpretative ideas.

> *He [the deviant] is then handed over for examination to the great scholars attending the court, who eventually agree that he must be a* luxus naturae—*a freak of nature. For in the face of a phenomenon that does not fit in with their preconceived ideas, the scholars make no attempt to revise their thinking, but only produce a meaningless formula that dismisses the phenomenon as an exception.*

Psychopathy

The Leopold-Loeb killing probably fits best with the concept of psychopathy, as it was then known, or sociopathy, as it later was named, or the antisocial personality, as the personality trait now tends to be labeled. Antisocial personality, the current designation, however, is tied directly to criminal acts and tends to fall heir to a considerable amount of tautological thinking; that is, inexplicable criminal activity is caused by those who have an antisocial personality and those who have such a personality are identified by means of their inexplicable criminal activity. This being so, we will stay with "psychopath," the earlier designation.

A psychopath has been defined by William and Joan McCord as "an antisocial, aggressive, highly impulsive person, who feels little or no guilt and is unable to form lasting bonds of affection with other human beings." Sir David Henderson, a British psychiatrist, who may have coined the term, observed that psychopaths "rarely if ever show any particle of remorse." Philippe Pinel provided the first clinical description of the condition, calling it *manie sans délire* (mania without frenzy). Another approach emphasizes that a psychopath is a person who lacks empathy, that is, an affective approach more appropriate to someone else's situation than one's own. The string of adjectives used by Hervey Cleckley for psychopaths includes egocentric, grandiose, manipulative, dominant, forceful, cold, impulsive, and sensation-seeking. Psychopaths are said to represent 3 to 4 percent of the male population and 1 percent of the female population.

The behavior also has been noted in other cultures. Among the Intuit Eskimos it is called *kunlangeta* and applied to a person who repeatedly lies, cheats, steals things, and takes sexual advantage of the women when the other men are out of the village. He is someone who does not pay attention to reprimands and who is always being brought before the elders for punishment. Other Intuits are likely to invite such persons to go hunting on an ice pack and then push them off into certain death in the freezing water.

David Rowe's explanation of psychopathy is among the more intriguing ideas. He believes that the condition possesses significant value for biological survival and therefore is likely to increase. Rowe maintains that psychopaths are high in terms of "mating effort," that is, in the amount of time and energy they devote to attracting, monopolizing, and defending sexual partners, a matter that contrasts with the "parenting effort," the time and energy devoted to nurturing offspring. The lack of emotional attachment to a current partner makes it easier to cheat on her, Rowe observes, and therefore psychopaths are likely to produce more offspring than "normal" people.

Psychopathy was catapulted into the limelight when Robert Lindner's book *Rebel without a Cause* (1944), a case history of a psychopath, was made into a movie that turned James Dean into a cult figure, particularly after his death in a sports-car crackup that seemed to verify the close fit between the motion picture role he had played and his own character. Psychopaths' public appeal lies in the attraction for many of us of the ingredients of a daredevil charm, a willingness to take risks, and the absence of a working conscience. It is our conscience that keeps most of us from doing the daring, exciting, and criminal things that psychopaths amiably do, things that could add so much zest to what is a good deal of the time our prosaic and routine existence.

The idea of psychopathy tends to be scorned by mainstream criminologists, who regard it as a concept without intellectual integrity. They see psychopathy as a diagnostic scrap-basket into which is placed a large variety of otherwise unclassified personality problems. Virtually all but a relatively small cadre of true believers in psychopathy would agree with Stephen Porter's recent statement that the term "represents an enigma that continues to baffle mental health professionals and the public."

Nonetheless, we must appreciate how closely Loeb's behavior fits the description of psychopathic action, especially when we see how the highly regarded explanations of crime fail to provide more than a scintilla of understanding of the killing of Bobby Franks. As psychopaths are said to be, Loeb was highly impulsive, a young man who felt little or no guilt, and one who was unable to form lasting bonds of affection with other human beings, at least others beside Leopold, who truly worshiped him. It is this emotional numbness that is said to characterize psychopaths. Note, for instance, Loeb's comment after he had been in jail for several weeks: "I know I should feel sorry I killed that young boy and all that, but I just don't feel it. I didn't have much feeling about this from the first. That's why I could do it. There was nothing inside of me to stop me. Of course, I'm sorry about my family, but not as much as I ought to be." It is possible that Loeb knew about conditions that were said to mark psychopathy and that he was seeking to provide a record of his abnormality in order to gain mercy from the court. But the manner in which he had acted throughout his life lends credence to his words.

But the concept of psychopathy can take us only so far. Lee Robins, for instance, found that antisocial behavior of the father was a common background factor for a psychopathic youngster and that Jews manifest a very low rate of psychopathy. In Cleckley's roster of criteria for determining psychopathy, "unexplained failure"—the fact that the psychopathic individual is unsuccessful in constructive activities—is prominent. Loeb? Leopold? As the vernacular has it: No way. The category of psychopathy may for many men be the equivalent of the tag "hysteria" that is so disproportionately put on women who show no manifest physiological malfunctioning.

Novelists on occasion have created—or relied on—persons with characteristics similar to Richard Loeb's, perhaps because such characters afford an opportunity to juxtapose social success with inherent evil. In *To Have and Have Not* (1937), Ernest Hemingway depicted such a person as possessing "an ability to make people like him without ever liking or trusting them in return, while at the same time convincing them warmly and heartily of his friendship; not a disinterested friendship, but a friendship so interested in their success that it automatically made accomplices; and an incapacity for either remorse or pity, had carried him to where he was now."

Much the same, but more detailed and chilling is the portrayal of James Steerforth almost a century earlier by Charles Dickens in *David Copperfield* (1850). David is magnetically attached to Steerforth, who singles him out for attention, meanwhile appropriating the money he possesses, when David first enters the brutal boarding school to which he has been banished by his stepfather. Literary critics see Steerforth as Dickens's perception of the decadence and dandyism of the English upper classes. One critic believes that Dickens intended to portray a "dissolute gentleman," but instead showed Steerforth as a "contemptuous cad." Few critics have appreciated the remarkable depiction of a personality type that would engage the attention of the best psychological and psychiatric minds in later years.

Though Steerforth violates rules and brutally injures people who are deeply important to David, David's emotional attachment to him never lessens. David saw Steerforth much the way that Leopold would portray Loeb.

There was an ease in his manner—a gay and light manner it was, but not swaggering—which I still believe to have borne a kind of enchantment with it. I still believe him, in virtue of this carriage, his animal spirits, his delightful voice, his handsome face and figure, and, for aught I know, some inborn power of attraction besides (which I think a few people possess), to have carried a spell with him to which it was a natural weakness to yield, and which not many persons could withstand. I could see how pleased [my friends] were with him, and how they seemed to open their hearts to him in a moment.

Steerforth, half a dozen years older than David, possessed, as Leopold often said of Loeb, a "natural gift of adapting himself to whomsoever he pleased, and making direct, when he cared to do it, to the main point of interest in anybody's heart." Both the real Loeb and the fictional Steerforth fit with the philosopher Albert Camus's definition of charm: the ability to get the answer *yes* without having asked the question. Interestingly, Steerforth insisted on calling David "Daisy" and told him: "If you had a sister, I should think she would have been a pretty, timid, little, bright-eyed sort of girl. I should have liked to know her."

One night at school David observes: "I thought of him very much after I went to bed, and raised myself, I recollect, to look at him where he lay in the moonlight, with his handsome face turned up, and his head reclining easily on his arm. . . . I admired and loved him, and his approval was return enough. It was so precious to me." When David and Steerforth reunite some years after their time at school, David is overcome with pleasure: "I grasped him by both hands, and could not let them go. But for the very shame, and fear that it might displease him, I could have held him round the neck and cried." David finds himself "glowing with pleasure that he had still this interest in me. . . . A dashing way he had of treating me as a plaything was more agreeable to me than any behavior he could have adopted." Later, when drunk, David expresses his deep feelings for Steerforth: "I said (in two words) 'Steerforth, you'retheguidingstarofmyexistence.'"

Steerforth seduces Little Em'ly, a charming, innocent young girl engaged to marry a member of the family of Peggotty, David's nursemaid. David comes to understand the core of Steerforth, but he knows that he never would have believed this until the evidence became unquestionable:

> *If any one had told me, then, that all this was a brilliant game, played for the excitement of high spirits in the thoughtless love of superiority, in a mere wasteful careless course of winning what was worthless to him, and next minute thrown away, I say, if any one had told me such a lie that night, I would have been indignant.*

Dickens has Steerforth drop a few hints of his totally unsavory character and the author himself offers an explanation of Steerforth's parallelism to what has been labeled psychopathy. "It would have been well for me (and for more than me)," Steerforth observes, "if I had had a steadfast and judicious father!" Steerforth's face, Dickens writes, had never before for David expressed such a dark kind of earnestness as when he utters these words. Despite Steerforth's terrible exploitation of Emily, David can condemn only intellectually; he cannot desert Steerforth emotionally: "Yes, Steerforth," he thinks to himself, "my sorrow may bear involuntary witness against you at the Judgment Throne; but my angry thoughts and reproaches never will, I know!" Note similarly Leopold's reflections long after Loeb's death:

> *Some people who have my welfare at heart tell me that I should not write as I do of Dick, that it hurts me, that it indicates that I am still influenced by what was amoral and mad in his character. . . . [But] the simple truth is that we cherish even when we don't emulate.*

Conclusion

The great wealth and social prominence of their families proved to be a double-edged sword for Nathan Leopold and Richard Loeb. The crime's notoriety led to a media feeding frenzy that kept their case from being handled as it might have been under more usual circumstances. Presumably, had the offenders been more lackluster, a life sentence probably would have been negotiated with little fanfare.

Though gruesome and virtually incomprehensible, the murder of Bobby Franks probably would have been recorded as but another more or less routine Chicago killing had the participants been part of the city's defined dross, the virtually anonymous cadre of lawbreakers. A lower-class Leopold would have been back on the streets in a much shorter time than the elite Leopold was. At the same time, without the kind of money that allowed the boys' families to employ so skillful an advocate as Clarence Darrow, it is very likely that Leopold and Loeb would have been hanged. The issue of the relationship between wealth and justice in the criminal courts is an issue that will come to the forefront again when we look at the trial of O. J. Simpson.

Leopold's personality, as formed before the murder and affected by the killing and by his prison experiences, is not easily reduced to a simple portrait. After Leopold's death, Elmer Gertz, an astute observer, tried to sketch with words the person he had known well but, he believed, had understood only imperfectly:

> *Though I was one of the two or three men closest to him in the last years of his life, I did not feel that I understand everything there was to know about him. I knew all the facts about essentials, and yet the inner truth escaped me. I knew that he had participated in one of the most notorious crimes of the twentieth century, yet I could not think of him as any sort of criminal, let alone a murderer. There was so much that was both appealing and unappealing in him—the gratitude that never dimmed, his utter impatience with those he regarded as inferiors, the continuing prejudice against blacks, the obsession with time and movement and activities, the refusal to accommodate himself to the necessities of his [medical] condition, the glaring contradictions in his character and temperament, the great intelligence mixed with naiveté.*

None of the usual theories to explain why Leopold and Loeb did what they did takes us very far, though Loeb at least fits very closely, albeit far from perfectly, with the kinds of people who are labeled psychopaths. But there are millions of people who equally well show the traits defined as psychopathic, and very few of them murder innocent youngsters.

Paula Fass, in her review of the twists and turns in the media's choreography of the Leopold-Loeb case, noted that "over time, the themes of childhood, psychology, and sexuality gathered sufficient strength to make us (almost) forget that in 1924 Leopold and Loeb were two rich kids who tried to get away with murder." Fass's prosaic summary offers perhaps the most sensible interpretation of what went wrong on the awful day in 1924 when two exceedingly rich and bright young men combined to kill a young boy by bashing him on the head with a chisel covered with adhesive tape so that they would not hurt their hands.

For Further Reading

Two books deal exclusively with the murder of Bobby Franks by Nathan Leopold and Richard Loeb. Maureen McKernan, a Chicago journalist, wrote *The Amazing Crime of Leopold and Loeb* (Chicago: Plymouth Court Press, 1924) shortly after the court's decision was handed down. McKernan's book is largely made up of verbatim reproductions of the psychiatric reports and the lead attorneys' arguments: a reissue of the book (Birmingham, Ala.: Notable Trials Library, 1989) contains a brief introduction by Alan Dershowitz, the Harvard Law School professor who later served as a member of the O. J. Simpson defense team. The second book, Hal Higdon's *The Crime of the Century: The Leopold and Loeb Case* (New York: Putnam, 1975), provides a thorough review of the events.

Nathan Leopold's autobiography, *Life Plus Ninety-Nine Years* (Garden City, N.Y.: Doubleday, 1958), is essential to an understanding of the case. In addition, John Bartlow Martin wrote a series of well-documented articles about Leopold's prison experiences a few years before Leopold was paroled. The articles appeared under the title "Murder on His Conscience" in the *Saturday Evening Post* on successive weeks: Part I on April 2, 1955, pp. 17–18, 86–88; Part II on April 9, pp. 32–33, 65–66; 71–72; Part III on April 16, pp. 36, 198, 201–202; and the final installment on April 23, pp. 28, 135–138. On the stabbing of Loeb see Gladys A. Erickson, *Warden Ragen of Joliet* (New York: E. P. Dutton, 1957).

More recently, Paula Fass has offered an excellent analysis of the shaping in popular culture of interpretations of the case in "Making and Remaking an Event: The Leopold and Loeb Case in American Culture," *Journal of American History*, 80 (December 1993):919–951.

There is a considerable literature on Clarence Darrow that includes discussion of his role in the Leopold-Loeb hearing. See in particular Irving Stone, *Clarence Darrow for the Defense* (New York: Doubleday, Doran, 1941), pp. 380–421; and Kevin Tierney, *Darrow: A Biography* (New York: Crowell, 1979), pp. 320–331. Darrow's autobiography, which goes over the Leopold-Loeb case lightly (pp. 226–243), is titled *Story of My Life* (New York: Scribner's, 1932). Darrow's speech before Judge Caverly has been reprinted numerous times. A good source is Arthur Weinberg, ed., *Attorney for the Damned* (New York: Simon and Schuster, 1957), which provides the speech's highlights (pp. 16–88) as well as an assemblage of Darrow's other writings and speeches. The full text of the speech can be found in Alvin V. Sellers, *The Leopold-Loeb Case* (Brunswick, Ga.: Classic Publishing Co., 1926), pp. 118–232, which also offers the statements of the prosecutors and Darrow's associate attorneys, and excerpts from the psychiatrists' reports. Most of the same material can be found in *Attorney Darrow's Plea for Mercy and Prosecutor Robert E. Crowe's Demand for the Death Penalty in the Loeb-Leopold Case, the Crime of the Century* (Chicago: Wilson Publishing Co., 1924). Another source for Darrow's presentation is *Clarence Darrow's Plea in Defense of Loeb and Leopold* (Girard, Kans.: Haldeman-Julius, 1926). A list of materials by and about Darrow can be found in Willard D. Hunsberger, *Clarence Darrow: A Bibliography* (Metuchen, N.J.: Scarecrow Press, 1981), with pages 150–160 detailing sources regarding the Leopold-Loeb case.

Elmer Gertz, who handled Leopold's parole appeal and became a close friend, discusses the case in *A Handful of Clients* (Chicago: Follett Publishing Co., 1965), pp. 1–192, and in *To Life: The Story of a Chicago Lawyer* (New York: McGraw-Hill, 1974; reprinted Carbondale: Southern Illinois University Press, 1990), pp. 189–199. *To Life* presents details about Leopold's life after his release from prison.

Additional material can be found in Francis X. Busch, *Prisoners at the Bar* (Indianapolis: Bobbs-Merrill, 1952), pp. 145–199; John Cassity, *The Quality of Murder* (New York: Julian Press, 1958), pp. 52–61; Alan Hynd, "The Case of the Curious Cubs," in Hynd, ed., *Murder, Mystery, and Mayhem* (New York: A. S. Barnes, 1958), pp. 47–56; William Kunstler, "The State of Illinois *versus* Richard A. Loeb and Nathan F. Leopold, Jr.," in Kunstler, *First Degree* (New York: Oceana, 1960), pp. 74–86; and, much less reliably, George Murray, *Madhouse on Madison Street* (Chicago: Follett Publishing Co., 1965), pp. 333–344. The book by Armand Deutsch, the first intended victim of Leopold and Loeb, is *Me and Bogie* (New York: G. P. Putnam's Sons, 1991).

The case is discussed from the viewpoint of mental health professionals in Maurice Urstein, *Leopold and Loeb: A Psychiatric-Psychological Study* (New York: Lecouver Press, 1924); Editorial, "The Crime and Trial of Loeb and Leopold," *Journal of Abnormal Psychology and Social Psychology*, 29 (October–December 1924):223–229; and Sheldon Glueck, "Some Implications of the Leopold and Loeb Hearing in Mitigation," *Mental Hygiene*, 9 (July 1925):449–468.

Meyer Levin's novel *Compulsion* (New York: Simon and Schuster, 1956) mixes fact with fiction, with a considerably larger proportion of the latter. The motion picture *Compulsion* (1959), made from Levin's book, wanders even further from the truth. Orson Welles, who played Darrow in the film, made a bit of motion picture history by delivering Darrow's speech in a monologue that lasted twelve minutes—a motion-picture record. Two other films—*Rope* (1948), an Alfred Hitchcock production, in which Farley Granger plays Leopold, and *Swoon* (1992)—also take considerable liberty with the facts.

Many of the private papers of Leopold and Gertz are held in the Special Collections section at Northwestern University in Evanston, Illinois; other papers of Leopold, including letters to and from many prominent criminologists of the time, are housed at the Chicago Historical Society. In writing this chapter, we also benefited from the kindness of Elaine Cressey Ohlin, who loaned us a treasure trove of material that included newspaper clippings and magazine stories about Leopold and Loeb and letters exchanged by Leopold with Edwin H. Sutherland and Donald Cressey.

Reviews of theories of crime include Ronald L. Akers, *Criminological Theories: Introduction and Evaluation,* 2nd ed. (Los Angeles: Roxbury Press, 1996); Francis T. Cullen and Velmer S. Burton, Jr., eds., *Contemporary Criminological Theory* (New York: New York University Press, 1994); Don C. Gibbons, *Talking about Crime: Problems and Issues in Theory* (Englewood Cliffs, N.J.: Prentice-Hall, 1994); and Marilyn McShane and Frank P. Williams III, eds., *Criminological Theory* (New York: Garland, 1997).

The vast literature on psychopathy can be sampled in three major treatises: Hervey M. Cleckley, *The Mask of Sanity: An Attempt to Clarify Some Issues about the So-Called Psychopathic Personality,* 3rd ed. (St. Louis: Mosby, 1955); Robert M. Lindner, *Rebel without a Cause: The Hypnoanalysis of a Criminal Psychopath* (New York: Grune & Stratton, 1944); and William McCord and Joan McCord, *The Psychopath: An Essay on the Criminal Mind* (Princeton, N.J.: Van Nostrand, 1964). For a recent overview see Stephen Porter, "Without Conscience or without Active Conscience: The Etiology of Psychopathy Revisited," *Aggression and Violent Behavior,* 1 (1996):179–189. The journal *Behavioral and Brain Sciences,* 18 (1995):523–599 offers a theme article on psychopathy by Linda Mealey and forty-two short responses by other scholars.

Interpretations of the relationship between David Copperfield and James Steerforth are found in William H. Marshall, *The World of the Victorian Novel* (New York: A. S. Barnes, 1964), pp. 169–185, and A. O. J. Cockshut, *The Imagination of Charles Dickens* (London: Collins, 1961), among other sources.

Chapter Three

Scottsboro (1931) and Racial Injustice

A posse of about fifty men, armed with shotguns, rifles, and pistols, and hastily deputized as sheriffs, lined the railroad tracks near the depot in Paint Rock, Alabama, early in the afternoon on March 26, 1931. They were waiting for the westbound forty-two-car Great Southern Railroad freight train. The train had begun its journey in Chattanooga, then moved through northern Alabama on its way to Memphis. At the town of Stevenson, Alabama, a group of a dozen young white men, one of them with a bleeding head, had reported to the station master that they had been thrown from the train by a larger group of blacks and that they wanted to press charges against their assailants. Members of the deputized posse had been ordered to arrest all blacks on the train and take them to the sheriff at nearby Scottsboro, the seat of Jackson County, a town of about 3,500 people.

Nine young black men—who forever after would be known as the Scottsboro boys—were rounded up when the freight train arrived at Stevenson. They ranged in age from thirteen to twenty. Eight of the nine were illiterate, unable to sign their names. Most of them, in this year of severe economic depression, had been riding the rails off and on for some time, getting a job here and there, sometimes stealing, and otherwise living by their wits.

Three other people also were found on the freight train. One was Orville Gilley, a white male. The other two were white women dressed in overalls and wearing men's caps. Ruby Bates at seventeen was the younger of the women; Victoria Price, twenty-four, already twice-married, was the older. After the black men had been put in the back of a truck to be taken to Scottsboro, Price told a deputy sheriff that she and her girlfriend had been raped by the nine blacks. This report triggered a series of events that would reverberate throughout the world and would include several perfunctory criminal trials, sentences of death, numerous appeals, and two landmark rulings by the United States Supreme Court. The Communist Party of the United States as well as several other national organizations would become deeply involved in the Scottsboro trials. The roster of those who would play a prominent part in the case included Samuel Leibowitz of New York, the most famous criminal trial lawyer of the time; a southern judge with unusual courage and integrity; and a very large number of persons who demonstrated how depressingly bad the administration of criminal justice can be when the aim is not to determine the truth of a matter but to uphold a way of life seen to be under siege.

The winding path that the Scottsboro case took in the courts as well as other events surrounding it can be a bit difficult to follow. To make it easier to track the case as it dragged its way for almost five years through what seemed to be interminable judicial proceedings, we have identified each of the trials by centered headings and then indicated subsequent appellate proceedings and other developments with sub-headings at the left-hand side of the page.

The First Trials: Scottsboro, April 1931

With lynch mobs threatening the suspects, they were moved from Scottsboro to a more secure jail in Gasden, a nearby town, and a National Guard unit was summoned to afford them protection. The four trials held at Scottsboro, which began less than two weeks after the arrests, were a judicial farce. An attorney from Chattanooga, secured by the black leadership in that city, and an over-the-hill member of the local bar were the only legal help the defendants had. Neither attorney had any preparation time except for a less-than-half-hour interview with the defendants. The attorney from Chattanooga, who carried the burden of the case, insisted that he was not to be regarded as the counsel of record, since he was not being paid, and that he was there only to help whichever local attorney would volunteer to carry the defense. A known alcoholic, the Chattanooga lawyer allegedly was intoxicated during much of the trial—so "stewed" he couldn't walk a straight line, one report said. He made only a feeble effort to rebut what often was contradictory and inconclusive evidence offered by the two young women and a handful of other state witnesses.

The trials were conducted before four separate juries—the state had asked for severances—and were completed in four days. Two of the young men—

Charlie Weems, at twenty the oldest, and Clarence Norris—were tried first. Their attorney cross-examined the few witnesses against the defendants listlessly and offered no closing argument. Particularly inculpating was the testimony of three of the Scottsboro young men that, though they had nothing to do with the rapes, they had seen others of the defendants having intercourse with the young women. This testimony would be repudiated later, accompanied by vivid tales of the threats and beatings that had prompted it.

The second trial, that of Haywood Patterson alone, got under way almost immediately after the first concluded, and it had not proceeded very far before the initial jury brought back a guilty verdict and a recommendation for death for Weems and Norris. Patterson's trial was also a parody of justice, and the jury reached a similar verdict with a similar sentence of death. Patterson would remember the moment of the jury's finding bitterly a quarter of a century later, when he cooperated in the composition of his biography: "I looked around," he said. "That courtroom was one big smiling white face."

Next came five defendants—Andrew Wright, Willie Roberson, Ozie Powell, Eugene Williams, and Olen Montgomery. Notwithstanding that Roberson had contracted syphilis and gonorrhea the year before and maintained that his genitals were so swollen he could not conceivably have had intercourse, the third jury quickly returned a verdict of guilty. All five defendants were condemned to die.

Leroy Wright, Andy's younger brother, only thirteen years old, was the defendant in the final trial. Because of his age, the prosecution asked for life imprisonment instead of death. The jury could not reach a unanimous verdict. Despite the state's specific request for a life sentence, newspaper reporters learned that seven of the twelve jurors had held out for death.

The four cases finished, the judge, with tears in his eyes (these were the first death sentences he had imposed in five years on the bench), declared a mistrial for Leroy Wright and then sentenced the other eight defendants to die.

THE AFTERMATH OF THE FIRST TRIALS

The Scottsboro case moved from the sleepy confines of its isolated Alabama venue onto the national scene when two organizations, the Communist Party, acting through its International Labor Defense (ILD) auxiliary, and the National Association for the Advancement of Colored People (NAACP), elected to rally to the convicted youths' cause. The NAACP was prodded by Clarence Darrow, Leopold and Loeb's defender, who was a member of its board of directors. For the Communist Party, which got on the case first and considerably more effectively, what had happened at Scottsboro represented an opportunity to advance its revolutionary agenda by championing blacks and seeking to persuade them that the defects of capitalism lay at the heart of racist justice. Cynics believed that the Communists in the end would be willing to sacrifice the boys in order to add drama to their contentions about the terrible defects of capitalism. An accurate judgment of the Communist role in the Scottsboro case later was expressed by an Alabama lawyer who said: "The communists made an acquittal impossible, but they kept the boys alive."

The tactics and antics involved in the tug-of-war between the Communists and the NAACP for control of the Scottsboro case might have been comic if the stakes had not been so high, with the lives of the youths in jeopardy. The Communists recruited many of the defendants' parents to their side, providing them with small stipends and inviting them to New York to address large audiences. The NAACP hired an outstanding southern lawyer and tried to convince the Scottsboro defendants that there was so much antagonism against the ILD that their appeal to the Alabama courts and, ultimately, to the governor would be rejected on that ground alone. At a court session in nearby Fort Payne arguing for a rehearing of the case, an ILD attorney, Joseph Brodsky, had been threatened by bystanders with death if he did not get out of town—and immediately.

The young men on trial would sign a declaration of allegiance to one group and then switch to the other when its representatives visited them. Finally, Darrow and two NAACP lawyers met with three ILD attorneys. Darrow's offer was that the attorneys act as a team of independent counsel, beholden to nobody but the clients. The ILD, though anxious to have Darrow's talents enlisted in its cause, would agree to cooperate only if it could retain the right to veto any strategy decision. At that point, negotiations broke down; the quest for justice was being undermined by politics and ideology. "Any real fight," the *Daily Worker*, the Communist newspaper, declared regarding the Scottsboro case, "must necessarily take the character of a struggle against the whole brutal system of landlord robbery and imperialist national oppression of the Negro people." Most fundamentally, the Communists sought to recruit masses of black people to their cause, something that, rather to their surprise, they so far had been unable to accomplish.

The appellate strategy focused on demonstrating that the trials had been a travesty. The cases had been inadequately prepared and hastily tried. The noise of the outside mob cheering the first guilty verdict, it was maintained, had unduly influenced the second jury. The defense attorneys also argued on appeal that statements of several of the young men had been offered only after they were told that they might go free if they would implicate others; if they would not do so, they were warned, they ran the risk of being lynched.

In addition, Hollace Ransdall, a young teacher-journalist-activist sent by the American Civil Liberties Union (ACLU) to Alabama, had discovered that both Victoria Price and Ruby Bates supplemented their factory wages by prostitution. A deputy sheriff told Ransdall that he didn't bother Price because she was a "quiet prostitute, and didn't go rarin' around cuttin' up in public and walkin' the streets solicitin', but just took men quiet-like." Despite this evidence, Price continued to say: "I hope to see every one of them burned to death," adding that the crime was particularly awful because she was a "virtuous woman." Price had recently been convicted of fornication and adultery, both misdemeanors, and spent time in jail for the offenses, but this information had been inadmissible at the trial because only state court verdicts involving felonies could be put into evidence.

Observers outside the South would claim that the trial of the Scottsboro defendants was another form of lynching, one that was being camouflaged as a judicial proceeding. Before 1929, lynchings had declined in the South from a high of about one hundred a year to a dozen or so annually, though there had been a rise during the Depression, from 1930 onward, to an annual rate of thirty. Southerners were aware of the poor image that lynchings gave them in the rest of the country. Many saw criminal trials as a route to accomplish the same thing and to mute outside criticism. Michael Meltsner, an attorney, interprets the situation in these terms: Southern justice became "a sham used not to grapple with tenacious questions of fact and law, guilt or innocence, but solely to maintain class and race power."

The Communist Party presumed, incorrectly as it turned out, that a huge mass of people, both blacks and whites, but particularly blacks, would so threaten and intimidate the Alabama appellate court judges that they would decide in favor of the Scottsboro defendants in order to save their own skin and that of other capitalists. The only thing that could stay the Alabama executioner, Communist Party leaders proclaimed, was the aroused anger of the workers. In the face of the people's protests, the court might decide that it was "better policy to hold off this cold blooded butchery so as to avoid arousing the masses to further fury." This proved to be pure bombast. While a following began to form in support of the Scottsboro defendants, it offered little if any direct threat to entrenched interests in Alabama.

ALABAMA SUPREME COURT, MARCH 1932

In late March of 1932 the Alabama Supreme Court, in separate opinions on each of the Scottsboro trials, voted to uphold the convictions of seven of the Scottsboro defendants, reversing Eugene Williams's sentence because he was a juvenile.

Arguing before the court for the state was Thomas G. Knight, Jr., the son of the justice who wrote the majority opinion in one of the cases. The younger Knight would personally handle the prosecutor's role in most of the later trials. Justice Knight compared the Scottsboro cases to the assassination of President McKinley in 1901, when retribution had been swift and severe. That case might have involved murder, Knight declared, but he was "of the opinion that something worse than death . . . happened to this defenseless woman, Victoria Price."

The court ruled that the verdicts were amply supported by evidence and that the proceedings had been fair. "The presence of the militia," the senior Knight wrote, "instead of having a coercive influence on the jury was a notice to everybody that the strong arm of the state was there to assure the accused a lawful trial." It also was the majority's opinion about the undue and unseemly rapidity with which the case had been tried that "if there was more speed . . . in the administration of the criminal laws . . . , life and property would be infinitely safer" and criminals would have greater respect for the law.

The majority thought that local newspaper coverage was not inflammatory and that stories in the Montgomery and Chattanooga papers, which it granted were less than impartial, probably did not circulate much in the Scottsboro region. Under Alabama law the character of Victoria Price had nothing to do with the charge, since rape "may be committed on an unchaste woman, even a common prostitute." The tumult outside the courtroom was nothing more than a band playing such tunes as "They'll Be a Hot Time in the Old Town Tonight" to promote the sale of Ford trucks. The trial record, the majority agreed, was more than ample to convince a reasonable person that the defendants had committed the offense with which they were charged, that "most foul and revolting crime, the atrocity of which was only equaled by the boldness with which it was perpetrated." The details of the case, in fact, were so "shocking" that they would not "admit of being repeated here."

The lone dissenter on the seven-judge bench was the chief justice, sixty-nine-year-old John C. Anderson. Anderson was said to "dominate" the Alabama court "by his sheer legal brilliance" and his "unassuming courtesy" during the thirty-six years he served on it, until his death on April 27, 1940. The seventh child in the family of a physician educated in Philadelphia, Anderson had been born during the Civil War. Most of his uncles served with the Confederate forces, though Anderson would note in an autobiography he wrote for his children, "my Alabama kin opposed secession."

While he could not bring his judicial brethren with him on this decision, Anderson's reputation and his leadership position on the court seem to have provided an important, and very possibly essential, background for the later decision of the U.S. Supreme Court favorable to the Scottsboro defendants. Had the Alabama bench been unanimous or had one of its lesser members written the dissent, there would not have been as much leverage for the reversal that constituted a thoroughgoing repudiation of the state high court majority opinion.

In his dissent, Anderson noted that "the record indicates that the appearance of the lawyers was rather pro forma than zealous and active . . . which is indicated by declination on the part of counsel to argue the case," a point that would find its way into the U.S. Supreme Court ruling. He objected to the swiftness with which the Scottsboro case had been tried, given that the "entire atmosphere was at fever heat." Anderson noted that all the defendants were given the same sentence—the statute prescribed a penalty that could be anywhere from ten years in the penitentiary to death—despite the fact that they differed in age, leadership, and other important elements of their alleged participation in the offense. For Anderson, this was evidence that the jurors were "coerced by public feeling or sentiment or actuated through passion or prejudice." Quoting a prior Alabama opinion that he had written in an especially brutal murder case in which a mob had threatened to break into the jail and lynch the offender, Anderson set forth what he believed should be a guiding principle:

> *No matter how revolting the accusation, how clear the proof, or how degraded, or even brutal, the offender, the Constitution, the law, the very genius of Anglo-American liberty, demand a fair and impartial trial. If guilty, let him suffer such penalty as an impartial jury, unawed by outside pressure, may under the law inflict on him. He is a human being and is entitled to this. Let not an outraged public, or one which deems itself outraged, stain its own hands—stamp on its soul the sin of a great crime—on the false plea that it is but the avenger of innocence.*

Using this guideline, Anderson was convinced that the defendants had not gotten an adequate trial. In justice to them, to the "fair name of the state of

Alabama, as well as the county of Jackson," he declared, "these cases should be retried after months of cooling time have elapsed and by their vigilant employed counsel."

THE U.S. SUPREME COURT, NOVEMBER 1932

The next step was the U.S. Supreme Court. This was a highly conservative bench—the "nine old men," some critics later dubbed them—that would drive Franklin Roosevelt to despair by refusing to uphold much of his New Deal legislation. In an ill-fated political misplay, Roosevelt unsuccessfully would seek to remodel the court by means of a law that would permit him to add a new court member when any of the incumbents reached the age of seventy.

Conservative though it was, in November 1932 the court, by a 7–2 vote in *Powell v. Alabama* (287 U.S. 45), overturned the Scottsboro jury's verdict on the ground that the defendants had not received the adequate legal counsel to which they were entitled under the Sixth Amendment. Justice George Sutherland, one of the most conservative judges sitting, was assigned to write the opinion after the chief justice, Charles Evans Hughes (in a move that made another justice, Harlan Fiske Stone, "furious"), would not allow the judges more time to study the case. Stone believed that Hughes wanted to bring a rapid end to the demonstrations that were being carried out in front of the court building by Communist supporters.

Sutherland's usual reluctance to interfere with state sovereignty had been highlighted earlier in *Meyer v. Nebraska* (262 U.S. 390, 412, 1923), in which he had dissented in a ruling that disallowed the state to prohibit the teaching of any language but English in either public or private schools. But Sutherland clearly was personally and judicially offended by what had taken place in Scottsboro, and he was determined to locate a basis for repudiating the jury verdict. In the *Powell* ruling he spelled out the reasoning behind his and his colleagues' decision to send the case back for another trial:

> *In light of . . . the ignorance and illiteracy of the defendants, their youth, the circumstances of public hostility, the imprisonment and the close surveillance of the defendants by the military forces, the facts that their family and friends were all in other states and communication with them necessarily difficult, and above all that they stood in deadly peril of their lives—we think the failure of the trial court to give them reasonable time and opportunity to secure counsel was a clear denial of due process.*

Justice Sutherland noted that the issue of adequate counsel had been handled at Scottsboro in a "casual fashion" and quoted at length the Chattanooga attorney's protestations that he was unprepared and was unfamiliar with Alabama procedure, was not being paid, and was merely appearing to offer what assistance he could to the defendants.

The ruling was a departure for the Supreme Court, which historically had maintained a hands-off attitude toward the way states carried out their criminal justice business. So flagrant was the injustice at Scottsboro against black Americans that the justices could not temper their outrage and write the events off as an unassailable prerogative of the Alabama courts. Commentators came to see the *Powell* case as a revolutionary extension to state proceedings of the rights guaranteed by the Sixth and Fourteenth Amendments. But Sutherland was too cautious and too conservative a judge to go quite that far. What he objected to, as a recent analyst of his legal thinking has noted, was the "bumbling nonchalance" and the "maddening tentativeness" about legal representation of the defendants at Scottsboro in a case in which lives were at stake. As Justice Cardozo would note later in *Palko v. Connecticut* (302 U.S. 319, 1937):

> *The [*Powell*] decision did not turn upon the fact that the benefit of counsel would have been guaranteed to the defendants by the provisions of the Sixth Amendment if they had been prosecuted in a federal court. The decision turned upon the fact that in the particular situation laid bare for us in the evidence that benefit of counsel was essential to the substance of a fair hearing.*

Felix Frankfurter, a Harvard law professor, and himself later a member of the Supreme Court, immediately recognized the import of the *Powell* ruling, calling it "the first application of the limitations of the Fourteenth Amendment to a state criminal trial." Thereafter, the federal courts would continue to broaden their selective incorporation of constitutional protections into state proceedings, though it was not until thirty years later that the court would grant an indigent defendant the right to have a lawyer appointed in any felony case (*Gideon v. Wainright*, 372 U.S. 335, 1963). This right was extended in 1972 in *Argersinger v. Hamlin* (407 U.S. 25) to misdemeanor cases in which imprisonment was a possible punishment. In 1966, in the pathbreaking *Miranda v. Arizona* (384 U.S. 436) decision, the court by a 5–4 vote reversed a conviction that involved the introduction into Miranda's trial of a confession secured by the police in the absence of counsel or without an effective waiver of counsel. The importance of the *Powell* decision can be seen from the result of a recent computer search that found 3,708 subsequent citations of it by American courts.

The Communists, nonetheless, were hardly placated by this victory. They noted that the court had ignored their claim that no trial in which blacks were excluded from the jury could possibly be fair. The *Daily Worker*, the official Communist Party newspaper, thought that all the court opinion accomplished was to instruct Alabama authorities "how to 'properly' carry out lynch schemes." Its cynicism aside, the party had achieved a crucially important goal. Speaking for his mates, Olen Montgomery wrote the ILD, "Since the Supreme Court have granted we boys a new trial I think it is my rite to express thanks and appreciation to the whole party for their care. . . . I my self feels like I have been born again from the worrying . . . I have had."

The Second Trials: Decatur, March 1933

For the new trials that the defendants were to receive, the Communist Party had agreed to hire as the chief defense attorney Samuel Leibowitz, a thirty-nine-year-old New York lawyer in Darrow's image, despite the fact that Leibowitz made it clear that he would not be beholden to Communist dictates.

Seven of the Scottsboro defendants meeting with their attorney, Samuel Leibowitz. Left to right are Deputy Sheriff Charles McComb, Leibowitz, Roy Wright, Olen Montgomery, Ozie Powell, Willie Roberson, Eugene Williams, Charlie Weems, and Andy Wright. AP/ Wide World Photos

The party leaders agreed to keep their class warfare propaganda more or less under wraps until the trials had concluded. The new defense lawyer sought to have the trials transferred to Birmingham to avoid the overwhelming tide of local opposition, but the judge would agree to move them only as far as Decatur, fifty miles to the west of Scottsboro.

In this new round, the first case heard was that of Haywood Patterson. Patterson, his black heritage mingled with one-quarter Creek Indian genes, was now regarded as the ringleader of the Scottsboro defendants. He was, in southern eyes, "an uppity nigger," a tough, independent-minded man who steadfastly refused to bend to the dictates of southern racial etiquette and who challenged and threatened the traditional rules.

Patterson often would fight when aggrieved. When they were to be moved from death row in the state's Kilby Prison before their second trial, the Scottsboro defendants began to pack their few belongings. Leave everything here, the warden told them, you'll be back. "That wasn't all we left," Patterson writes. "We had our opinions of the death house and we left them in the beds and covered them with sheets. . . . They had put it on us and we put it on them. In hell, if the guests get a chance, they don't treat the devil any better than he treats them."

To build a record on which to appeal, Leibowitz opened this second set of trials by arguing that blacks had been illegally excluded from the grand jury. As expected, the judge ruled against him, and again ruled for the prosecution when Leibowitz sought to demonstrate that, contrary to the requirements of the U.S. Constitution, blacks had been excluded from petit jury service. He called a number of witnesses, all of whom granted that they had never seen a black person on a jury in the county. The court reporter, who had not missed a session in twenty-four years, testified to the same effect.

After that, Leibowitz took on Victoria Price, the state's prime witness, in cross-examination. Years later, he would grant that in his long courtroom practice he had rarely met so formidable an opponent as Price. She often gave him back as good as she got. Once, when Price said from the witness stand, "I do know one thing, those Negroes and this Haywood Patterson raped me," Leibowitz stared at her dramatically for a long moment. "You are a little bit of an actress," he said slowly. Price responded quickly: "You're a pretty good actor yourself."

Evidence presented by Leibowitz documented the confrontation between whites and several of the blacks on the freight train. The whites had thrown rocks and shouted "black sons of bitches." The blacks had gathered support from throughout the train and thrown off all but one of the white youngsters. Orville Gilley had been spared, all agreed, because the train had picked up speed and nobody wanted to see him seriously injured or perhaps killed. After the fight, the blacks said that they dispersed to the various cars in which they originally had been riding.

The scientific evidence was very strong in favor of the defendants. Dr. R. R. Bridges, a gynecologist, pointed out that it had been necessary to insert a swab as far back as the neck of Price's cervix to locate enough semen for a slide smear. He maintained that if she had been raped, as she claimed, by six young, healthy men and had not douched it was impossible for him not to have found very large quantities of semen in her vagina. Nor were there bruises, cuts, or other signs in her vaginal area congruent with an allegation of rape. Also, the floor of the gondola car had been covered with a thick layer of chert, a fine quartz gravel used as track ballast and around railroad stations, yet there were no cuts or other indications that Price had been manhandled on that rough surface.

Defense testimony was offered by Leslie Carter, who said that he had intercourse with Ruby Bates in a hobo camp the night before the train ride while, nearby, Jack Tiller had been doing the same with Victoria Price. Carter said that Price had manufactured the rape story to avoid being arrested for vagrancy and for crossing a state line with a man for immoral purposes. Her boyfriend in fact had refused to ride the rails with her for fear of being arrested for precisely that latter offense. "What the hell do we care about Negroes," Carter had Price saying to him.

Then came the defense's greatest hope. Ruby Bates, who had been reported missing, was dramatically ushered into court and testified that everything she had said in the initial trials at Scottsboro was a lie, that her words there had been thrust upon her by Victoria Price. Both Carter and Bates, however, made poor witnesses. Both were, for one thing, too well dressed. The prosecution got them to admit that they had been outfitted and subsidized up North—in New York City—by the Communist Party. Carter was shrill and flamboyant; Bates had trouble trying to reconcile her previous testimony with her new version of what had taken place and often was evasive under cross-examination. Almost half a century later, Victoria Price would tell a *Washington Post* reporter with a certain glee that when Bates left the courtroom that day bystanders threw tomatoes at her: "There was three bushels of tomatoes on her face, on her dress and down the front of her." Price added, "I was standin' in the window watchin' and yellin' 'Hallelujah, Hallelujah.'"

A final argument to the jury by Wade Wright, the county solicitor, turned ugly. Bates, Wright said, had been misled in New York by "Jew language." Referring to Carter's time in the North, Wright wondered if he might have changed his name to Carterinsky. "Did you watch his hands?" Wright asked. "If he had been with Brodsky another two weeks he would have been down here with a pack on his back a-trying to sell you goods." Then he roared at the jurors: "Show them," he said, pausing for effect. "Show them that Alabama justice cannot be bought and sold with Jew money from New York." Both remarks, over Leibowitz's furious objections and his call for a mistrial, seemed to find favor with the jurors and court spectators.

The verdict was preordained. The jury found Patterson guilty and sentenced him to death in the electric chair.

The judge, James Edwin Horton, Jr. (he looked like a picture of Abe Lincoln, Patterson would write in his memoir), had increasingly become convinced of the innocence of the Scottsboro boys and postponed the trials of the other defendants until the ugly local mood had calmed down. Horton, fifty-five years old at the time, came from an aristocratic southern background; his maternal grandfather, John Branch, had been the governor of North Carolina and secretary of the navy under Andrew Jackson.

Back in New York, where he was welcomed as a hero, Leibowitz would lose his temper, injuring what few chances he might have had in the later trials of the Scottsboro defendants. A newspaper reporter asked him how the Alabama jury could have ignored the persuasive evidence of innocence. You would not have to ask how they could reach that verdict, Leibowitz said, descending to the same level as his opponents, if you had seen "those bigots whose mouths are slits in their faces, whose eyes pop out like frogs', whose chins drip tobacco juice, bewhiskered and filthy." After two weeks in Decatur, Leibowitz declared, he needed "a moral, mental, and physical bath."

Rallies for the accused blacks burst out all over the northern states, and 3,000 persons came to Washington, D.C., to protest the Decatur verdict in front of Franklin D. Roosevelt's White House. Roosevelt, dependent on the traditional support of southern white voters, pled urgent other business as an excuse not to address the crowd or to receive its emissaries.

The Communist control of the case drew continuous fire from both supporters and enemies of the Scottsboro boys. The Communists by far had been the dominant force rallying support for the defendants, but there always was suspicion that they were not fundamentally concerned with the defendants' fate but with the party's own political and financial prospects. Southerners, who almost uniformly despised the Communists, were more than willing to sacrifice the defendants rather than line up behind what they regarded as a despicable, alien political threat. Nonetheless, southern newspapers, especially in metropolitan areas such as Birmingham and Montgomery, began to shift a bit in their views, now at times maintaining that the evidence against the Scottsboro defendants was at best inconclusive.

At the end of June, lawyers for both sides met in Athens, Alabama, Judge Horton's hometown, to present arguments regarding a possible rehearing of the Patterson case. Horton preempted discussion of the issue, and, to the surprise of all, he read a long, formal statement in which he said that he had become convinced that the verdict against Patterson was not based on satisfactory evidence of guilt. Therefore, he was ordering that it be set aside and a new trial held. Horton's carefully crafted words represent the essence of what the Scottsboro case fundamentally was about:

> Social order is based on law, and its perpetuity on its fair and impartial administration. Deliberate injustice is more fatal to the one who imposes than to the one on whom it is imposed. The victim may die quickly and his suffering cease, but the teachings of Christianity and the uniform lessons of all history illustrate without exception that its perpetrators not only pay the penalty themselves, but their children throughout endless generations.

Horton declared that "the evidence greatly preponderates in the favor of the defendant," insisting that the medical findings demonstrated conclusively that there had not been a group rape of Victoria Price. Price's testimony, he insisted, was not only uncorroborated but also improbable and contradicted by the doctors' reports. Horton did not reveal what must have been a powerful impetus for his conclusion. During the trial, the prosecutor had asked him to excuse Dr. Marvin Lynch from testifying, since Lynch merely would repeat what Dr. R. R. Bridges had said. But Lynch subsequently had asked for a private conference with the judge, and, as Horton revealed many years later, Lynch confided that he was convinced that the rape charges had been manufactured. "I looked at both the women and told them they were lying, that they had not been raped—and they both laughed at me." But Lynch believed that it would be the death of his medical practice if he testified against the claims of rape.

The rape allegedly had occurred, Judge Horton noted, during the thirty-eight miles between Stevenson and Paint Rock. Victoria Price maintained that during this time she had sexual intercourse with at least six of the black youths in a railroad car whose bottom was filled with a jagged quartz rock. Yet when she was carefully examined by a doctor an hour or so after she was taken from the train, there was no evidence of marks on her body, no live semen in her vagina, no scalp wounds, though she said that she had been viciously hit on the head. Nor was there any mention in the court records of the presence of the slightest amount of semen on the clothing of any of the defendants.

Unfortunately, to support his decision, Horton went into such gynecological detail that the Alabama press refused to print most of the material he discussed on the ground that it was not fit family fare. Alabamans who might have been persuaded by Horton were thus denied access to the specific grounds on which he had reached his conclusion. As for Horton himself, he was unsuccessful in his attempt to retain his position as circuit court judge in the 1934 election, and he returned to the private practice of law and gentleman farming until his death at the age of ninety-five in March 1973. While it is obvious that his defeat at the polls was a direct result of Horton's decision to

Dr. R. R. Bridges testifies during the Scottsboro trial. His finding that the medical evidence contradicted the accusations of rape failed to sway the jury. AP/Wide World Photos

overturn the jury verdict, it should be noted that Wade Wright, the Jew-baiting county solicitor, also failed in his reelection bid, while Chief Justice Anderson was returned to the state supreme court several more times despite his dissent in the first Scottsboro case.

The Third Trial, Decatur, November 1934

The state, though stung by Horton's decision, persisted, perhaps in part because the prosecutor had his eye on being elected governor of Alabama and could not politically afford to back away from the case. In late November 1934, seven of the Scottsboro boys again faced a Decatur jury; the cases of Roy Wright and Eugene Williams had been transferred to juvenile court. The state had maneuvered to get a new judge, William Washington Callahan, a seventy-year-old curmudgeon who let it be known that he had little patience with drawn-out attempts to present or extend what he regarded as unnecessary defense evidence.

The judge frustrated Leibowitz at every turn. Callahan was peremptory and impatient, underlining his distaste for the defense's case by severe looks, sighs of disbelief, and tones of voice and facial expressions that would not be discernible in the transcript, which reported only what was said during the trial. When it came to his summary of the case, Callahan introduced a statement that appalled the defense lawyers:

> *Where the woman charged to have been raped, as in this case, is a white woman, there is a very strong presumption under the law that she will not and did not yield voluntarily to intercourse with the defendant, a Negro; and this is true, whatever the station in life the prosecutrix may occupy, whether she be the most despised, ignorant and abandoned woman of the community, or the spotless virgin and daughter of a prominent home of luxury and learning.*

Callahan found it impossible to believe that any white female would permit a black man to have sexual intercourse with her: "the fact that she [Price] might have been convicted or had relations with white people does not mean in any sense of the word she would submit to the embraces of a Negro." The ugly racist nature of the trial judge's words is compounded by the fact that the statement was beside the point. The defense was not arguing that Price had consented to intercourse, but that none had taken place.

Predictably, the jury again returned a guilty verdict and again recommended death in the electric chair.

AFTERMATH OF THE THIRD TRIAL

Two things were becoming increasingly apparent. Though he had carried out the defense of the Scottsboro seven with consummate skill and dedication, Leibowitz was so despised in Decatur, as an outsider, a Jew, and the man who had ridiculed the town's citizens, that it was questionable whether he was more of an asset than a handicap to the case. The same could be said of the ILD: its brash Communist propaganda tended to drown out whatever else it might be saying about the defendants' case. The ILD tended to ignore details of the charge against the Scottsboro boys and men and to concentrate on the more generic task of broadcasting the horrors of the political system that was condemning them. The ILD also devoted much of its energy to recruiting party members and raising money to finance the Communist cause.

The marriage of convenience between Leibowitz and the ILD was further shaken when two ILD lawyers were ensnared by the Alabama authorities while offering Price a bribe to change her testimony. They had suggested $1,000, then gone up to $1,500 when she demurred. Price reported the offer to the police, who advised her to play along. Law enforcement officers were at the scene in Nashville when the ILD attorneys arrived there to hand over the money. The attorneys were arrested and then left the state, forfeiting their $500 bail.

ALABAMA SUPREME COURT, JULY 1934

Everyone interested in criminal justice, after becoming familiar with the trial transcript of the Decatur proceedings, ought to read the decision of the Alabama Supreme Court in *Norris v. State*. The opinion will prove infuriating to fair-minded people. It demonstrates the ability of the highest court in a sovereign state to reach a conclusion that is so out of line with the facts before it that a reader has to wonder how the justices could conceivably have endorsed the decision with a straight face (without at least crossing their fingers to indicate that, after all, guys, this is a political and social decision that has nothing to do with justice).

The issue the appellate court wrestled with was whether Leibowitz and his colleagues had demonstrated that blacks were systematically excluded from Alabama grand and petit juries. The justice who wrote the decision insisted that "the jury commissioners made no exclusion of any negro from the jury roll on account of his race or color." This is what the commissioners had said and the justices could find no reason to doubt them. It was only that somehow blacks had not been suited for "such important service." The jury commission-ers said that they paid no heed to race, and therefore they could not testify whether there was a single black on the jury rolls, though Leibowitz had been willing to go through the entire roster name by name. Besides, plenty of whites were excluded from jury duty because they failed to meet the standards; therefore, it hardly would be surprising if every black proved deficient. The court noted that the editor of the local newspaper, who granted that he knew some "good Negroes," was unwilling to say whether any truly possessed the necessary qualifications to serve on a jury that required "good judgment." For "such high service," the Alabama Supreme Court decision declared, one needed "men of intelligence, character, and sound judgment"; this could not be stressed too greatly. The appeal had to be denied since it was evident that the failure to have blacks on the jury represented nothing more than the conscientious manner in which the commissioners had followed the laws and could not be deemed to demonstrate any racial animus or bias.

U.S. SUPREME COURT, APRIL 1935

The U.S. Supreme Court thought otherwise. The rupture between Leibowitz and the ILD led to his pursuing Norris's appeal, while the ILD handled that of Patterson. Leibowitz focused on the failure of Alabama authorities to place blacks on the jury rolls and pointed out that they later had forged the names of several blacks in the jury register to seek to defuse his contention. He demon-strated that no black had served on a jury in Decatur for more than sixty years. The trial record showed, as the Alabama Supreme Court opinion had noted, that the editor of the Scottsboro newspaper had granted that he had seen no blacks on any jury during the two dozen years that he had attended court sessions. This was, he insisted, because blacks lacked "sound judgment." Asked by Leibowitz what he meant, the editor had said: "I know some good Negroes as far as Negroes go, but I think that 'sound judgment' part of the statute—I think they can't get around that." It was common knowledge, he said, that most Negroes steal: "They're not trained you know, and I might say the same applies to women."

So compelling was Leibowitz's claim that Supreme Court Chief Justice Hughes asked to examine the forgeries in the Alabama county jury roll, an extraordinary move on the part of a court that confines itself to deciding questions of law and not to determining the accuracy of evidentiary allega-tions.

Leibowitz's argument persuaded the Supreme Court, in *Norris v. Alabama*

(294 U.S. 587, 1935), to reverse the conviction of Norris and to order the Alabama Supreme Court to do the same for Patterson (*Patterson v. Alabama*, 294 U.S. 600, 1935) on the ground of exclusion of blacks from the grand and trial juries. "In the light of the testimony given by the defendant's witnesses," Chief Justice Hughes ruled, "we find it impossible to accept such a sweeping characterization of the lack of qualifications of Negroes in Morgan County." Hughes quoted the Alabama jury commissioner who had said: "I do not know of any Negro in Morgan County over twenty-one and under sixty-five who is generally reputed to be honest and intelligent and who is esteemed in the community for his integrity, good character and sound judgment, who is not an habitual drunkard, who isn't afflicted with a permanent disease or physical weakness which would render him unfit to discharge the duties of juror and who can read English and who has never been convicted of a crime involving moral turpitude."

The chief justice in his decision regarded this claim as utter nonsense: "It is so sweeping and so contrary to the evidence, as to the many qualified Negroes, that it destroys the intended effect of the commissioner's testimony."

The Fourth Trial, Decatur, January 1936

Despite this setback in the U.S. Supreme Court, the state of Alabama refused to back away from the Scottsboro case. Thomas Knight, the ever-persistent prosecutor, was now lieutenant governor, but he had himself appointed a special prosecutor so that he could again try the Scottsboro case. Meanwhile, a major realignment of the defense's support groups had taken place. The ACLU, the NAACP, the ILD, the League for Industrial Democracy, and the Episcopal Federation for Social Service had agreed to form the Scottsboro Defense Committee (SDC) with no one group to have a dominant voice. They appointed Allan Knight Chalmers, a thirty-eight-year-old minister of considerable ability and total dedication, to run the committee. Chalmers, admired by all, selflessly followed the principle he would set forth in the self-effacing story of his work on the Scottsboro case.

> *There are enough staid people in the world holding things as they are. We need no more of them. What we need is people caught by the truth that no one is free when anyone is bound. That is not an easy idea to have get a hold on you. It has to be applied person by person, not just in the pious generalities of the resolutions good people pass when they gather for a moment and separate without effective action.*

Leibowitz agreed to keep a low profile in future trials, which would be led for the defense by Clarence Watts, a highly regarded local attorney with traditional southern views on the proper relationship between the races, but a man with a firm belief that Victoria Price had never been raped.

This time one black man was placed on the fourteen-person grand jury that brought back an indictment against Haywood Patterson. Since only a two-thirds vote was needed to indict, there is no record of the position that black man took.

During Patterson's trial, Judge Callahan mercilessly hassled the defense. A correspondent from the *Nation* captured what went on: "Judge Callahan said that if such and such things were true, in a tone implying they probably were, then the defendant was a 'rapist' and should be convicted." When Callahan uttered these words, the reporter observed, "he glared over at the defendant in fury, his lips drawn back in a snarl, and he rolled out the word 'r-r-rapist' in a horrendous tone." The judge employed such tactics "hour after hour and day after day in an already prejudiced courtroom." Typical was this courtroom interchange:

> *Prosecutor: If we let this nigger go, it won't be safe for your mother, wife, or sweetheart to walk the streets of the South.*
>
> *Leibowitz: Your Honor, must we continue to try this case in a welter of such inflammatory appeals?*
>
> *Prosecutor (hurt): I ain't done nothing wrong. Your Honor knows I always make the same speech in every nigger rape case.*
>
> *Judge: Objection overruled.*

The jury again returned a verdict of guilty, but this time, largely due to the obstinacy of one member, the sentence was set at seventy-five years instead of death.

AFTERMATH OF THE FOURTH TRIAL

As three of the manacled defendants were being driven back to the state prison, Ozie Powell stabbed a deputy sheriff (who would recover) and he himself then was shot in the head, destroying some brain tissue, which impaired his mind for the remainder of his life. Powell was sitting on the right-hand side of the car, and slashed the deputy's throat with his free hand. Clarence Norris, who sat in the middle of the back seat of the car, shackled to the other two defendants, said that the deputy had been cussing out Powell, castigating the "Communist, Jew, northern lawyers" who were defending him. Powell had "sassed" the deputy by saying that he thought they would do a "damn sight" better with what they had than with some southern lawyers. The deputy then slapped him across the mouth. Powell had purchased a pocket knife in the prison, and kept it hidden during shakedowns by placing it in the extra lining of the fly on his pants that ran straight along the buttons, a place where custodians never would search. The driver managed to bring the car to a halt, jumped out, and then fired back into it, hitting Powell in the head.

In prison, the Scottsboro defendants were placed in solitary confinement, where their mental health deteriorated noticeably. Several of the men, most notably Patterson, often had been involved in prison disciplinary actions. Of all the defendants, Patterson had become the most "adjusted" to prison: he was shrewd and enterprising, and could be defiant or humble, as his best interests dictated. Patterson often conned the defense committee out of money, which he lent to fellow inmates at high interest rates, and he maintained homosexual relationships with several other inmates, taking the role of a "wolf" who protects "gal-boys" and takes his reward in sexual favors.

There were signs by 1936 that officials and the Alabama public were wearying of the bitingly negative publicity their state was receiving throughout the world because of the Scottsboro case. The nerve ends that the original accusations had exposed had become numb. The governor offered to see that a mild sentence was imposed if the men would plead guilty to miscegenation—that is, having sexual relations with members of the white race—an offer the defense turned down. Birmingham's leading newspapers wondered in print whether all the fuss on behalf of "two hook-wormy Magdalenes" was worth the trouble. When Knight died early in 1937, hopes rose for some kind of a settlement, but Judge Callahan refused to budge.

The Fifth Trial, Decatur, July 1937

On June 14, 1937, the Alabama Supreme Court again upheld Patterson's conviction and his sentence. The appeal had largely concentrated on what the defense claimed was the trial court's unreasonable refusal to allow the case to be transferred to a federal court. The state supreme court found no merit in that claim nor had it changed its mind about not permitting Victoria Price to be interrogated about her sexual behavior prior to the alleged rape.

A month later Clarence Norris was put on trial, found guilty, and sentenced to die in the electric chair. Callahan had so badgered the southern lawyer,

Clarence Watts, that Watts became emotionally distraught and had to with-draw from the remainder of the cases. In the Andy Wright trial, which fol-lowed, the state reduced the penalty it sought to ninety-nine years imprison-ment. "I'm entitled to an acquittal in this case and I ask you men in all seriousness to do what you swore at the outset you would do," Leibowitz told the jurors. That case was lost, too.

At the end of the Weems trial (the state had asked for and obtained a seventy-five-year sentence), Leibowitz, overwhelmed by the impossibility of his task, abandoned any pretense of dignity and tact and assailed the court procedure: "I'm sick and tired of this sanctimonious hypocrisy," he shouted. "It isn't Charlie Weems on trial in this case, it's a Jew lawyer and New York State put on trial here by the inflammatory remarks of [the assistant attorney general]." The prosecutor, paying no heed to what Leibowitz said, scolded him for jeopardizing the chances of his clients with his outburst.

The state decided to prosecute Ozie Powell only for the knife assault on the deputy sheriff, to which he pleaded guilty and received a twenty-year sentence. Then, stunningly, the prosecutor asked the court to drop the charges against the remaining four defendants and set them free. These defendants were then released despite the fact that the evidence against them was precisely the same that had been used to convict the others. As one northern observer sarcasti-cally noted, the decision left Alabama in the "anomalous position of providing only 50 percent protection for the 'flower of Southern womanhood.'" The state declared that it had concluded that Roberson and Montgomery probably were not guilty, one because of his venereal disease and the other because he was almost blind, and also because they had been seen in freight cars other than where the rape allegedly had taken place. There was no explanation why, if this was true, they had been locked up for six and a half years, despite their innocence.

After the trial, the governor reduced Norris's sentence from death to life imprisonment. Subsequently, there were numerous maneuvers and meetings, some delicate, others heavy handed, seeking to persuade Alabama's governor to exercise clemency on behalf of the Scottsboro defendants still in prison and thereby to put an end to the continuing charade of justice. At first, it looked as if this would happen, but the state's chief executive, despite gentle pressure from President Franklin D. Roosevelt, developed cold feet, fearing that releas-ing the Scottsboro prisoners would end his political career.

Meanwhile, up North the freed men were a continuing source of concern to their sponsors, who feared that if they got into trouble it would harm the chances of the others for release. Montgomery was particularly worrisome, drinking heavily, drifting across the country, and in and out of trouble with the law.

Then Charlie Weems was released by the parole board in November of 1943 and Andrew Wright and Clarence Norris the following January. Though required to stay in Alabama on parole and work in a factory, both soon fled north, but they agreed to turn themselves in to the authorities to avoid hurting the release and parole prospects of the remaining Scottsboro defendants. They were returned to prison, but Norris was released again in late 1946 along with Powell. In the summer of 1948, after being incarcerated more than seventeen years, Haywood Patterson escaped from the prison farm, and using a harrowing series of tactics to evade the guard dogs that were set on his trail (he drowned two of them), Patterson worked his way north to Detroit, where he later was apprehended by the FBI. Michigan's governor refused to extradite him. Finally, on June 9, 1960, Andy Wright, the last of the Scottsboro defendants, walked out of Kilby Prison on parole after having served nineteen years and two months for a crime that he had not committed.

A reporter asked Wright how he felt. "I have no hard feelings toward anyone," Wright said. Someone else asked him about Victoria Price. "I'm not mad because the girl lied about me," he said. "If she's still living, I feel sorry for her because I don't guess she sleeps much at night." Then, without waiting for any more questions, Wright turned and walked away.

The nine men accused of rape at Scottsboro suffered different fates as their lives proceeded and then wound down. Andy Wright, the last released, was again accused of rape, largely, he believed, because of his reputation as a Scottsboro boy. This time he was acquitted. His younger brother, Roy, returned from a voyage as a merchant marine sailor in 1959, twenty-two years after his release, and discovered his wife at the home of another man. He stabbed her to death and then went back to their apartment and killed himself. Patterson was sentenced to prison for manslaughter in Detroit in 1951 after stabbing a man fatally in a barroom brawl. He died in prison of cancer the following summer. Olen Montgomery reportedly died in Alabama in 1974 and Ozie Powell in Atlanta a year later.

Clarence Norris was the last survivor the group. He had acquired a considerable taste for gambling in prison and that, plus a quick temper (he stabbed a girlfriend once but she did not press charges), often got him into trouble. Or, as Norris puts it: "Over the years I have been arrested and fingerprinted so many times I have lost count." Nonetheless, law enforcement authorities never tumbled to the fact that, seeking to avoid apprehension as a parole violator, he was using his brother Willie's name and his brother's identification papers. Finally, Norris, then living in New York City, got "the best job I ever had," working for the city, cleaning and waxing the floors of a warehouse. "I was my own boss, with nobody hovering over me, telling me what to do." After congressional pressure and much negotiation, Norris finally was granted a full pardon on November 29, 1976, forty-five years after his arrest in Paint Rock, Alabama. He died early in 1989 in New York, at the age of seventy-six. Victoria Price and Ruby Bates disappeared from public sight. Bates, after a speaking tour for the ILD, had gone to work in an upstate New York spinning factory.

NBC v. Victoria Street

Then in 1976 there was a national television show, NBC's "Judge Horton and the Scottsboro Boys," viewed by some forty-one million people. It won numerous prizes, including the Peabody Award for playwriting and awards from the Screenwriter's Guild and the American Bar Association. The show had been produced with the assumption, reported in the first edition of Dan Carter's monumental study of the Scottsboro case, that both Price and Bates were dead—indeed, that they had died in 1961 within thirty miles of each other. The television drama mercilessly portrayed Price as a whore, perjurer, and suborner of perjury.

But Price, married for the preceding twenty-eight years to a sharecropper named Walter Street, was very much alive and had been residing for thirty-five years in the small Tennessee town of Flintville under the name of Katherine Victory Street; on her Social Security card, issued in 1936, she had added "Queen" before Katherine and insisted that this was what she had been christened. She lived on a tobacco farm in a dwelling, a *Washington Post* reporter wrote, "that most people would call a shack." She claimed her correct name always had been "Victory," and that the court had got it wrong in the Scottsboro trial. She sued NBC for $6 million in damages.

In the trial, after the plaintiff had presented her evidence, the judge declared a mistrial on the ground that there existed no material evidence upon which the jury could find in Price's favor on claims of slander or invasion of privacy. When all the evidence had been heard, the same result was reached in regard to the libel claim. On appeal, in a lengthy and difficult decision, the court concluded that Price had remained a "public" person and therefore, on the basis of judicial precedent, she did not have the right to recover damages for defamation. "[O]nce a person becomes a public figure in connection with a particular controversy, that person remains a public figure thereafter for purposes of later commentary or treatment of that controversy." A case that was relied on was *Gertz v. Robert Welch, Inc.* (418 U.S. 323, 1974), involving the Chicago lawyer who, readers may remember, had befriended Nathan Leopold and successfully quarterbacked Leopold's effort to be paroled.

Later, when the U.S. Supreme Court agreed to hear an appeal of the Price case, NBC settled for an amount that remains confidential as part of the agreement. Disregarding her attorney's advice, Price accepted the offer and used the money to buy a small house, a dream she said she had carried with her all her life.

Price, according to one of the lawyers who handled her defamation case, died in 1983 in Lincoln County, Tennessee, about twenty or so miles north of Huntsville, Alabama, where she had been brought up. "She was a pretty good ol' lady," the lawyer recalls. The second attorney who worked with her on the defamation suit retains vivid memories of his client. She had showed up in his office the day after the NBC television show, and her first words were "Does the name Victoria Price mean anything to you?" Taken aback, he blurted out, "But they said you were dead."

Still the mistress of retort, Price answered, "Do I look dead?"

Price was, the lawyer says today, a "country woman, highly intelligent, but feisty and, well, mean-spirited." Price never would say forthrightly that she had not been raped, but the attorney saw in her a certain "swagger," an attitude that conveyed that the Scottsboro boys would not have dared to touch her, combined with a certain pride that she had played the part she chose for herself so well. Ruby Bates Schut, who also filed suit against NBC, was living with her carpenter husband in Washington State; she died on October 27, 1976, in a Yakima hospital, before the appellate court delivered its opinion.

Reporters covering the suit against NBC located two of the men who had served on the jury in the first Decatur trial. Both remained convinced that the defendants were guilty. Franklin Stewart, seventy and still working at the same hardware store that had employed him three decades earlier, dismissed Ruby Bates's recantation. "She was all dressed up," he remembered, "and she was just a country girl. The other side got to her." Arch Earwood, eighty-one, said his vote for guilt came because he was certain that Victoria Price was truthful since "she told her story just like a pig a-trotting."

As They Saw It: Patterson and Norris

Two of the nine Scottsboro defendants would in time produce books that depicted how they felt about this ugly miscarriage of justice. Haywood Patterson, in collaboration with Earl Conrad, devotes virtually all of *Scottsboro Boy* to describing in notably vivid detail the grim and brutalizing conditions that characterized the Alabama prisons in which he did his time. There were casual murders of inmate by inmate and inmate by officer, terrible and relentless beatings of prisoners by guards, and constant humiliations. Patterson tells of his existence in these terms:

> *You had to move through the prison like a cat waiting for other cats to jump on you. The cat might be a guard or a prisoner. You had to see through the back of your head. You had to move your eyes from left to right to see who would come at you. . . . One night I was on the fourth floor leaning off the banister looking down on the main floor. All of a sudden a guy eased up on me with a tenpenny nail sharpened in icepick style. He had driven the nail through the end of a broomstick and it made a devilish dirk.*

Patterson says he jumped out of harm's way just in time. "I knew who he was. He was crazy. He had no reason to jump on me and he needed none. The prison was his reason."

Patterson was in constant trouble for flouting the rules (though it never was clear which rules were meant to be observed and which were mere window dressing). He could be obsequious, skilled in playing the Uncle Tom role to perfection when he deemed it necessary, equally skilled at boldly defying the authorities when he regarded it as essential to his survival or tactically worthwhile.

Patterson had learned to read in prison. He notes that part of his fare was pulp magazines such as *True Detective* and *Inside Detective*. Then, almost as an aside, he uses the contents of these magazines for virtually the only discussion of his own case that he offers:

> *I listened to the prisoners and read the stories and saw that what worked against the Negro was circumstantial evidence. That one thing. This can point to a person's guilt when he is not guilty. The circumstances of a white person's word against a black's, that is evidence in the South. It is the reason why a great many Negroes are in jail. The law of the white folks in the South is, "Don't you dispute my word, nigger." If a white person says you did something, you did it.*

Then Patterson offers a commentary on the only method he knew that would have allowed a black person in the South at that time to combat this condition with any hope of success:

> *There's only one way a Negro can get out of it when this kind of evidence,* white testimony, *is brought in. That is to have rich white folks or labor organizations fronting for you. I saw that in my case. Nine of us were sentenced on the strength of one woman's say-so.* Nobody *backed her up.* Her word *was enough in an Alabama court.*

Then Patterson tells us why he believes this happened:

> *Color is more important than evidence down there. Color is evidence. Black color convicts you. A light Negro stands a better chance in court than a real black one like me. . . . And what is in back of that? They just want us to work for nothing. They do this perfect to us in prison.*

Clarence Norris did not get along well with Patterson at first, though he was close to the other defendants. "Haywood was the type of guy that always kept a lot of bullshit going. There is only so much you can do if you have your head in the mouth of a lion. He did a lot of things against himself."

Norris makes many of the same general points as Patterson in his autobiography, *The Last of the Scottsboro Boys.* Of Kilby Prison, where he was incarcerated, he writes: "I knew I was there because I was a 'nigger.' An animal to be locked up as in a zoo. Except that zoo animals are treated much better than the black men in Kilby Prison. I thought I was a goner and it was only a matter of time." Norris also combines plaintiveness with a sense of the cynical self-serving manner in which he and the other Scottsboro defendants were being used by politicians. "I wondered how much longer the state of Alabama would spend its money to prosecute nine innocent boys in order to send them to their deaths. I couldn't understand it then or now, the hatred." Then he looks for possible motives: "And most of the officials involved with the case tried to use it as a stepladder to success; reputations were won and lost. Organizations became larger and better known. Newspapers sold better, deputies became sheriffs, elected officials were reelected and went on to bigger and better positions. All they had to do was scream, 'Kill those Scottsboro niggers.'"

Rape and the Long Shadow of Scottsboro

The Scottsboro cases exercised a profound influence on the way that criminal justice came to be administered in the United States forever after. It is one of the ironies of political life that persons strongly identified with an ideological position can accomplish things contrary to that position, things that could not be done by those on the other side of the political fence. Richard Nixon, for instance, was able to resume American relationships with Communist China only because Nixon was so notoriously hostile to communism that nobody could sensibly regard his negotiations as a sellout to the forces of evil.

So too with the Scottsboro case. That a deeply conservative Supreme Court could twice overturn the Alabama trial verdicts, and dramatically extend federal constitutional protections to defendants in the state courts, testifies to the powerful impact that the cases exercised. Before we consider their significance for the administration of criminal justice we need to look briefly at issues concerning the crime of forcible rape, the charge that triggered the Scottsboro case.

For several centuries there was a deeply embedded premise in Anglo-American law that women were likely to claim falsely that they had been raped if they found themselves in a tight situation from which they thought such an allegation could extricate them. This position was most strongly enunciated by Sir Matthew Hale, a seventeenth-century English jurist, who wrote in his *Pleas of the Crown* about a man with a hernia that dropped his stomach to his knees, making sexual intercourse impossible. Nonetheless, this man, Hale wrote, was falsely accused of rape. Hale's conclusion on the issue was framed in words that would be later read to juries in California and many other states in every case of sexual assault: Rape, it ran, is "a charge which is easily made and once made, difficult to defend against, even if the person is innocent. Therefore, the law requires you to examine the testimony of the female person named in the information with caution."

Ironically, despite overwhelming evidence regarding the absurdity of the charges, Hale himself imposed a sentence of death on two women accused of witchcraft at the Bury St. Edmunds assize in 1662. Witchcraft, unlike rape, represented an accusation that truly is easily alleged and virtually impossible to defend against. How do you satisfactorily demonstrate that it is not your spirit that is flying about the rafters of the courtroom on a broomstick and tormenting your accusers?

Susan Brownmiller in her classic study of rape, *Against Our Will*, connects the powerful survival of this archaic juridical doctrine into contemporary times to Scottsboro, at least in regard to interracial rape. "If one case convinced the American public—and international opinion—that lying, scheming white women who cried rape were directly responsible for the terrible penalties inflicted on black men, the name of that case was Scottsboro." The case, Brownmiller writes, remains "damning proof to liberals everywhere of Eve incarnate and that the concept of Original Sin was a no-good, promiscuous woman who rode a freight train through Alabama."

But Brownmiller offers her own spin on the case, noting that Victoria Price and Ruby Bates were *kept in jail* (the emphasis is hers) with possible vagrancy and prostitution charges hanging over them. Brownmiller believes that "[t]he singular opportunity afforded Price and Bates [to cry rape] should be appreciated by every woman." She implies that charging rape constitutes a weapon, the power of which is (or should be) appreciated by all women—and presumably is irresistible if conditions become sufficiently threatening for women. But this is not Brownmiller's only didactic theme. She wonders whether, if women had been allowed on the Scottsboro case juries, they might have seen through the facade of the rape allegation. Would they, Brownmiller asks rhetorically, have been better able to understand the import of dead, immobile sperm in Victoria Price's cervix? For Brownmiller, Victoria Price and Ruby Bates, like all women, were "movable pawns" of the male power structure. "They were corralled by a posse of white men who already believed a rape had taken place. Confused and fearful they fell into line." It was men who led the women to accuse other men, though she grants that the women did so "to save their own skins."

The actual situation, taking the Scottsboro case as a whole, would appear rather more complicated than Brownmiller makes it. The blacks were rounded up at Pine Rock on the basis of the accusations of the whites they had earlier fought with and bested. It is arguable whether either Price or Bates would have come under legal scrutiny; after all, riding the rails was also what the white males had been doing and they most certainly would not be legally detained. One could also argue that the rape charges, though perhaps fueled originally by self-protection, were continued out of self-interest and probably a certain pleasure from being in the limelight.

If Price was lying, and there seems to be no doubt that she was, the case may offer some contemporary concern about the limiting of cross-examination of women who bring rape charges. If a woman has been "unlawfully violated," Callahan observed, "she may appeal to the courts with an abiding faith that no accusing finger can be pointed to her erring past or hopeless future, as an excuse for denying to her full and adequate protection of the law." At Scottsboro, therefore, how Victoria Price had come by the small amount of nonmotile semen in her cervix was deemed irrelevant, and jury members therefore could more readily conclude that it was the product of the alleged rape.

Judge Callahan at Decatur frustrated Leibowitz's incessant efforts to show that Victoria Price had sexual relations with her boyfriend in the hobo camp. The trial transcript shows several interactions such as this one:

> *Q to Price: Did you go to the hoboes' jungle with them [Bates's and Price's boyfriends]?*
>
> *Mr. Knight objected to the question. The court sustained the objection. Mr. Leibowitz said: Will you let me tell your Honor what I would like to prove by the witness by this question? The court refused: I adhere to my ruling. I can imagine what you want to prove. Mr. Leibowitz reserved an exception.*

In the realm of rape accusations, Scottsboro is something of an aberration, though much less so for an interracial rape with a white accuser. In the United States, men guilty of rape often go free because the details of a rape are known only to the participants, and the accusers are unable to convince the authorities or a judge or jury beyond a reasonable doubt of the accused's culpability. This happens despite the fact that rape charges are likely to be based on fact. But what are we to do with the likes of prosecuting witnesses such as Victoria Price? At what point do newer evidentiary rules, such as those that can restrict evidence of previous sexual conduct, push toward the kind of consequence that befell the Scottsboro defendants? Perhaps time has taken the edge off the fierce fear of interracial sexual relationships that marked southern etiquette and the false front of protecting "southern womanhood" that closed jurors' minds to overwhelming evidence of the accused's innocence. Rape ceased to be a capital offense in the United States in 1977 (*Coker v. Georgia* 433 U.S. 584) on the ground that the penalty was disproportionate to the offense. But its equitable prosecution—the law's ability to convict the guilty and acquit the innocent—continues to present some of the most difficult dilemmas in the administration of criminal justice.

Scottsboro and Constitutional Rights

The decision in *Powell* regarding adequate legal representation and that in *Norris* regarding the inclusion of blacks on juries had profound implications for the fair administration of criminal justice, primarily because they initiated close federal court scrutiny of state practices. These decisions, one commentator has pointed out, were a principal landmark in "a new liberty which gives the nation a bill of rights against state action." Particularly noteworthy was the response at the time the *Norris* decision was handed down of Alabama Governor Bibb Graves, a strong segregationist. Graves sent a letter to each of the state's trial judges regarding the Supreme Court's ruling. He was notably tactful. "I do not assume or intimate that the contents of the jury boxes in any way fail to conform to all legal requirements," Graves noted, pussyfooting around the obvious truth that they did not do so. Nonetheless, Graves stood fast for justice: "Holdings of the United States Supreme Court," he wrote, "are the supreme law of the land. Whether we like the decisions or not, it is the patriotic duty of every citizen and the sworn duty of every public official to accept and uphold them in letter and spirit."

For its part, the Supreme Court took a monumental step toward increasing fairness in criminal proceedings. The vague words of the Fourteenth Amendment in the past had been used to protect property rights and to nullify New Deal legislation. Now a set of conservative justices applied the constitutional doctrine for the purpose for which it had been adopted, to protect black people from oppression. To do so, they had to intrude themselves into the practices of a sovereign state, a juridical penetration that would have great significance for upgrading the quality of criminal justice throughout the country.

At the same time, the Supreme Court highlighted starkly the appalling inadequacy of a major premise on which criminal justice operates: that if procedural regularities are observed scrupulously (or more or less scrupulously) justice will prevail. Provide an adequate attorney for the defendants and allow their peers to sit on the jury and a just verdict will be reached. In truth, though, as the Scottsboro case vividly demonstrated, these matters were, at least in this instance, quite beside the point. A rural Alabama jury was going to convict the Scottsboro defendants because it was beyond reason to reject the claim of a white woman, of whatever sexual notoriety, that she had been raped by black men.

For Stephen Landsman, the Scottsboro case was a pivotal event that propelled legal developments in the United States in a positive direction. "The tales a society tells about great trials can help identify the central conflicts of an era." Then he adds:

Critical cases often involve a clash between governing authority and those who would consciously challenge it. In such proceedings, those in control seem willing to ignore fair play in order to suppress a perceived threat. Yet often, at least in democracies, the opposition is powerful enough to challenge this behavior, and the rulers are uncertain enough of themselves to have second thoughts about their chosen course of action. Out of the ensuing clash of forces, a set of lessons, or a story, may emerge that leads to a reordering of the legal process or even of relations in a society as a whole.

However grandiose such an interpretation, it undoubtedly has a ring of truth in regard to the judicial tribulations and terrors that befell the nine black men arrested at Paint Rock in 1931 for a crime that they had not committed. They paid an unconscionably huge personal price for whatever changes their situation may have produced in the world about them. Nor by any means have the questions the Scottsboro case raised—most particularly the relationship in the United States between the ruling whites and the black minority—reached a settled and satisfactory state. Memories of the case dig deep, and it is not surprising that a recent essay on a murder trial two-thirds of a century later would be titled: "From Scottsboro to Simpson."

What Else Might Have Happened?

The story of Scottsboro presented here dovetails with interpretations found in every responsible report of that sensational case. But there remain a number of perplexing elements that challenge the acceptance of conventional wisdom about what happened—or, more accurately, what did not happen. Nobody can reasonably dispute that all nine of the Scottsboro defendants clearly were not guilty of the alleged rapes of Victoria Price and Ruby Bates. It is chilling too to appreciate that had Price and Bates confined their accusations to one person each, it is very likely that the individuals they named would have been tried summarily and executed, and the case would have become one of innumerable barely noticed instances of awful racial injustice.

At the same time, commentators on the Scottsboro trials have not pursued all the implications of information that suggests—though it certainly does not prove—that the gondola cars were not an uneventful site as the train moved toward Paint Rock. Nor does it seem unlikely that the prosecution and perhaps the defense were aware of a scenario different from what either offered in court, and that they appreciated that it was to neither's advantage to probe some issues more deeply.

The involvement of Orville Gilley (a.k.a. Carolina Slim) in the trials is one piece of the puzzle. Gilley, the white man drawn back into the car by the blacks for his own safety because the train had picked up considerable speed, was the only eyewitness with no alleged involvement in the rapes. Price testified that she had been "lying on Gilley's lap" for about five or ten minutes before the train stopped at Paint Rock. We also know that the night before boarding the train Price had sexual relations with a man named Tiller and then spent the evening sleeping by Gilley's side in the hobo camp. Add to this Bates's testimony that before the white boys had been thrown off the train Price had said that if she knew that Gilley and another man were not likely to return to the chert car soon, she and Ruby "would go over there and make some money from these boys."

Gilley reportedly had denied before the grand jury Price's allegations of rape. He made a cameo appearance in one of the trials at Scottsboro, saying only that he saw five blacks in the gondola car, while he lay huddled in a corner. He did not testify about rape and was not cross-examined. Gilley was in California during the first Decatur trial, but played a prominent role in the second. On the stand, he maintained that he saw Price and Bates being raped, though his depiction of the scene differed in several important respects from Price's story. The defense was barred by the judge from questioning Gilley about any other sexual involvement that he or others might have had with Price or Bates. It also came out that Gilley and his mother had been receiving money from the prosecutor's office prior to the trial. Gilley did not appear in the subsequent Decatur trial; he was in prison for assaulting and robbing two women.

If truthful, would Gilley have said that Price and Bates had had consensual intercourse with the blacks, or perhaps, though very much less likely, that one or two of them, with Patterson and Norris the most reasonable choices, had taken the women by force? Had he himself had sex with the women, or had some of the white boys who had been thrown from the train? Testimony along these lines at a minimum would have led to the release of at least seven of the Scottsboro defendants. It also could have jeopardized the prosecution's case by exposing Price as promiscuous and a blatant liar in terms of her statement that five or six (the number varied) of the young black men had raped her. Gilley was a loose cannon, and the state's tactic might have been to keep him muzzled until he could be depended on to tell the "right" story.

The sequence in which the defendants were tried and the order in which they were released also seem to tell a story. Norris and Weems were the first defendants in the trials at Scottsboro; at Decatur, Patterson was the only person tried before Judge Horton called an end to the proceedings. At later trials the focus was largely on Patterson and Norris, and sometimes Weems.

Undoubtedly, the prosecutor believed that his strongest case was against these men, particularly since virtually the only identification evidence Victoria Price offered was that her first assailant had been a big and strong man: a description that fits Patterson, Norris, and Weems far better than it would the other defendants. Patterson was never released; he had to escape from prison, and Norris was one of the last of the defendants to be paroled.

Why too did the state later offer the Scottsboro boys a plea bargain that would have them admit to the criminal offense of miscegenation in exchange for reduced sentences, most of which they had already served? Miscegenation, charged almost exclusively in black-white marriages or ongoing liaisons, invariably indicated a consensual relationship. Was the state willing to abandon its position about the white-woman purity of Price and Bates and align the penalty with a truer reading of what it knew to be the facts of the case?

The evidence regarding sperm in the vaginal tracts of the two accusing women is not altogether clear-cut. At the first trial, Dr. Bridges said that he had found "a very great amount" of sperm when he examined Victoria Price and Ruby Bates. At all later trials, he would maintain that he had difficulty locating any sperm, and most of what he did find had lost its motility. Why did the doctor take such contradictory positions? Could he have balked after the first trial at the prospect of the nine defendants being executed on the basis of what he had said?

The testimony at the first trial by some Scottsboro defendants, including Patterson, that several of their number, but not they themselves, had raped Price and Bates certainly may have been the result of earlier threats by their interrogators. But they also could have known that something untoward had happened and been concerned only that the finger of guilt not be pointed at them.

Finally, there are the diverse stories of Ruby Bates. First, she joined Price in supporting her allegations of rape. Then, after a trip north, she recanted, providing the defense (and commentators on the trial) with powerful evidence that the whole story was fabricated, that nothing had gone on in that gondola car. But matters did not end there. Between the first and second trials, writing to a boyfriend whose attentions were wandering, Bates in January 1932 offered the following exculpatory statement about her sexual involvement with blacks. It read in part:

> *i want to make a statement too you Mary Sanders is goddam lie about those Negroes jassing me those police made me tell a lie that is my statement because i Want to clear*

my self that is all to it if you Want too Believe ok. if not that is ok. . . . those Negroes did not touch me or those white Boys i hope you believe me the law dont.

A few sentences later came a rather different statement:

. . . it is the gods truth i hope you Will Believe me i was jazed But those white Boys jazed me i Wish those Negroes are not Burnt on account of me it is these white Boys fault that is my statement. . . .

Finally came a postscript: "P.S. this is one time that I might tell a lie. But it is the truth so god help me." Hauled off to the police station the following day, Bates was pressed to sign a paper saying that she was drunk and didn't know what she was doing when she had written this letter.

Many years later in her old age (she had changed her first name to Lucille and married a man named Schut), Bates offered another version of her story, saying that Price had been raped by the largest of the men, presumably Patterson, perhaps Norris or Weems. The report of this claim came by way of William Bradford Huie, a writer who in *Mud on the Stars* had movingly deplored in fiction the execution in the electric chair in Alabama of a young black man who had been convicted of the rape of a white woman who encouraged their relationship. (In *The Execution of Private Slovik*, Huie told the story of a wimpy Michigan boy, enlisted in the U.S. Army during the Second World War as an alternative to a jail term. Slovik was emotionally unfit for combat but, because nobody in the chain of command had the guts to halt it, he was executed by an army firing squad for cowardice in refusing to fight, the only person so dealt with by the U.S. Army since the Civil War.)

It was to Huie at his home in 1964 and at her home a dozen years later (as Huie told a *Birmingham News* reporter) that Ruby Bates said that she had been raped. She said she had changed her testimony because people up North had convinced her that it would cause her personal misery if it was believed that she had been raped by a black man. Huie had met Bates when she was hired as a practical nurse to look after his dying mother-in-law.

In 1976, Huie visited Bates in Tacoma and asked her point-blank whether she had been raped. She first said, "What do you think?" Then she added that she hadn't been raped because she was wearing overalls, while Price was wearing a dress—hardly an accurate statement. After that, when her husband had left the room, Bates turned to Huie and said: "You remember what I told you before." This last conversation, however, has to be considered in its context: it took place while Bates was suing NBC for damages, and it was to her advantage to reassume the role of victim.

What can we make of these teasing clues? We suspect that something sexual probably happened in the gondola car before it reached Paint Rock. We suspect that both Price and Bates had consensual sexual intercourse, perhaps with one or two of the blacks, perhaps with the white boys and Gilley alone or as well. Whether they did so, if they did, for money or for play we do not know. We also accept as reasonable the judgment regarding our speculations by Dan Carter, the leading historian of the Scottsboro case. What we suggest, Carter notes in a letter, is "not impossible," and, though "we can assert until hell freezes over, none of us will ever know with absolute certainty what happened."

For Further Reading

The most comprehensive report on the Scottsboro case is Dan T. Carter, *Scottsboro: A Tragedy of the American South* (Baton Rouge: Louisiana State University Press, 1969; rev. ed., 1979). The revised edition adds (pp. 416–422) a detailed report of Victoria Price's suit against NBC. Carter meticulously combed archives and employs with telling effect excerpts from many of the letters that the Scottsboro boys wrote to those seeking to free them. The book is based on his 1967 Ph.D. dissertation at the University of North Carolina, "The Scottsboro Case, 1931–1950," which contains additional details.

It is worth noting a letter that Carter wrote to Clarence Norris years later, when Norris sought vindication from Alabama:

> *There is today an organization called the "Flat Earth Society." Its thousands of members believe that the earth is flat and no amount of proof or persuasion can convince them otherwise. Well, I spent the better part of two years researching and writing an account of that [Scottsboro] case. I read over 10,000 pages of trial transcripts; I went over hundreds of newspaper accounts and first-hand reports. I read through the correspondence of every major organization involved in the case. Finally, I reviewed the medical testimony with several experts in the field. And I tell you flatly that I would join the Flat Earth Society before I would accept the notion that Victoria Price and Ruby Bates were raped on March 25, 1931.*

More recently, in *Stories of Scottsboro* (New York: Pantheon Books, 1994), Harvard historian James E. Goodman brings together in collage style different perspectives on the ingredients of the Scottsboro case. Goodman focuses not only on details of the case itself and how persons interpreted them, but also on the broader implications of the Scottsboro trials for race relations in the North and in the South.

The Alabama viewpoint, with a scalding diatribe against Communist interference with their local affairs, appears in Files Crenshaw, Jr., and Kenneth A. Miller, *Scottsboro: The Firebrand of Communism* (Montgomery, Ala: Brown Printing Co., 1936). The book contains long verbatim transcripts of the various trials that, though somewhat partially selected, provide a strong sense of the courtroom proceedings.

An excellent short report on the Scottsboro case for younger readers is James Haskins, *The Scottsboro Boys* (New York: Henry Holt, 1994). The history of the town of Scottsboro is set out in W. Jerry Gist, *The Story of Scottsboro, Alabama* (Nashville, Tenn.: Rich Printing Co., 1968), which includes a very one-sided (the state of Alabama's side) account of the trial, pp. 185–243. Decatur's history can be found in William H. Jenkins and John Knox, *The Story of Decatur, Alabama* (Decatur: Decatur Printing Co., 1970). Though largely reprinting excerpts from the trial transcripts, Gillian White Goodrich's master's thesis in history, "James Edwin Horton, Jr.: Scottsboro Judge" (University of Alabama, 1974), offers some useful biographical information about its subject.

Allan K. Chalmers tells of his untiring efforts to free the Scottsboro defendants when he was head of the Scottsboro Defense Committee in *They Shall Be Free* (Garden City, N.Y.: Doubleday, 1951). Two of the Scottsboro defendants later collaborated on books that provide valuable details of their experiences and attitudes: Haywood Patterson and Earl Conrad, *Scottsboro Boy* (Garden City, N.Y.: Doubleday, 1950); and Clarence Norris and Sybil D. Washington, *The Last of the Scottsboro Boys* (New York: G. P. Putnam's Sons, 1979). The Norris-Washington book incorporates several reproductions of trial transcripts and court decisions. More recently, Kwando Mbiassi has published the results of a series of interviews he conducted with Norris in *The Man from Scottsboro: Clarence Norris and the Infamous Rape Trial in His Own Words* (Jefferson, N.C.: MacFarland, 1997).

Shorter essays on the case include a well-written early article, "The Freight-Car Case," by Edmund Wilson in the *New Republic*, August 26, 1931, pp. 38–43; and Arthur Garfield Hays's *Trial by Prejudice* (New York: Da Capo Press, 1970), pp. 25–150. Hays was an associate counsel with Clarence Darrow during their ill-fated negotiations with the ILD for control of the case. Another report is Dee Garrison, ed., *Rebel Pen: The Writings of Mary Heaton Vorse* (New

York: Monthly Review Press, 1985), pp. 148–152. Vorse was present at the first Decatur trial. Legal implications of the case are briefly addressed in Robert F. Martin, "The Scottsboro Cases," in John W. Johnson, ed., *Historic United States Court Cases, 1690–1990: An Encyclopedia* (New York: Garland, 1992), pp. 382–388. The quarrel between the ILD and the NAACP is reviewed in detail in several articles by Hugh T. Murray, Jr., including "Aspects of the Scottsboro Campaign," *Science and Society*, 35 (1971):177–192, and "The NAACP versus the Communist Party: The Scottsboro Rape Case, 1931–1932," in Bernard Sternsher, ed., *The Negro in Depression and War: Prelude to Revolution, 1930–1945* (Chicago: Quadrangle, 1976), pp. 267–281. Murray also discusses literary and artistic offspring of the case in "Changing America and the Changing Image of Scottsboro," *Phylon*, 38 (1977):82–92.

There are three biographies of Leibowitz that put the Scottsboro case into the context of his career as a lawyer and a trial and appellate court judge in New York: Leibowitz's son, Robert, wrote *The Defender: The Life and Career of Samuel S. Leibowitz, 1893–1933* (Englewood Cliffs, N.J., 1981), in which pp. 185–249 deal with the Scottsboro case, largely by reprinting verbatim sections of the transcript of the first trial in Decatur. The other books are Quentin Reynolds, *Courtroom: The Story of Samuel S. Leibowitz* (New York: Farrar, Straus, 1950), especially pp. 248–314 on Scottsboro; and Fred D. Pasley, *Not Guilty!: The Story of Samuel Leibowitz* (New York: G. P. Putnam's Sons, 1933), with pp. 226–278 devoted to the Scottsboro case.

The appellate court decisions provide useful information: for the trial in Scottsboro see *Patterson v. State*, 224 Ala. 531, 141 So. 195 (1932); *Powell v. State*, 224 Ala. 540, 141 So. 201 (1932); and *Weems et al. v. State*, 224 Ala. 524, 141 So. 215 (1932). The Supreme Court decision appears as *Powell v. Alabama*, 287 U.S. 45 (1932). The decisions on appeals from the first Decatur trial can be found in *Norris v. State*, 229 Ala. 226, 156 So. 556 (1934); *Patterson v. State*, 229 Ala. 270, 156 So. 567 (1934); *Norris v. Alabama*, 294 U.S. 587 (1935); and *Patterson v. Alabama*, 294 U.S. 600 (1935). The second Decatur trial is considered in *Patterson v. State*, 234 Ala. 342, 175 So. 371 (1937). Certiorari was denied by the U.S. Supreme Court, 302 U.S. 733 (1937).

The decision on Victoria Price's claim against NBC is reported in *Street v. National Broadcasting Company*, 512 F. Supp. 398 (E.D. Tenn. 1977), *aff'd* 645 F.2d 1227 (6th Cir.), *cert. denied* 454 U.S. 1095 (1961), which also includes a complete transcript of Judge Horton's ruling mandating a retrial after the first Decatur trial. Raymond W. Fraley, Jr., and Don Wyatt were the two Fayetteville, Tenn., lawyers who talked with us about Price and the case they handled for her. Fraley very kindly supplied his file on the case for our use.

Particularly good interpretations of the Supreme Court decision in *Powell v. Alabama* are provided in Francis Heller, *The Sixth Amendment to the Constitution of the United States* (Lawrence: University of Kansas Press, 1951), pp. 121–127; and Hadley Arkes, *The Return of George Sutherland: Restoring Jurisprudence of National Rights* (Princeton, N.J.: Princeton University Press, 1994), pp. 262–273.

Chapter Four

Bruno Richard Hauptmann (1932),
Public Outrage,
and Criminal Justice

Bruno Richard Hauptmann, thirty-six years old, an illegal German immigrant in the United States, was executed in the electric chair at the New Jersey State Prison in Trenton on April 3, 1936. Hauptmann was pronounced dead at 8:47 P.M. by the doctor in attendance. He had been sentenced to die for the felony-murder of the twenty-month-old child of Anne Morrow Lindbergh and Charles A. Lindbergh, probably the most idolized couple in the United States.

Lindbergh, thirty years old when his child was kidnapped, was a daredevil pilot who had broken the time record for transcontinental flight and then captivated the world in May 1927 by becoming the first person to fly solo nonstop across the Atlantic Ocean, from New York to Paris. He was greeted on landing at Paris's Le Bourget Aerodrome in the middle of the night by more than a hundred thousand people. The 3,614-mile flight had taken thirty-three hours and thirty minutes: at one point, Lindbergh flew only five feet above the ocean waves so that their spray would keep him awake. His fragile single-engine craft, the *Spirit of St. Louis,* which had no sextant, no radio, and no port window, can be seen today suspended as a large mobile from the ceiling in the main gallery of the Smithsonian Institution National Air and Space Museum in Washington, D.C.

Lindbergh had a Swedish-American background. His father had been a congressman from Minnesota. His mother, separated from Lindbergh's father when Charles was fourteen years old, taught high school chemistry in upscale Grosse Point, Michigan. Lindbergh's good looks, his lanky frame that led to the nickname Slim, his dignity, and his shy diffidence combined with an aloofness and a mere hint of disdain endeared him to the public. His wife, twenty-five years old at the time of the kidnapping, would later become a highly regarded poet and evocative writer. She was the daughter of Dwight Morrow, a J. P. Morgan banking company partner and one of America's richest men.

There were numerous delays that night before Hauptmann was executed, as his attorneys frantically sought to halt the proceedings. New Jersey's governor had postponed the execution twice, believing that others had been involved with Hauptmann and that, facing imminent death, he might trade his coconspirators' names for a life sentence. Gabriel Heatter, a prominent radio news broadcaster, was forced to improvise on the air for an extra hour until the signal was given inside the prison for the executioner to pull the switch, sending two thousand volts of electricity through Hauptmann's body. Among those with strongly imprinted memories of Heatter's radio broadcast more than sixty years ago is one of the present authors, who still can recall Heatter's sudden dramatic sign-off:

"Bruno Richard Hauptmann is dead," he intoned.[1]

Hauptmann died proclaiming his innocence. His execution, like the killing of Lee Harvey Oswald by Jack Ruby years later, ended any possibility of hearing from the mouth of the alleged perpetrator what had happened. A desire for clear-cut resolution of murky circumstances is characteristic of notorious crimes. (Note most recently the attempt to elicit a "true confession" from James Earl Ray, the convicted assassin of Martin Luther King, Jr., before Ray died.)

There are strikingly different judgments about whether justice was served in the Lindbergh case. These differences are conveyed in the two following quotations, one expressing satisfaction that justice had been done, the other equally certain that the Hauptmann case made a mockery of the search for truth.

A lawyer, Francis X. Busch, in a burst of emotional tabloid-style prose, saw the case this way:

> *The kidnapping and killing of the Lindbergh baby stirred the emotions of the American public as no other crime has done in the last fifty years. From one end of the country to the other, fathers and mothers shared the anxiety of the beloved and distracted parents*

---

1. There has been some mild slippage in that memory, however. In his autobiography, Heatter indicates that what he said was: "Ladies and gentlemen, Bruno Hauptmann is dead. Good night."

during the supposed negotiations for their child's safe return. When, after more than two years, the culprit was discovered and put on trial, the day-to-day proceedings in the little old courthouse at Flemington, New Jersey, claimed top priority in every newspaper and news radio program in the nation. This discovery, as the result of one of the most amazing investigations in criminal history, of an incredible concatenation of incriminatory facts and circumstances, the intelligent and forceful presentation of the technical and unusual aspects of the case to a law jury, and the celerity with which the appeal from the judgment of conviction was fully and dispassionately considered and disposed of by the court of last resort increased public confidence in the effectiveness of the judicial process.

Anthony Scaduto, a journalist, writing two decades after Busch, reaches a very different conclusion:

Richard Hauptmann was the victim of men who distorted truth and manufactured evidence and rushed him into the electric chair. That Hauptmann was made a scapegoat because of police frustrations, because of an obsession to punish someone, anyone, for committing such a foul act upon the child of the hero Lindbergh, upon Lindbergh himself, is evident. The proof is overwhelming. There was no conspiracy per se to convict Hauptmann, but Hauptmann was the victim of something more dreadful. He was the victim of individual perjurers who believed they were acting justly, morally— with God on their side—in twisting to make more perfect the case against the man they believed guilty. It was a classic instance of the weakness of the adversary system of justice.

These last sentiments are echoed by the crime writer Noel Behn: "I had become convinced," he observes, "that Hauptmann's trial was a raucous tragedy, that with few exceptions prosecution witnesses had either distorted the truth or committed flat-out perjury, that the state police had tampered with physical evidence, and, in many cases, suppressed vital information."

What, then, do we have here? Do we have the framing of an innocent man, at least innocent of the felony-murder charge? Or is this yet another implausible set of conspiracy theories of the kind that seem to arise in the wake of sensational and complicated cases in which loose ends inevitably hang out—as in the Kennedy assassination, the killing of Martin Luther King, Jr., and, as we shall see, the O. J. Simpson case?

The fact that much evidence pointing toward the railroading of Hauptmann was not entered into the trial record but uncovered many decades later complicates presentation of the details of the case. Hauptmann's attorney, Edward J. Reilly, was hired by the Hearst newspapers, who were certain of Hauptmann's guilt. Reilly, often drunk, talked with Hauptmann in jail for less than an hour during the four months before the trial. Two years after the trial Reilly would be confined to a mental hospital and die there from the ravages of syphilis. We will not seek at first to compensate for Reilly's inadequacy, but generally will present the evidence as the jury heard it and reserve for later pages subsequent challenges to its accuracy.

The Crime and the Search for the Perpetrator(s)

On March 1, 1932, Charles A. Lindbergh, Jr., a handsome, pudgy child with blond ringlets, was taken from the upstairs nursery room of his parents' fourteen-room country house. The house had been built in a vaguely French-manor style and was situated amid dense woods and a meadow on almost four hundred acres of land in rural Hunterdon County in New Jersey, twenty-one miles southwest of Trenton, New Jersey's capital, and about sixty miles from New York City. The child's absence was discovered at about ten o'clock in the evening by Betty Gow, his Scottish nursemaid, when she went to check on him before retiring. She and Anne Lindbergh, who was three months pregnant, had put the child to bed at about six o'clock, after Betty Gow had sewn a high-necked flannel shirt for him and daubed it with Vicks VapoRub to treat his chest cold.

There was no sign of a struggle or of a forced entry into the nursery. Because of warping, one of the three windows in the room had not been secured. There was a clump of yellow clay on a trunk near the window, and the top crib sheet remained fastened with safety pins, suggesting that the child had been lifted from his bed. No one had heard the baby cry, nor had there been any barking by the family's black-and-white fox terrier, a matter later variously charged to its old age and amiable nature, to the fact that it was on the other side of the house, or to the noise of howling winds and rain that drowned out any other sound.[2]

One item in particular would continually bedevil those seeking to explain the Lindbergh kidnapping case. The Lindberghs never had stayed at their country house on a Tuesday evening that year: they always went to Anne Lindbergh's widowed mother at Day Hill, her nearby fifty-two-acre estate.

---

2. The disconcerting inability of those who investigated and those who wrote about the Hauptmann case to agree on facts is illustrated in a small way when Noel Behn says the dog was named Wahgoosh, Edward Oxford reports its name as Skean, and the FBI files identify it as Trixie.

This time they had decided not to move the infant because of the nasty weather and the fact that he still showed signs of his three-day-old cold. The kidnapper must have learned—somehow—that the Lindberghs would be in their own house this particular Tuesday and must have been told, or figured out, which room the baby slept in and when he might be unattended. It was also difficult to understand why the kidnapper had taken the child before the people in the house had gone to bed, after which he could have been more certain of not being interrupted, though he might have known that two bedrooms were close to the nursery. In addition, oddly, Lindbergh was at home that evening because he had failed to remember that he was one of the two guests of honor at a New York University alumni dinner for 1,800 persons at the Waldorf-Astoria Hotel to celebrate the school's hundredth anniversary.

After summoning the police, Lindbergh showed them part of a folding ladder that was lying about seventy-five feet from the house. Two other portions of the ladder, as well as a dowel pin and a chisel, were discovered nearby. The chisel apparently had been carried to pry open the nursery window. The slender, homemade thirty-eight-pound ladder was of an unusual design: the middle and top sections could be folded into the bottom part so that it could be carried easily. Marks on the outside wall showed where the ladder had been propped against the house. Rather inexpertly constructed, the ladder had broken, presumably when the kidnapper was carrying the extra weight of the Lindbergh child on his way down from the window. Other possible clues outside the house soon were eradicated as mobs of people descended on the estate once the news of the kidnapping became public.

An envelope, first opened in the presence of the police, had been left in the nursery. It contained a demand for $50,000 in ransom money (the equivalent of about one and a half million dollars today) and instructed Lindbergh not to alert the police. The letter was marked by a distinctive set of symbols, two interlocking circles and an egg-shaped oval where they overlapped. The circles were outlined in blue, the oval was solid red, and three square holes were punched in a horizontal line into the three parts of the design. That symbol later was said to have been printed on targets used by German machine- gunners during the war. The ransom note, printed in large block letters, read as follows:

Dear Sir!

Have 50000$ ready 25000$ in 20$ bills 15000$ in 10$ bills and 10000$ in 5$ bills After 2–4 days we will inform you were to deliver the mony We warn you for making anyding public or for notify the Police The child is in gut care.

Indication for all letters are singnature and three holes.

It seemed very likely that the letter had been written by a person still steeped in a European culture (thus the dollar sign after the amounts) who at times used phonetic spellings (as in mony and singnature). Specifically, the writer probably was German (thus gut for good). Of course, the letter might have been dictated or it might have been a shrewd attempt to throw its recipients off the trail. Each succeeding ransom letter was filled with similar kinds of errors. Difficult words, though, tended to be spelled correctly, suggesting that the writer had looked them up in a dictionary.

Public outrage in the wake of the kidnapping was enormous, and there was deep sympathy for the parents, who received more than thirty-eight thousand pieces of mail during the weeks after their child was taken. Organized crime figures were among the first suspects, and Lindbergh hired several persons with presumed links to criminal gangs to try to obtain the return of his child. At the same time, a number of police forces, including local, state, and federal agencies, never well coordinated, picked at different aspects of the case. Overall responsibility lay with the superintendent of the New Jersey State Police, H. Norman Schwarzkopf, whose recognition for his work on the Lindbergh kidnapping case would be eclipsed by the exploits of his warrior son, also named Norman, who would command the coalition forces in Operation Desert Storm in the Persian Gulf War in 1991. The senior Schwarzkopf, a graduate of the U.S. Military Academy, had seen active service in the First World War as an artillery officer. Then, in 1921, when he was twenty-six, he had been named to head the newly formed New Jersey State Police Force.

Initial efforts to solve the Lindbergh kidnapping case took three major forms. First, there was the attempted liaison with organized crime. Nothing came of this, though several extortion plots were hatched by imaginative con-men that ate up a good deal of the time and energy of those seeking to locate the child. Second, there was a strenuous effort to trace the ladder by finding the original site where the wood had been milled and the resale companies to which it had been shipped. Evidence about the ladder that was painstakingly developed later would prove highly incriminating. The third approach focused on the household servants employed by the Lindberghs. The police zeroed in on a maid, twenty-eight-year-old Violet Sharpe. She had been seeing Finn Henrik ("Red") Johnson, a Norwegian working on the *Reynard*, a yacht owned by the millionaire Thomas Lamont. Sharpe had told Johnson before the kidnapping that she could not keep a date with him because the family unexpectedly would be remaining overnight at the Lindbergh house that Tuesday. She at first lied to her interrogators regarding her date with Johnson, perhaps because she was being courted by the butler in the Lindbergh house and did not want him to learn of her dalliance. She was pressed incessantly by the police during a series of very tough sessions. On the evening of another scheduled interrogation, Sharpe opened a can of cyanide chloride that was used for polishing the household silverware, poured the crystals into a glass, added water, swallowed the mixture, and staggered down the stairs. By the time a doctor could reach the scene, she was dead.

Soon after the kidnapping, Lindbergh issued a statement that he wished to establish personal contact with the kidnappers. He said that he would make no attempt to apprehend them when and after they returned his child. The Lindberghs also released to the newspapers details regarding the baby's diet and his special needs if he became ill; his heartbroken mother pleaded for his abductors to take good care of him. The next ransom note, identifiable by the distinctive symbol on the bottom, assured the parents that a nurse was caring for the child and that the instructions about dietary requirements were being scrupulously followed.

Lindbergh was powerful—that is, he was rich, famous, and strongly opinionated—and by now he had become accustomed to having his own way. He made it very clear from the beginning that he was calling the shots in the kidnapping investigation. Understandably, his sole focus was on recovering his child alive. But the matter was not straightforward. The question that was never addressed, both out of compassion and because of Lindbergh's standing, was this: Would it not encourage further kidnappings if the ransom demand was met and the kidnapper permitted to go his way untouched? The year after the Lindbergh kidnapping, the governor of New York proposed a penalty against those who privately negotiated with kidnappers, arguing: "We cannot afford to consider the feelings or interest of an individual when it conflicts with the safety and welfare of the people as a whole." The New York measure did not succeed, but many years later governments, most notably the Israelis, made it plain—and with considerable success—that they would not negotiate with anyone who used kidnapped hostages as bargaining chips.

A second ransom note arrived four days after the kidnapping and raised the ante to $70,000 on the ground that the situation had been made more hazardous because of the involvement of the police and the press. Meanwhile, in a quixotic endeavor, Dr. John F. Condon put a personal advertisement in the *Bronx Home News*, an afternoon newspaper with a circulation of about 100,000 that covered the borough north of Manhattan, saying that he would add $1,000 of his own money for the kidnapper and would serve as the go-between for the return of the baby. Condon forever after would be known as "Jafsie," a code name derived from the phonetic sound of his initials and would be used for his communications with the ransom-note writer. Condon was a physically impressive seventy-two-year-old former Bronx school principal; adorned with a gray walrus mustache, he was a bit of an eccentric and something of a windbag, but also a man with a strong social conscience. Why Condon presumed that the kidnapper would notice his advertisement in so obscure an outlet as the *Bronx Home News* would remain one of the more puzzling questions about the case, leading to speculation that he himself was part of the kidnapping scheme.

The advertisement elicited a letter to Condon with the same identifying insignia as that on the earlier ransom letters. It was addressed to "Mr. Doctor John F. Condon," a standard German form, and had such misspellings as "cace" (for case), "handel," and "gett." Condon, after first contacting the Lindberghs and receiving their authorization to enter into negotiations, put further notices in the local newspaper and talked to the kidnapper on the telephone, insisting that he heard a voice in the background say in Italian, "Statti zitto!" In English this would be "Shut up."

A first meeting between Condon and the person with whom he had been in contact took place in the Woodlawn Cemetery in the Bronx and lasted for an hour, with Condon allegedly pleading with the man, who identified himself as "John," to return the baby. Several times Condon asked the man what his mother would say if she knew that he was mixed up in a thing like this. John ignored the comment, said that the baby was being well cared for on a boat, and that he was one of a group of six who had planned the kidnapping for more than a year. He correctly identified the pins from the Lindbergh baby's crib that Condon had brought with him, and later he would send to Condon a package that held the baby's yellow Dr. Denton sleeping suit as proof that he had the child, though he complained that the demand for the garment had forced him to spend $3 for a replacement. The police had released an inaccurate description of the suit to be able to weed out pretenders. Subsequently, Condon would brood over a passing question by John during their cemetery conversation: "Would I burn if the baby is dead?" he had asked.

Lindbergh's identification of the nightdress pushed forward plans to meet the ransom request. Despite Lindbergh's initial objections, federal agents and J. P. Morgan bankers prevailed upon him to have the serial numbers on the ransom bills recorded and $35,000 of the ransom money made up of more readily identifiable gold-backed notes. The banknotes—5,150 bills—were placed in a distinctive box in the hope that it could be identified later in the possession of the kidnapper.

On April 2, 1932—a month and a day after the kidnapping—Lindbergh drove Condon to another cemetery in the Bronx, Saint Raymond's, and waited in the car while the money was handed over. Lindbergh said that he heard someone say: "Hey, Doctor, over here!" in a distinctive voice—high, nasal and reedy, and with a strong accent. At the last moment, Condon had decided to hold back $20,000, apparently thinking that the kidnapper had gotten too greedy; he did not realize that the money he withheld included a sizable portion of the more easily identifiable gold-backed notes. He told the other man that Lindbergh had been unable to raise more than the amount of the original demand. To find the child, Condon was told, he should locate "the boad Nelly," a twenty-eight-foot-long vessel said to be moored between Cape Cod and Martha's Vineyard. John said that there were two persons on the boat, and that both of them were innocent of knowledge of the kidnapping. Later, the police would be severely criticized for not having taken steps to follow the kidnapper once contact had been established. Their defense was that Lindbergh had insisted that they not do so.

The directions to find "the boad Nelly" prompted a wild and frantic effort as Lindbergh and others flew up and down the coast in amphibious planes looking for the vessel. The Coast Guard sealed off the area but the intensive search, increasingly fueled by desperation, produced nothing.

Then, on May 12, 1932—more than two months after the kidnapping—the badly decomposed body of a child was discovered in a shallow grave about four miles from the Lindbergh house. The left leg was gone from the knee down, both hands were missing, and most of the internal organs had been carried away by animals. The body was dressed in the flannel undershirt that Betty Gow had stitched. The sleeping suit was missing; presumably, the offender either had cold-bloodedly taken it when the baby died, presuming that it would prove useful for identification, or had returned to remove it from the body when evidence was needed to show that he truly was the kidnapper.

The child's body had been discovered by a truck driver delivering lumber who had stopped by the side of the road and walked about seventy-five feet into the woods to urinate. Identification was based on the child's teeth, his distinctive toes, with the little toe on his right foot curled up under the one next to it, and the remnants of clothing on the body. After the autopsy, Lindbergh had the child's body cremated so that its grave would not become a site of public desecration. Before that was done, the morgue owner allowed two newspaper photographers to open the casket and take pictures of the remains. Lindbergh was told that the newsmen had broken into the morgue through a window; his embittered belief that they had done so is said to have seared itself onto his mind, reinforcing his belief that there was too much license and not enough discipline in the United States.

Now it became a question of waiting to see if the ransom money would turn up. A fifty-seven-page circular listing serial numbers had been sent to a quarter of a million banks and agencies throughout the country. A few bills soon surfaced and the police marked each location where they were discovered on a map, seeking to discern a pattern. Most of the first notes put into circulation were of lower denominations, and some were folded tightly in a distinctive manner, lengthwise through the center, then through the center crosswise, and crosswise again through the center. Such a folded note would fit into a watch pocket, a common feature of men's trousers at the time. Meanwhile, President Franklin Roosevelt, desiring to remove the United States from the gold standard in the face of a drain on U.S. gold reserves prompted by the Depression, issued an executive order directing that all gold coins, gold bullion, and gold-backed notes be deposited at a federal reserve bank before May 1, 1933. After that, at least technically, these bills would not be legal tender, though in fact they usually were accepted and exchanged for newer currency. But with many fewer of them about, the bills would be more likely to be noticed when passed.

The largest deposit of ransom money—$2,980—was made on May 1, the date that the bills were supposed to be turned in. The depositor signed the name J. J. Faulkner and provided an uptown Manhattan address. No such person lived at the address given, and no one ever came forth to reclaim the deposit after the newspapers reported the story. Who Faulkner might have been remains one of the tantalizing puzzles of the Hauptmann case: the handwriting on the deposit slip clearly was not the same as that on the ransom messages.

The mapping of the areas where ransom notes had surfaced showed a concentration in the Bronx, though some bills were recovered in places as distant as Maine and California. The police also put together a sketch of the kidnapper, based on descriptions by Condon and Joseph Perrone, a taxi driver who had been given a ransom letter to deliver to Condon's house. The sketch was shown to persons who had received ransom banknotes, including a movie-theater cashier in Manhattan who said that it matched the looks of a customer who had purchased a ticket from her. Her testimony, like much of the evidence against Hauptmann, conflicted with a plausible alibi: the night the bill was passed at the movie theater was Hauptmann's birthday, and there were witnesses who insisted that he had spent the evening at home in their presence.

The case broke wide open on September 18, 1934, more than two years after the ransom had been paid. Gas station proprietors had been requested to write down the license plate numbers of customers who paid with gold-backed currency. A Bronx filling station owner, thinking the gold certificate a customer had given him might be counterfeit, had penciled 4U-13-41 in a margin on the back, then added the state initials, N.Y. A bank officer, handed the bill by a teller who wondered if it should be accepted, found the serial number on the ransom currency list. He notified the police.

The license number was for a dark blue 1930 Dodge registered to Richard Hauptmann, living at 1279 East 222nd Street, on the second floor of a house in the Bronx. Hauptmann was a carpenter, and his apartment was ten blocks from the lumber mill that had been identified as one of the places that had sold the kind of wood from which the kidnap ladder was constructed. He also lived near the cemetery where the ransom money was paid. Hauptmann had no arrest record in the United States, though he had entered the country illegally. He had been caught twice as a stowaway on a ship, but succeeded on a third attempt, hiding in a coal bunker and then walking casually off the ship when it arrived in New York in 1923, allegedly on his twenty-fourth birthday. He had no passport and only a few cents in his pocket.[3]

Hauptmann had served as a machine gunner in the 177th Regiment of the German army during the last stages of the First World War and had been slightly wounded twice. Two of his three older brothers were killed in combat. After being demobilized, Hauptmann had been arrested for a series of burglaries, all committed within a six-day period, as well as an armed robbery. One burglary, done with a friend who had been in Hauptmann's regiment, involved using a ladder to enter a second-story window in the home of the burgomaster in a nearby town and stealing cash and a silver pocket watch. The robbery was of food from the perambulators of two housewives. Hauptmann brandished a gun at the women, shouting: "We'll shoot! We're radicals!" He had spent three years of a five-and-a-half-year sentence in prison for these crimes. His attorneys would claim that the offenses were only reflections of desperate postwar

---

3. The ship on which Hauptmann stowed away has been variously identified as the S.S. *Portia*, the S.S. *Hannover*, and the S.S. *George Washington*. A check in the *New York Times* of ship arrivals in the city on the day of Hauptmann's twenty-fourth birthday and a few days on either side indicates that none of the named ships came into port at that time.

times in a poverty-stricken country, of the fact that Hauptmann could not obtain work.

The decision was made by the New York and New Jersey police not to arrest Hauptmann in his home. Nine police officers in three cars followed him when he left early on the morning of September 19, hoping that he might lead them to coconspirators. Then, fearful of losing him in traffic, they surrounded his car and took him into custody. Another gold note was found in his wallet, apparently lying flat, though some sources indicate that it was folded in the same distinctive manner as many of the recovered bills had been. The police tore apart Hauptmann's apartment, in time recovering a hidden hoard of ransom money and, vitally, though considerably later, a floor plank in the attic from which eight feet of wood had been sawed—wood that, it would be claimed, had been used to fashion one of the rungs of the kidnap ladder.

The interrogation of Hauptmann was pitiless. He was questioned without an attorney by relays of officers for twenty straight hours. He maintained stolidly that he had been given the money for safekeeping by a friend, Isidor Fisch, a fur trader who had returned to Germany and died of tuberculosis in the charity ward of a Leipzig hospital. Wits skeptical of this explanation would ridicule it ever after as a "Fisch story." Hauptmann's wife, the police determined, was unaware of the kidnapping: Hauptmann had not told her about the existence of the ransom money. He willingly provided dozens of handwriting samples. The samples duplicated the misspellings in the ransom requests, such as "rihgt" for "right." But during his trial, Hauptmann would claim that he had merely written the words the way the police had spelled them for him. He also said, and there was subsequent proof of his claim, that the police had beaten him severely: "They turned the lights out so that I couldn't see who was hitting me. They punched me and kicked me. They strapped me to a chair and kicked me in the chest and stomach." The strategy used by the police was to call in a doctor who examined Hauptmann and declared officially that his body was unmarked, then to beat him afterward.

The police also found Dr. Condon's telephone number penciled on the door trim in an unlighted attic closet. Hauptmann disingenuously said that, though he didn't remember writing it, he might have put the number there because it was his habit to scribble down things that interested him and that he probably saw the number in the newspaper.

The seemingly strong case against Hauptmann encountered a detour when Condon was asked to pick the person he had met in the cemetery out of a lineup. He focused on Hauptmann but then stated: "I would not say that he is the man." Condon's failure to provide positive identification stunned the police, and he was not invited by the prosecutor to testify before the grand jury when an indictment was secured. Later, at the trial, Condon would maintain that he had merely wanted Hauptmann to relax and that he presumed that in a subsequent person-to-person talk he could cajole him to confess and to name his accomplices.

Hauptmann was charged in the Bronx with extortion, a crime carrying a maximum sentence of twenty years. During his interrogation, according to an FBI agent's report to headquarters that was disclosed much later, the district attorney directed an outburst against Hauptmann that conveys the intensity of the feeling against him:

> *Your wife is being held in the Women's jail with a lot of prostitutes. She is separated from your baby. It has no one who loves it, to take care of it. It may die of undernourishment. Your wife is hysterical. She will probably become an imbecile over*

Bruno Richard Hauptmann, in the center looking at the camera, during an extradition hearing in the Bronx. AP/Wide World Photos

the shock of this. If you have any speck of manhood in you, you will come clean on this. . . .

But I can see you're just an animal. You don't care what happens to your wife and baby. . . . You're the lowest human being I have ever had before me. . . . The other night down at the police department, a mob were trying to get at your wife to hang her.

Hauptmann's wife, who had not been detained in the women's jail, now secured a lawyer for him, and Hauptmann remained adamant that he had been given the money by Fisch and had spent a portion of the cache because Fisch owed him $7,000; he had loaned Fisch money for stock market speculation. The Bronx grand jury indicted Hauptmann on the extortion charge after hearing from thirty-two witnesses, including Albert S. Osborn, the country's leading handwriting expert who, after initial hesitation, said that he was certain that Hauptmann had written the ransom note. Hauptmann told the grand jury that on the day of the kidnapping he had worked as a carpenter at the Majestic Hotel in Manhattan. The records for the hotel first were reported missing and later were said to have been altered. The job foreman, who initially testified otherwise, subsequently declared that Hauptmann had not worked at the Majestic on the day of the kidnapping. When the grand jury indicted Hauptmann, his bail was set at $100,000 and he was placed under a twenty-four-hour suicide watch that would continue throughout his trial.

New Jersey sought to have Hauptmann extradited so that he could be tried on a capital charge in connection with the death of the Lindbergh child. Possession of the ransom money was considered sufficient grounds for the extortion case, but it was a considerably more complicated matter to place Hauptmann in New Jersey and to tie him to the child's death. Control of the case in New Jersey was assumed by the attorney general, thirty-eight-year-old David T. Wilentz, who had come to the United States from Latvia with his parents when he was six years old. Wilentz, opposed to capital punishment, had been appointed attorney general in 1933 and had never prosecuted a criminal case, although he often had served as a defense counsel.

The first step was to secure a grand jury indictment in New Jersey. Wilentz chose to do so in Hunterdon rather than Mercer County, where the body had been discovered, because he believed Hunterdon citizens were more likely to favor the prosecution. Once again, Dr. Condon was omitted from the roster of those who testified before the grand jury.

Unresolved questions about the cause of death and the location of the alleged homicide nagged at the prosecution's grand jury presentation. If the child had been killed during the kidnapping itself, either accidentally or with criminal intent, then the crime of murder or that of felony-murder (a death ensuing from the commission of a statutory felony) took place in Hunterdon County. If the death had occurred in Mercer County, where the body was discovered, then that was where the case should be tried. The coroner had declared that a skull fracture had been the cause of death. But it was uncertain whether death had ensued when the kidnapper dropped the child after the ladder broke or from a blow that had been inflicted after he had gone some distance from the Lindbergh house.

Besides, a peculiar quirk of New Jersey law required that if a crime was the result of a conspiracy, the state would have no right to try Hauptmann unless all those who participated in the conspiracy were joined with him or it was shown that he himself had struck the blow that killed the child. These legal requirements had the prosecution walking on juridical eggshells as it tried to frame a satisfactory charge.

Wilentz carefully crafted an indictment alleging felony-murder, but mentioned no specific felony. Subsequently, the felony would be pinpointed as burglary, based on breaking and entering the house and the theft of the child's sleeping garment. Kidnapping was not alleged. That offense had carried a death penalty in New Jersey until 1928, when the law was amended to decree a sentence of thirty years to life. Nor was kidnapping one of the enumerated felonies that would support a charge of felony-murder and the possibility of a death sentence. Extortion was not mentioned in the New Jersey indictment, since that offense had occurred in the Bronx. Besides, the prosecutor did not want to foreclose the possibility of a later trial for extortion should the felony-murder prosecution falter.

In the archaic legalese of the time, the twenty-three-member Hunterdon County grand jury returned the following indictment on October 9, 1934:

> *The grand inquest for the State of New Jersey in and of the County of Hunterdon upon their respective oaths present that Bruno Richard Hauptmann on the first day of March, in the year of our Lord one thousand nine hundred and thirty-two, with force and arms at the township of East Amwell, in the County of Hunterdon aforesaid, and within the jurisdiction of this court, did willfully, feloniously and of his malice aforethought, kill and murder Charles A. Lindbergh Jr., contrary to the form of the statute in such case made and provided and against the peace of the State, the government and the dignity of the same.*

The indictment represented a high-risk strategy for the prosecution. If a trial jury was convinced that others were involved in the kidnapping or responsible for the killing, or that the death of the child occurred after March 1,

1932, or by accident, it could reject the prosecution's theory of the case and vote to acquit or to recommend mercy, a recommendation that the judge by law was prevented from denying. Besides, preempting a trial for extortion in the Bronx could have proven to be a wrong-headed and premature tactic. Hauptmann likely would have been convicted of that charge and might have implicated others in the kidnapping. Nonetheless, on the basis of the Hunterdon County indictment, the governor of New York signed an extradition order turning Hauptmann over to the New Jersey authorities. In calmer times, critics would find severe deficiencies, if not outright perjury, in the extradition hearing. But whatever errors there were in the Bronx proceedings, once Hauptmann had been transported to New Jersey these became so much water under the constitutional bridge.

The Trial

The trial of Bruno Richard Hauptmann[4] in the small courtroom in Flemington, New Jersey, began on January 2, 1935. Eighty people could comfortably be seated; two hundred were jammed into the court. Three hundred news reporters and more than one hundred cameramen covered the trial. Forty-five direct telegraph lines ran from a room above the court, and special teletype machines were connected to Berlin, Paris, Melbourne, and Buenos Aires. The trial was the first to be broadcast live; one of the commentators was Samuel Leibowitz, the defense attorney in the Scottsboro case. On one day more than twenty thousand people lined up in biting winter cold in the hope of getting inside the courtroom, or at least catching a glimpse of the major participants. As George Waller, an early chronicler of the case, noted: "A phrase that hardly seemed inflated traveled from mouth to mouth, and back again: this was to be the trial of the century." H. L. Mencken, a mordant iconoclast, would blasphemously label the trial "the greatest story since the Resurrection," while Edna Ferber, a novelist covering the case, conveyed the emotions the hate-filled mob surrounding the courthouse produced in her: "It made you want to resign as a member of the human race."

The jury was composed of eight men and four women from diverse backgrounds and with an average age of about forty. Jury members were paid $3 a

---

4. Hauptmann preferred the name Richard after he came to the United States, and that is what his wife called him. Prosecutors, however, called him Bruno because that usage played into the antipathy toward Hitler and the German people.

day (payment had risen to $5 daily sixty years later at the O. J. Simpson trial). They were sequestered two to a room on the top floor of the four-story, fifty-room Union Hotel, located across the street from the courthouse. Jurors could easily hear what the broadcasters were saying in the studio on the floor below them, and they constantly were exposed to comments such as "Kill the German" and "Burn Bruno Burn" from people in the streets as they made their way to and from the courtroom. They were shielded during meals in the hotel dining room by a flimsy screen, but those on the other side of the screen often talked loudly in order to make their observations audible to the jurors.

Wilentz proved to be a talented prosecutor. When questioning defense witnesses, he was initially casual, almost indifferent, first putting them somewhat at ease, but then ferociously pinpointing inconsistencies in their stories. Hauptmann sat stolidly through it all, expressionless, exuding an air of confidence and unconcern, though on rare occasions he would burst out with accusations of "Liar!" during the testimony of a prosecution witness.

This time, Dr. John Condon stated that the man who had identified himself as John in the Bronx cemetery most certainly was Bruno Richard Hauptmann: he vividly remembered the darkish blond hair, the deep-set blue eyes, the high cheekbones, small mouth, pointed chin, and, of course, the heavy accent. He had not been certain at the time whether the accent was German or Scandinavian.

Then Albert S. Osborn, the nation's leading handwriting expert, and his son, Albert D. Osborn, who collaborated with him, testified that the similarity between Hauptmann's handwriting, particularly his spelling, and the ransom notes was beyond any possible question. The Osborns also maintained that in his application for a driving license Hauptmann had made some of the same spelling errors, and that the handwriting on the driving application was the same as that in the ransom notes.

The evidence offered by Arthur Koehler, a wood expert—or in fancier terminology, a xylotomist—went a long way toward convicting Hauptmann. Koehler, employed by the U.S. Department of Forestry at its Madison, Wisconsin, laboratory, had disassembled the ladder and analyzed each segment of it. He wrote to every lumber mill in the country asking if it had processed wood of the particular type and cut used to construct the ladder. He then visited numerous mills to try to find a match between the ladder wood and what they sold, seeking to pinpoint the site that had a plane that cut a distinguishing pattern into the wood. Ultimately, Koehler traced the wood to a McCormick, South Carolina, mill and from there to a number of lumberyards, including one near Hauptmann's house. The most impressive piece of wood evidence was the claim that Hauptmann, a bit short of material to finish the ladder, had removed a board from his attic and used it for what became known as Rung 16. Displaying blown-up pictures, Koehler sought to convince the jury of the exact match between that ladder segment and the piece missing from the Hauptmann attic.

The defense tried to undermine this evidence by challenging the prosecution's failure to document meticulously who had control over the ladder as evidence from the time it was discovered to the time that it was exhibited in court, implying that what eventually was displayed may have been faked.

Hauptmann was the first witness the defense called to the stand. He underwent six hours of direct examination by Reilly and eleven more of cross-examination by the prosecutor. He remained adamant that he had received the ransom money from Isidor Fisch and denied emphatically that he had kidnapped the Lindbergh child and that he had met with Condon. Hauptmann claimed that the considerably improved lifestyle that he had enjoyed following the date of the ransom exchange was the result of sound investments made by him and Fisch in the stock market. But he did very poorly on some phases of the cross-examination. Wilentz ripped into his tale of stock market success and entered into the record some of Hauptmann's personal papers, which showed that before the kidnapping he had also misspelled words such as "right" (rihgt) and "boat" (boad). Only once did Hauptmann lose his poise. He seemed to smile when Wilentz observed that, though dunning letters showed he was hard up for cash, he didn't make any effort to determine how much money Fisch had left with him. The interrogation then took this turn, with Wilentz speaking first:

> *"This is funny to you, isn't it?"*
> *Hauptmann stopped smiling. "No."*
> *"You're having fun—smiling at me . . ."*
> *"No."*
> *"You think you're a big shot . . ."*
> *Hauptmann, angrily and contemptuously: "Should I cry?"*
> *". . . bigger than everybody, don't you?"*
> *"No—but I know I am innocent!"*

The prosecutor next accused Hauptmann of being proud of his willpower. "You wouldn't tell if they murdered you?" he said. Hauptmann's answer was spat out, the most emotional moment in all his time on the witness stand.

"No," he said, and then added: "I am innocent. That keeps me the power to stand up!"

Wilentz's summation to the jury was both venomous and vile. The most jolting aspect of his remarks involved a focus on Hauptmann's ethnicity: "What type of man would murder the child of Charles and Anne Lindbergh?" the prosecutor asked rhetorically and then provided an absurd answer: "He wouldn't be an American. No American gangster and no American racketeer ever sank to the level of killing babies. Ah, no! An American gangster that did want to participate in a kidnapping wouldn't pick out Colonel Lindbergh."

Wilentz's tone became more impassioned as he proceeded; rather than concentrate on the evidence, he relentlessly portrayed Hauptmann as a snake, a piece of vermin, "an animal lower than the lowest form in the animal kingdom"; seemingly, the defendant's demeanor, with a hint of arrogance, and a categoric refusal to give ground regarding his innocence in the face of Wilentz's attack, had instilled in the prosecutor a hatred that carried him well beyond the requirement of his job, which he failed to remember was to seek justice in a fair and impartial manner. Surrounded by the blinding glare of public attention and the near-universal belief in Hauptmann's guilt, neither Wilentz nor others who might have been able to take a principled stand were willing to do so. Wilentz, one newspaper reporter noted, was "beating himself to pieces with his own desperate conviction of Hauptmann's guilt."

In New Jersey in 1935, judges were permitted to comment more openly than in most states regarding their beliefs about evidence, a practice also followed in England. Thomas W. Trenchard, the impressive-looking seventy-one-year-old judge at the Hauptmann trial, made full use of this prerogative. He would carefully outline a defense position and then ask scornfully: "Do you believe that?" Not only the words, but his manner of saying them—which would not be reflected in the trial transcript—were significant. Trenchard's emphases made the sentence more in the nature of "Do *you* believe THAT?" Of Condon's testimony, the judge said: "Upon the whole, is there any doubt in your mind as to [its] reliability?" Of the defense idea that an underworld gang might have done the kidnapping, he asked mockingly: "Now do you believe that? Is there any evidence in this case whatsoever to support any such conclusion?" Typical was Trenchard's observation: "If the ladder was not there for the purpose of reaching the nursery window, for what purpose was it there?"

The trial had spanned more than six weeks. In New Jersey at the time jurors could be made to remain where they deliberated until they reached a verdict or reported that they were hopelessly deadlocked, even if they had to discuss the case through the night. The Hauptmann jurors asked the chief constable to obtain a magnifying glass, arousing all forms of speculation regarding why they wanted it. Then they returned to the court after eleven hours and fourteen minutes, a return heralded for serious cases such as this by the customary tolling of the 125-year-old bell in the courthouse steeple.

The jury's verdict was that Hauptmann was guilty. There was no recommendation, as there could have been, that the defendant receive a sentence of life imprisonment instead of death. Rumors had it that the initial ballot had been seven for death and five for life imprisonment; those in the minority had gradually been persuaded to adopt the majority position.

Hauptmann's subsequent appeal to the New Jersey appellate court raised issues that continue to plague those who study the case. His attorney argued that the trial court had not established its jurisdiction over the matter since no adequate proof had been offered that the child's killing had taken place in Hunterdon and not Mercer County, where the body had been discovered. The appeal disputed the legality of the felony-murder charge, arguing that it was verbal gymnastics to say that the house had been entered with the intent to steal a sleeping garment of no proven value. It was further claimed that there had been no proof of jimmying the window nor even that the window had been the point of entry. Nor was intent to steal the garment established, since it had been returned to its owners. Finally, no proof had been offered that it was Hauptmann who had committed the alleged burglary.

Hauptmann's appellate attorney also argued that the evidence strongly supported the conclusion that no single person alone could have done all the things involved in the kidnapping, a conclusion reached then and now by virtually every person who has closely examined the evidence. In addition, there was a picking away at the reliability of the evidence; for instance, when Hauptmann had been shown the ladder and asked if it was his, he had contemptuously shaken his head: "I am a carpenter," he said, then sarcastically noted that the ladder looked "like a music instrument." There also was an objection to the daily appearance of Lindbergh in the court, constantly offering the jurors a vivid picture of a bereaved father whose sorrow had to be redressed.

Unimpressed, the New Jersey appellate court unanimously rejected Hauptmann's appeal. The evidence, it ruled, though circumstantial, was so conclusive in so many different ways, that it left no room for reasonable doubt.

The only two openings left to Hauptmann were an appeal to the eight-member New Jersey Board of Pardons and an appeal to the U.S. Supreme Court. The Board of Pardons was chaired by Harold G. Hoffman, who had been elected governor two years earlier at the age of thirty-six, making him the youngest state chief executive in the nation and a much-mentioned possible candidate for the presidency or vice presidency. Hoffman believed that Hauptmann had not acted alone and that much of the evidence used against him was tainted, but he was not permitted by law to commute Hauptmann's term by himself as governor, a right granted most state executives.

Besides the governor, the Board of Pardons was made up of five judges, a retired butcher, and a newspaper publisher. The panel rejected Hauptmann's appeal by a seven-to-one vote; the one holdout was the governor. After that, Hoffman secretly visited Hauptmann in prison late one night, hoping for a confession but getting none. Nevertheless, he granted Hauptmann a thirty-day reprieve (which would lengthen into two months because rescheduling the execution at the end of the reprieve had to be to a time at least a month later). During that period, Schwarzkopf and other investigators, though sorely displeased, were ordered to investigate much more strenuously what Hoffman saw as loose ends in the case. This quest for additional evidence so spurred New Jersey's best-known crime hunter, Ellis Parker, a close associate of Hoffman's, that Parker arranged a bizarre kidnapping and torturing of Paul Wendel, a disbarred attorney with a history of mental troubles, to force Wendel to sign a confession saying that he had killed the Lindbergh baby. Wendel signed the "confession," but by saving laundry receipts and etching his initials on the wall where he had been held captive he was able to prove his story of abduction. Parker and his collaborators went to jail.

During this time, too, Samuel Leibowitz was hired to try to get the "true story" from Hauptmann. He made three visits to him in his cell, painstakingly pointed out each item of evidence that he had failed to address satisfactorily, and impressed on Hauptmann that he was utterly doomed if he did not confess. None of this swayed Hauptmann from his protestations of innocence. Neither did an offer from a newspaper of $75,000 to be given to his widow and young son if Hauptmann would write out for the paper the details of the kidnapping and death of the child, a story that it promised to publish only after Hauptmann was executed.

Meanwhile, in December 1935, the Lindberghs left the United States for a life of exile in England, where they believed they would be granted more privacy and where there had never been a reported kidnapping for ransom. In contrast, between 1929 and 1934, more than two hundred people (some sources say several thousand) had been kidnapped in the United States. The *New York Herald Tribune* thought that Lindbergh's departure was a judgment, almost biblical in nature, on American ways:

> *The departure of Colonel and Mrs. Lindbergh for England, to find a tolerable home there in a safer and more civilized land than ours has shown itself to be, is its own commentary upon the American social scene. Nations have exiled their heroes before; they have broken them with meanness. But when has a nation made life unbearable to one of its most distinguished men through a sheer inability to protect him from its criminals and lunatics and the vast vulgarity of its sensationalists, publicity-seekers, petty politicians and yellow newspapers? It seems as incredible as it is shocking. Yet everyone knows that this is exactly what happened.*

Albert Einstein, like Hauptmann an immigrant from Germany, agreed, though without generalizing the blame to the entire country. The kidnapping, he told an interviewer, was "a sign of lack of sanity in social development." The most pointed and poignant comment was that of Anne Morrow Lindbergh: "Fame," she observed, "is a kind of death."

Time finally ran out for Hauptmann. On April 3, 1936, he was taken to the execution chamber at the New Jersey State Prison. His attorney read the 109-word statement that Hauptmann had written. "I am glad that my life in a world that had not understood me has ended," it began. He proclaimed again that he was "an innocent man," and said that his death would not be in vain if it served to help abolish capital punishment, especially a death penalty inflicted on the basis of only circumstantial evidence.

Hauptmann's head had been shaved and his trousers slit at the ankles so that electrodes could be set in place. There were fifty-five witnesses. At 8:44 P.M. the executioner sent 2,000 volts of electricity through Hauptmann twice in the space of sixty seconds; then, to be sure, another 1,000 volts were sent in the second minute. Hauptmann's body became rigid, his lips jarred apart, and his hands clenched the sides of the electric chair. Wisps of smoke rose from his head. Then the doctor stepped up and officially pronounced him dead. Four years plus one month and two days had gone by since the Lindbergh baby had been stolen from its crib.

New Jersey law at the time decreed that no religious service could legally be performed over the remains of a person executed. But Hauptmann's body was

Charles Lindbergh, perhaps the most admired of all Americans of his time, returning to the courtroom during the Hauptmann trial. Some thought his daily presence at the proceedings unduly influenced the jury against Hauptmann. AP/Wide World Photos

taken to New York, where two ministers offered prayers before the corpse was cremated.

Was Hauptmann Guilty?

Over the ensuing years, the case against Hauptmann has come under heavy fire as additional information has been uncovered, much of it found in the 33,391 pages of material secured through the Freedom of Information Act from the internal FBI files. The adulation of Lindbergh, the anti-German sentiment of the Hitler period, and the extraordinary public pressure for revenge no longer control considerations of the case. Operating in calmer times, revisionists have provided powerful reasons to seriously doubt that justice was served in that Flemington, New Jersey, court almost two-thirds of a century ago.

It is incontrovertible that Hauptmann was in possession of the ransom money, possibly all or virtually all of it. But his "Fisch story" explanation, however suspicious, could have been true. The ransom money evidence was buttressed by testimony repudiating Hauptmann's alibi that he was at work on the day of the crime, the eyewitness testimony of Condon, the taxi driver, and two New Jersey men who said they saw him at the crime scene, as well as the powerful earwitness testimony of Lindbergh. Add to these the incriminating evidence of the ladder with Rung 16 traced to Hauptmann's attic and the handwriting analyses, and Hauptmann was doomed, particularly since he lacked funds to follow up exculpatory evidence satisfactorily and his lead attorney often performed in a lackadaisical and perfunctory manner.

The strong, persisting belief that the kidnapping could not have been done by one man alone underlay the challenge to the verdict by Governor Harold Hoffman. But the governor too was caught in political turmoil. Going as far as he did and insisting that he only wanted to be more certain before a man was killed very likely cost Hoffman any hope he might have entertained for higher political office.

But uneasiness about the Hauptmann verdict persists. In later years, a pair of writers—Noel Behn and Anthony Scaduto—published new material questioning aspects of the case against Hauptmann. But both made the serious mistake of believing that they also were obligated to show who actually had committed the crime. The scenarios they offered were singularly farfetched, detracting considerably from the overall credibility of their material.

Then, in 1985, Ludovic Kennedy tackled the Hauptmann case, spurred to the task after seeing Anna Hauptmann movingly proclaim her husband's innocence during a 1981 television program. Kennedy had written three earlier books on miscarriages of justice that resulted in official government pardons to men he demonstrated had been falsely convicted. The book that resulted from his probes into the Lindbergh case led the *New Statesman* to say that he had "proven beyond doubt that Hauptmann was innocent," a view echoed by the *Christian Science Monitor* in much the same words: "Kennedy presents a strong and believable case for Hauptmann's innocence."

For Kennedy, the emotions surrounding the kidnapping of the Lindbergh child drove the verdict: the crime, he observes, "was not only known in detail but had shocked and outraged almost everyone in the country, filling them with a deep personal loathing of the perpetrators and a desire, almost an obsession, to see them caught and destroyed." When Hauptmann, an illegal German immigrant, was found with the ransom money, Kennedy believes, he became a ready-made object for previously unfocused rage and disgust. "No one was of a mind to doubt."

Kennedy demonstrates that the identifications of Hauptmann were highly suspect. One of the two eyewitnesses placing Hauptmann near the kidnapping scene was eighty-seven-year-old Amandus Hochmuth, a Hunterdon County man who swore in court that he could identify Hauptmann as the person in a car carrying a ladder who had driven by his house on the day of the kidnapping. Later, it would be discovered that Hochmuth was partially blind because of cataracts. When he came to the governor's office to collect the $1,000 that was his share of the reward money, Hochmuth identified an eighteen-inch-tall vase with flowers on top of a file cabinet ten feet from him as a woman's hat. Noting the puzzlement of those in the room, he changed his answer: it was a bowl of fruit "sitting on a piece of furniture."

The other New Jersey eyewitness was Millard Whited, illiterate and very poor, and uniformly regarded by his neighbors as a chronic liar. When first questioned the day after the kidnapping, Whited said that he had seen nothing suspicious in the neighborhood. Seven weeks after that he made a formal statement to the police restating his lack of any information regarding the kidnapping. He changed his story after the police told him that he had a good chance to receive a share of the $25,000 reward money. Now he identified Hauptmann as having ridden by on the day of the kidnapping with a ladder in his car. The police also had given Whited $150 in cash and $35 a day for expenses and showed him two photographs of Hauptmann before he was asked to pick him out of a lineup.

The other two eyewitnesses, from the Bronx, also offered hardly ironclad stories. Condon had refused to identify Hauptmann, though he singled him out in a fourteen-man lineup that contained thirteen burly policemen and one very bedraggled suspect who had been continuously questioned and deprived of sleep—and was the only person in the lineup who spoke with an accent. The taxi driver who said that Hauptmann was the man who had paid him to deliver a ransom note to Condon had similarly identified a variety of people and was at first declared by Schwarzkopf to be a totally unbelievable witness, since he initially had said that he could not see the man well enough to know him were he to see him again.

Kennedy's skepticism about the reliability of the eyewitness testimony finds support in the work of two New York newspapermen who at the time of the Hauptmann trial carried out a crude experiment. Using photographs of nine famous people, they interviewed a group of Lindbergh's neighbors. They asked if the neighbors had seen any of the people in the photographs in the vicinity at the time of the kidnapping. A picture of the head of the federal National Recovery Administration drew responses such as "I remember him all right. He was coming up the road dressed as a tramp," and "Isn't that the Whatley fellow, the English butler of the Lindberghs?" The neighbors also identified New York Mayor Fiorello LaGuardia as a man driving near the Lindbergh estate with a ladder on the back of his car.

Besides his reservations about the eyewitness sightings, Kennedy also doubted that two years after it had happened Lindbergh, who had been sitting in a car some eighty to one hundred feet distant, could say with any assurance that he recognized a voice that he had heard saying, "Hey, Doctor, over here!" Yet Lindbergh's identification as well as his daily attendance at the trial, jurors would later say, was very important in impelling their verdict.

The writing in the attic that Hauptmann granted might have been his, though he had no memory of having penciled Condon's number on the door in a dark closet, also proved to be a spurious piece of evidence against him. Three newspapermen who had covered the trial each independently said years after that the telephone number had been placed there by a reporter from the New York *Daily News* who wanted to create an eye-catching story for the next edition of his paper.

There also was serious concern that the rung of the ladder said to have come from Hauptmann's attic involved evidence manufactured by the police. For one thing, experts on wood later testified that closer examination showed that there was a mismatch between the specimen and its possible use as Rung

16. It was pointed out that the place from which the piece of wood in the attic had come had not been noticed during nine earlier examinations of the site, though it surely would have been obvious. After their initial searches, the police had rented Hauptmann's apartment for several months, providing ample privacy and opportunity to manufacture evidence. Why, Hauptmann's later defenders would ask, would Hauptmann have ripped up the attic floor in a rented apartment when he had plenty of satisfactory pieces of lumber in his garage that he could have used?

Disputes have also arisen over the Osborns' assertion that the ransom notes and the samples of Hauptmann's writing matched. For one thing, it is noted that the senior Osborn hesitated about reaching that conclusion until he learned that the ransom money had been located on the Hauptmann premises. In addition, comprehensive and sophisticated reviews of handwriting analysis have since concluded that it is a very imprecise endeavor and have argued that such testimony ought not be admissible in a criminal trial. (In 1971—thirty-five years later—the son and grandson of the Osborns who testified at the Hauptmann trial, as well as four other "experts," would say that there was not "the slightest question" that writing said to be that of another flying celebrity, Howard Hughes, was genuine. The third-generation Osborn added that "it was impossible as a practical matter, based on years of experience, that anyone other than" Hughes could have written the letters in question. Another handwriting expert insisted that the chances were less than one in a million that someone other than Hughes might be the writer. Not long after, Clifford Irving confessed that he had forged the letters.)

Hauptmann's alibi that he had been employed as a carpenter at the Majestic Hotel collapsed when the defense could not produce records that might have indicated his work there on the day of the kidnapping. The records later were found, though they obviously had been doctored in an attempt to demonstrate that he had not started work until near the end of the month. As did so many other prosecution witnesses, the timekeeper at the Majestic came under some heavy police pressure to testify against Hauptmann.

Later consideration also disputed the medical judgment that the Lindbergh baby had died from a fractured skull. The body was so badly decomposed, it was said, that the crude autopsy was totally inadequate. It was performed by the funeral home owner with the coroner, a medical doctor, looking on; the doctor's hands were so riddled with arthritis that he could not do the autopsy himself and feared that he would lose his job if this became public knowledge. Finally, evidence was suppressed by the prosecution. The footprint under the window where the ladder was said to have been raised and the footprint found where Hauptmann allegedly had stood in the Bronx cemetery never were introduced into the trial.

The huge discrepancy in resources and talent available to the state and to the defendant emphasized the extreme disadvantage suffered by an impoverished and despised person accused of a heinous crime. A suggestion offered at the time still has merit: "In a case like Hauptmann's," Arthur Reeve, a criminologist, declared, "the best attorney available should have been appointed by the court and have been granted the time and funds necessary to meet the points raised by the state in order that the defendant's guilt or innocence should be established beyond any reasonable doubt."

"So ended the brief life of Bruno Richard Hauptmann," Kennedy concludes, "guilty beyond a doubt of appropriating monies not his (yet part of which he believed was due him); but of kidnapping, extortion and murder as ignorant, and innocent, as you and I." Perhaps. A careful scrutiny of the Lindbergh case leads us to a different conclusion. We suspect that having brilliantly exonerated several other persons who had been declared guilty, Kennedy was too determined to establish Hauptmann's innocence. Our reading of the record would endorse only the judgment that, whatever else, the untainted evidence against Hauptmann did not support a verdict of guilt beyond a reasonable doubt of the charge against him.

The Death Penalty and Other Criminal Justice Issues

Tension is created in the criminal justice system when a defendant such as Hauptmann steadfastly declares his innocence, though circumstantial evidence might point, even very strongly, to his guilt. As Louis Seidman has noted: "Both critics and defenders of the Hauptmann verdict share a common failing: they cannot tolerate ambiguity and overestimate the ability of institutions operating under great pressure to act upon the truth." There always is the possibility that the defendant truly is innocent, an unnerving prospect for those seeking to put him to death. That tension was heightened in the Hauptmann case because of the exalted status of the Lindberghs and the enormous wave of public horror at the crime, particularly since the victim was a child, a circumstance that almost invariably arouses protective emotions.

Hauptmann may have been guilty—the evidence is very strong that he was guilty of something—but it is clear that a good argument can be made that he was not legally guilty of the offense for which he was executed. Most trial courts and appellate tribunals today would look much more critically at the highly questionable stretching of the felony-murder doctrine. At the time, though, the idea of derailing the process of moving Hauptmann toward a date with the electric chair carried altogether too much political peril. Whatever its ideals, the criminal justice system, when severely pressed, is too likely to adjust its ways to mollify public outrage.

The Death Penalty

The course of capital punishment has followed an erratic pathway in the United States, with states dropping the penalty from their statute books, then reinserting it years later. Appeals courts, particularly when confronted with evidence that the penalty is applied unreasonably and most often to the detriment of minorities and the poor, have put brakes on how death is to be determined by trial courts and juries. At the moment, the trend in the United States in keeping with public opinion is strongly toward much greater use of capital punishment, and this in the face of the disappearance of the penalty in virtually all nations of the world.

The 1930s, when Bruno Richard Hauptmann was executed, was the decade with the highest number of executions in the century except for the 1910–1920 period. Maybe the Hauptmann case gave pause to the death-dealing drive in New Jersey: there had been six executions there in 1935, two plus his in 1936, but there was none in 1937. By 1938, however, the level had risen to seven. New Jersey abolished capital punishment in 1972 but reinstated it ten years later. No one has been executed in the state since 1963, though there are several persons now on death row awaiting the outcome of appeals.

The Gallup Poll began surveys of public opinion on the death penalty in December 1936 in the wake of the unprecedented level of public attention directed toward Hauptmann's execution. At that time, 61 percent of those questioned supported the death penalty and 39 percent were opposed. Since then, the pattern of responses on the question has oscillated. The percentage of those favoring capital punishment declined through the 1950s and early 1960s. Support reached its lowest point in 1966 with only 42 percent approving, and peaked in 1988 when 79 percent of Americans expressed support. In the 1990s the pro–capital punishment sentiment has hovered near 70 percent.

When capital punishment was reestablished in New Jersey in 1982, kidnapping was included among the offenses that could be tied to a felony-related charge of capital murder. In New Jersey criminal law a statute dating back to

1898 allowed what is called a *non vult* (literal meaning: not willed) plea in a murder case. If the defendant so pleads and admits guilt, and the prosecutor permits, the defendant will not be executed. It was in regard to this provision that Hauptmann was continually pressed to confess and thereby to save his life. The *non vult* plea no longer exists: it was declared to be unconstitutionally coercive for capital cases in 1972. There has been another change. State law at the time of Hauptmann's trial in New Jersey allowed a jury to decide guilt and punishment in one verdict. Now the determinations must be by separate actions.

Felony-Murder

Legal scholars today typically take exception to the doctrinal legitimacy of the criminal charge that led to Hauptmann's conviction and execution. They maintain that it was the circumstances of the case—the hysterical need to find and punish a scapegoat—that led the prosecutors, the trial court, and the appellate court to ignore the obvious inadequacy of the evidence to uphold a felony-murder conviction.

There was no reliable proof that placed Hauptmann in New Jersey on the night of the kidnapping, and it was a very considerable stretch to tie the theft of the sleeping garment to the allegation that Hauptmann also was responsible for the child's death. Clarence Darrow, the attorney who had saved Leopold and Loeb from the hangman's noose, put this matter succinctly: "Just the fact that Hauptmann had the ransom money on him," he stated, "doesn't prove that he had anything to do with the murder." Also, the burglary, even if it had been alleged or proven, could be said to have been completed before the death of the child occurred, thus removing its eligibility to support the crime of felony-murder.

Had Hauptmann's case been tried forty-five years later he could not have been executed for felony-murder, since a New Jersey law enacted in 1982 specified that the death penalty could be imposed only on those who committed the murder themselves or who paid another person to do so. Hauptmann's position also would have been stronger had he been able to have counsel prior to the police interrogation, as he could now, and had he been allowed to learn all the details of the police investigations. In addition, partly in response to the Hauptmann case, New Jersey governors in 1947 were given the right to grant executive clemency on their own rather than having the decision made by the Board of Pardons.

In a particularly thoughtful appraisal of the use of the felony-murder doctrine in the Hauptmann trial, James E. Starrs, a law professor, calls it an example of "prosecutorial shenanigans," marked by "overreach and unpersuasiveness." He notes that the "blunderbuss" indictment against Hauptmann was a juridical subterfuge that would not pass muster today. Hauptmann could not have been indicted for stealing the child, since such a "theft" would not qualify under New Jersey law as larceny, the essential element of burglary. Starrs believes that it was nothing more than wordplay to insist that stealing the child's nightdress rather than the child was sufficient to sustain a charge of burglary.

The felony-murder doctrine has been controversial ever since its creation—"an unsightly wart on the skin of the criminal law," according to some legal scholars. In the United States, the felony-murder rule can lead to the conviction for murder of, say, two robbers who literally scare their victim to death: the victim dies from a heart attack presumably brought on by his confrontation with the felons. In a case where one robber kills the victim, much to the other's horror, the second robber—called a nonslayer participant—can be held responsible for the murder. An arson of a barn that takes the life of a transient sleeping hidden in a corner (unbeknownst to the arsonist, who has searched the site) could become a death-eligible homicide under the felony-murder doctrine. Those seeking to demonstrate the truly illogical reach of the felony-murder doctrine are wont to cite cases in which a law enforcement officer kills a fleeing felon and the felon's accomplice is charged with the murder on the ground that the death would not have occurred had not the pair been engaged in a felonious act.

The Federal Kidnapping Law

The most prominent criminal justice consequence of the Lindbergh case was the passage of a federal kidnapping statute on June 22, 1932, just a month after the child's corpse was discovered. First labeled the Cochran Bill, after its sponsor, but soon and ever after known as the Lindbergh Law, the measure set a penalty of death for kidnapping and stipulated that if a child was not returned three days (later lowered to a single day) after a presumed kidnapping, the FBI was authorized to assist in the search. After seven days, there would be an assumption that the victim had been taken across a state line and the FBI could assume jurisdiction. Objections in Congress to the measure had focused on the bill's encroachment on state rights and the concomitant centralization of too much power in the federal government.

The idea to make kidnapping a federal offense had largely been instigated by the fact that St. Louis was a favorite site for organized-crime kidnappings and that victims often were immediately moved across the state boundary into Illinois, where there were many organized-crime strongholds. The 1934 amendments also escalated the possible penalty for kidnapping "for ransom, reward, or otherwise" to death. There was a further proviso in the 1934 enactment indicating that a sentence of death should not be imposed if, prior to its imposition, the kidnapped person had been liberated and was unharmed. In time, kidnappings, the notable crime of the Lindbergh period ("a very dangerous way to raise money," in Paula Fass's words) became much less common.

More generally, the Lindbergh Law prefaced a series of enactments that over the years would reflect special legislative concern to protect young children. "We get hit in the gut by those cases in which a child is the victim," Fass, a history professor at the University of California, Berkeley, has observed, "and that makes it much easier for laws to get passed." Besides the Lindbergh Law, she specifies what is known as Megan's law, mandating release of information about sexual offenders, which grew out of the sexual murder of Megan Kanka in northern New Jersey, and the so-called three-strikes laws, decreeing sentences of twenty-five years to life for persons convicted of a third offense. The three-strikes laws were passed after the murder of Polly Klaas in California. But there can be another, though rare side to this situation. In Massachusetts, the initial second-degree murder conviction of Louise Woodward, a nineteen-year-old au pair from Britain, for the death of her eight-month-old charge so impressed a legislator with its unfairness that he changed his vote in favor of reinstituting the death penalty, sending the measure down to defeat. Woodward shortly after had her conviction reduced to manslaughter and was sentenced to time spent in custody—279 days.

Life after the Deaths

The Lindberghs would have five more children. They returned to the United States in April 1939, after having lived peacefully for more than three years in England and France. Lindbergh became sympathetic to the Hitler regime, receiving from Hermann Goering, Hitler's deputy, the Service Cross of the German Eagle with the Star, the highest decoration the Third Reich could award a civilian. Before the December 1941 Japanese attack on Pearl Harbor, Lindbergh was the leading crusader for American isolationism and appeasement, much to the chagrin of his early admirers. His incessant theme was that the United States ought to protect its own borders, not waste resources on a fraternal European quarrel. Germany, Britain, France, and Italy, he main-tained, had too much in common to be at war: they should be encouraged to unite to prevent white civilization from being overrun by the yellow and black hordes in the Soviet Union, Africa, and Asia. In an infamous speech in Des Moines, Iowa, on September 11, 1941, Lindbergh blamed the British, the Jews, and the Roosevelt administration for pushing America toward war. Harold Nicolson, an Englishman and close friend of Lindbergh until they split over their different ideological positions, would blame the kidnapping for Lindbergh's tolerance of fascism. "The suffering which that dreadful crime entailed upon . . . himself and those he loved pierced his armor. He identified the outrage to his private life first with the popular press and by inevitable association with freedom of speech, and then with freedom. He began to loathe democracy."

His political views were used to keep Lindbergh from reclaiming his Air Force Reserve commission during the Second World War, but he nonetheless made outstanding contributions to the design of American fighting aircraft and, though a civilian adviser, flew several combat missions in the Pacific theater of war, allegedly in the process of testing aircraft. After the war, he was forgiven, almost, for his isolationist stand. He died of lymphatic cancer on August 26, 1974, at the age of seventy-two on Maui in the Hawaiian Islands, where his family had a home. Anne Morrow Lindbergh celebrated her ninety-first birthday in 1998.

Harold Hoffman, in part because of his role in the Lindbergh case, failed to win reelection as governor in 1938. In 1954, largely through the investigative work of Schwarzkopf, Hoffman was found to have embezzled $300,000 from a state agency he headed. He died six weeks later, on June 5, 1954, of a heart attack in a hotel room that he maintained in New York City.

David Wilentz and Anna Hauptmann, in addition to Anne Morrow Lind-bergh, were hardy survivors among those closely involved in the Lindbergh kidnapping case. Wilentz served as New Jersey's attorney general until 1944, then entered private practice. He became the most influential figure in the state Democratic party organization, "a personality of near legendary impor-tance," a later governor would say. He died in July 1988 at the age of ninety-three. His son would become chief justice of the New Jersey Supreme Court.

In 1981 Anna Hauptmann unsuccessfully petitioned the New Jersey courts to reopen her husband's case and to reverse the earlier decision on the ground that it violated his civil rights. Her case was based on material presented in Kennedy's book, in many instances supported by evidence obtained from the FBI files. Mrs. Hauptmann argued that the prosecutor, in collaboration with the police and others, had suppressed evidence, suborned perjury, manufactured evidence, knowingly presented false evidence, and otherwise violated her husband's civil rights. The court dismissed the action on the ground that a prosecutor, even if he had done what was claimed, was immune from a civil action.[5] Other of Anna Hauptmann's claims, such as those alleging illegal search and seizure, were dismissed on the ground that they were personal to Hauptmann, and still others because the statute of limitations had expired.

Anna Hauptmann died in New Holland, Pennsylvania, on October 10, 1994, less than four months after O. J. Simpson was accused of murdering his former wife and her ill-fated friend. Her ashes were scattered over the cemetery in the German town where she had grown up. A local newspaperman observed that Anna had never remarried, had not changed her last name, had never lost her belief in her husband's innocence, and refused to say the words "with liberty and justice for all" when she recited the pledge of allegiance at public gatherings.

For Further Reading

Two comprehensive reports of the Lindbergh kidnapping are George Waller, *Kidnap: The Story of the Lindbergh Case* (New York: Dial Press, 1961), and Jim Fisher, *The Lindbergh Case* (New Brunswick, N.J.: Rutgers University Press, 1994). Waller's book is used in William A. Prosser, "The Lindbergh Case Revisited: George Waller's 'Kidnap,'" *Minnesota Law Review*, 46 (1961):383–391, as a sounding board for a vigorous and colorful critique of authors who find fault with the Hauptmann verdict.

Revisionist examinations of the trial include Gregory Ahlgren and Stephen Monier, *Crime of the Century: The Lindbergh Kidnapping Hoax* (Boston: Branden Books, 1993), who argue that the baby was killed when Lindbergh accidentally dropped it while playing one of the practical jokes that characterized his behavior. After that, everything was an attempt to cover up his guilt. The book is correctly said by a reviewer to have "not one shred of evidence to support the notion . . . and plenty of evidence to show it as preposterous as it is poisonous."

Noel Behn in *Lindbergh: The Crime* (New York: Atlantic Monthly Press, 1994) offers the equally bizarre idea that the child was killed out of envy by Anne's

---

5. *Hauptmann v. Wilentz*, 570 F. Supp. 351 (D. N.J., 1983). The U.S. Supreme Court plans to reexamine the traditional legal position of prosecutorial immunity during its 1998 session. The case, *Kalina v. Fletcher*, involves a suit brought by a man who was jailed based on allegedly false statements by a prosecutor seeking an arrest warrant.

eldest sister Elisabeth three days before its absence was announced. Behn claims that his informant had obtained affidavits from servants in the Lindbergh household supporting his position, but these, alas, were thrown away by a janitor when they became waterlogged during a storm. He also maintains that Jacob Nosovitsky, who often used the initials J.J. as part of his numerous aliases, wrote the later ransom notes after he had obtained a copy of the original one. Nosovitsky, it is claimed, passed the money to Fisch, who then gave it to Hauptmann. Theon Wright's *In Search of the Lindbergh Baby* (New York: Tower, 1981) insists, quite unbelievably, that the body found in Mercer County was not that of the Lindbergh child.

Anthony Scaduto, *Scapegoat: The Lonesome Death of Bruno Richard Hauptmann* (New York: Putnam, 1976), and, most especially, Ludovic Kennedy, *The Airman and the Carpenter: The Lindbergh Kidnaping and the Framing of Richard Hauptmann* (New York: Viking, 1985), both indicate the considerable flaws in the police work and the shortcomings and fabrication of some of the evidence on which Hauptmann was convicted. But Scaduto's claim that Paul Wendel was the actual kidnapper seems very farfetched.

Anthony K. Dutch, *Hysteria: Lindbergh Kidnap Case* (Philadelphia: Dorrance, 1975), argues that the emotional reactions to the kidnapping overcame rational judgment, a view echoed by Helen M. Hughes in "The Lindbergh Case: A Study of Human Interest and Politics," *American Journal of Sociology*, 42 (1930):32–54. Hughes illustrates how the case was used by the Communist and German media to further ideological ends.

Sidney B. Whipple, who covered the trial for the United Press, reconstructs the evidence in *The Story of the Lindbergh Kidnapping* (New York: Blue Ribbon Books, 1935) and *The Trial of Bruno Richard Hauptmann* (Garden City, N.Y.: Doubleday, 1937). The latter includes extended quotations from the trial transcript as well as a copy of the indictment. John Brant and Edith Renaud, *The True Story of the Lindbergh Kidnapping* (New York: Kroy Wen Publications, 1932), offer a fairly flimsy early examination of the case. The tools of his trade are employed by Dudley D. Schoenfeld to support a highly speculative analysis of Hauptmann's personality in *The Crime and the Criminal: A Psychiatric Study of the Lindbergh Case* (New York: Covici-Friede, 1936). To be read with considerable caution is John F. Condon's *Jafsie Tells All! Revealing the Inside Story of the Lindbergh-Hauptmann Case* (New York: Jonathan Lee, 1946).

The three best studies of Charles Lindbergh's life are Kenneth S. Davis, *The Hero: Charles A. Lindbergh and the American Dream* (New York: Doubleday, 1959); Walter S. Ross, *The Last Hero: Charles A. Lindbergh*, 2nd ed. (New York: Harper and Row, 1976); and A. Scott Berg, *Lindbergh* (New York: Putnam, 1998).

A good brief overview of Lindbergh's life and career can be found in Perry D. Luckett, *Charles A. Lindbergh: A Bio-Bibliography* (New York: Greenwood Press, 1986). Wayne S. Cole details Lindbergh's prewar noninterventionist stand in a sympathetic treatise, *Charles A. Lindbergh and the Battle against American Intervention in World War II* (New York: Harcourt Brace Jovanovich, 1974).

Anne Morrow Lindbergh depicts the anguish of the kidnapping in *Hour of Gold, Hour of Lead: Diaries and Letters of Anne Morrow Lindbergh, 1929–1932* (New York: Harcourt Brace Jovanovich, 1973). Books about her writing career also contain material regarding her reactions to the kidnapping and death of her child. Particularly solid is Dorothy Hermann, *Anne Morrow Lindbergh: A Gift for Life* (New York: Tichnor & Fields, 1992), pp. 86–112 and 146–160. For another first-rate overview of the kidnapping case see Joyce Milton, *Loss of Eden: A Biography of Charles and Anne Morrow Lindbergh* (New York: HarperCollins, 1993), pp. 209–275, 287–347, and 475–479.

A comprehensive collection of legal and other writings on capital punishment is Bryan Vila and Cynthia Morris, eds., *Capital Punishment in the United States: A Documentary History* (Westport, Conn.: Greenwood, 1997). See also William J. Bowers, Glenn L. Pierce, and John F. McDevitt, *Legal Homicide: Death as Punishment in America, 1964–1982* (Boston: Northeastern University Press, 1984), and Mark Costanzo, *Just Revenge: Causes and Consequences of the Death Penalty* (New York: St. Martin's, 1997). A comprehensive legal analysis is provided in Leigh B. Bienen, "The Proportionality Review of Capital Cases by State High Courts after *Gregg:* Only 'The Appearance of Justice,'" *Journal of Criminal Law and Criminology,* 87 (1996):130–314. C. Ronald Huff, Arye Rattner, and Edward Sagarin's *Convicted but Innocent: Wrongful Conviction and Public Policy* (Thousand Oaks, Calif.: Sage, 1996) examines possible errors of justice in capital cases. On the same subject see Hugo Adam Bedau and Michael L. Radelet, "Miscarriages of Justice in Potentially Capital Cases," *Stanford Law Review,* 40 (1987):21–179, later expanded, with Constance E. Putnam, as *In Spite of Innocence: Erroneous Convictions in Capital Cases* (Boston: Northeastern University Press, 1992).

An excellent review of the felony-murder doctrine as it affected the Lindbergh case is James E. Starrs, "The Prosecution of Bruno Richard Hauptmann: An Imitation of Falconry," *Journal of Forensic Sciences,* 28 (1983):1083–1107. On the felony-murder rule in general see Norval Morris, "The Felon's Responsibility for the Lethal Acts of Others," *University of Pennsylvania Law Review,* 105 (1956):50–88, and George P. Fletcher, "Reflections on Felony-Murder," *Southwestern University Law Review,* 12 (1981):413–429.

Other noteworthy material on the Lindbergh case can be found in Gabriel Heatter, *There's Good News Tonight* (Garden City, N.Y.: Doubleday, 1960), pp. 65–80; and Edward Oxford, "The *Other* Trial of the Century," *American History*, 30 (July 1995):18–27, 66–69. Paula S. Fass discusses the moral issue of paying ransom in terms of the Lindbergh case in *Kidnapped: Child Abduction in America* (New York: Oxford University Press, 1997), pp. 95–131. See also Ernest K. Alix, *Ransom Kidnapping in America, 1874–1974* (Carbondale: Southern Illinois University Press, 1978). On the kidnapping laws that emerged in the wake of the Hauptmann case, see Robert C. Finley, "The Lindbergh Law," *Georgetown University Law Journal*, 28 (1940):908–942.

A solid account of the excesses of the trial and an analysis of whether Hauptmann would have had constitutional protection forty years later is Louis M. Seidman, "The Trial and Execution of Bruno Richard Hauptmann: Another Case that 'Will Not Die,'" *Georgetown University Law Journal*, 66 (1977):1–48. An excellent critique of handwriting analysis is D. Michael Risinger and Michael J. Saks, "Science and Nonscience in the Courts: *Daubert* Meets Handwriting Identification Expertise," *Iowa Law Review*, 82 (1996):21–74.

Arthur Koehler tells of his work to identify the ladder in "Technique Used in Tracing the Lindbergh Kidnapping Ladder," *Journal of Criminal Law and Criminology*, 27 (1937):712–724. A thorough and strongly supportive review of Koehler's work is Shirley A. Graham, "Anatomy of the Lindbergh Kidnapping," *Journal of Forensic Sciences*, 42 (1997):368–377. The expert evidence in the trial is thoroughly examined in terms of what is now known in a series of articles in the *Journal of Forensic Sciences*, 28 (1983):1035–1107. The second-guessers largely concur with the state's witnesses, though Michael Baden, who came to play a prominent role in the trial of O. J. Simpson, indicates that the autopsy work "left much to be desired."

Transcripts of the case and court decisions include the following: *State v. Hauptmann*, 180 Atl. 809 (1935), is the opinion of the New Jersey Court of Errors and Appeals that affirmed the trial court verdict. The U.S. Supreme Court denied certiorari in *Hauptmann v. New Jersey*, 296 U.S. 649 (1935). *Hauptmann v. Wilentz*, 570 F. Supp. 351 (1983), is the decision in the post-execution civil rights case brought by Anna Hauptmann. The full transcript of the Hauptmann trial can be found in volumes 1373–1376 (1935) of the records of the New Jersey Court of Errors and Appeals and in the library of the Northwestern University School of Law. There are also very extensive holdings on the case in the Lindbergh Archives at the New Jersey State Police Museum and Learning Center in West Trenton.

Chapter Five

Alger Hiss (1948), the House Un-American Activities Committee, and the Courts

Alger Hiss, almost blind, died at the Lenox Hill Hospital in New York City on November 15, 1996, four days following his ninety-second birthday. The cause of death was cardiopulmonary complications following a lung infection. Hiss took to his grave the answer to a question that has bedeviled many people for many years: Had he truly been engaged in espionage for the Soviet Union, America's cold-war enemy, or was he the victim of a plot to discredit him and to advance the political fortunes of, among others, Richard Nixon, the thirty-five-year-old first-term congressman from California who leapfrogged to the presidency in considerable measure because of the visibility he obtained when he set in motion the process that sent Hiss to prison? When Nixon ran for the U.S. Senate after masterminding the Hiss case, his victory margin exceeded that of every other Senate winner in the country.

Nixon was by far the most intelligent and hardworking member of the congressional committee that choreographed Hiss's downfall; indeed, it in no way stretches the truth to describe the other House Un-American Activities Committee members as disasters: typically bigots, rabble-rousers, clowns, and embarrassments to the more respectable members of Congress. Nixon also enjoyed an advantage not shared by his committee colleagues. The FBI regularly fed investigative results about possible Communist subversives to the Reverend John F. Cronin, a Catholic priest who had dedicated himself to identifying security risks in government. Cronin, impressed by Nixon, was passing along relevant information, some of it about Hiss, to the congressman. This stacked deck that Nixon used in the HUAC hunt for Communists was essential to his skyrocketing career, which, a biographer points out, was marked during the Hiss episode by "hard work and shrewd instinct, political calculus, and courage."

Neither Hiss nor Nixon ever budged from his original position about the case. Hiss spent the remainder of his life seeking vindication. He and his supporters insisted that he was an innocent man convicted by postwar paranoia about Communism. Nixon maintained that if the American people knew the truth about Alger Hiss, they would boil him in oil.

The Temper of the Time

Commentaries on Hiss's death emphasized that his trial reflected the mood of the time, that it took place in a period of "Hissteria" and that it was "the first morality play of the red-baiting era." "If God plays games," a *Time* magazine essay noted, "having Alger Hiss die during the O.J. trial was one of 1996's best; the principal of one generation's Trial of the Century left the stage exactly one week before the principal of another generation's Trial of the Century ascended the witness stand for the first time."

The *Time* essayist believed that the Simpson case reflected deep racial divisions in the nation; he saw the Hiss case as mirroring the ideological divisions of its time. The 1940s, when the case erupted, was a period of fierce political anger and unease. The country's mood is not readily conveyed in words: emotions are best felt, not described. And the emotions underlying the prosecution of Hiss were extraordinarily intense. "It is hard to recreate the dreadful atmosphere which suffused the late 1940s in America," a Hiss obituary writer noted. A British historian has called the period "The Great Fear." Today the relationship between the United States and Russia is placid: Americans are indifferent and condescending toward a country, then the kingpin of an empire, that is experiencing a high degree of instability and economic difficulty, and seems like a weary, toothless tiger. But at the time of the Hiss trial, Soviet Communism was regarded as an ominous, encroaching threat to the integrity of the United States, even to the continuance of the country's democratic freedom.

This searing concern can be better understood by remembering a few historic landmarks. A Communist government took control of czarist Russia by revolutionary means in 1917, after the country's military collapse near the end of the First World War. The new regime held out the promise of reforms that on paper had great appeal to people who regarded American capitalism as repressive and who saw economic and social inequality among Americans as hypocritical and intolerable. Few in the United States who supported the Soviet Union actually had experienced life there firsthand, even for relatively brief periods: there were no jet airplanes, there was careful screening of those admitted to the Soviet Union, and those few handpicked American visitors, typically lacking foreign language skills, were unable to communicate with ordinary Russians. The totalitarian Soviet government controlled the media and few Russians were courageous—or foolhardy—enough to criticize the regime.

Soviet Communism, with full employment and a bias toward promoting the welfare of the working class, seemed to some, particularly American intellectuals, to represent a contemporary Eden, the best hope for better human conditions. There were great cynicism and weariness in America after the First World War. For its part, the Soviet Union seemed intent on fomenting populist revolution around the globe, adhering to Marx's precept that the workers of the world should unite and throw off their shackles.

The sympathy of some Americans for the Soviet regime increased dramatically during the worldwide Great Depression of the 1930s, when signs of economic failure and devastation, including massive unemployment, appeared everywhere. Estimates are that one of every four Americans was unable to find work in March 1933, when Franklin Roosevelt was sworn in as president. Breadlines and soup kitchens issuing free food were common sights: vendors, often former white-collar workers, sold apples on the streets for five cents each. But these paltry efforts were inadequate. Many starved; many died without medical care. In the 1930s, Hiss's wife volunteered to work in a tent city where the homeless and unemployed camped in tarpaper shacks on the streets and parks along swanky Riverside Drive in New York City. There were no safety nets—no social security and no unemployment insurance.

The temporary alliance during the Second World War between Hitler's Nazi Germany and Stalin's Soviet Union disenchanted many American Communists. But when the Germans turned on their momentary allies and invaded Russia, support swung back toward the Soviets, particularly when they fought with such extraordinary bravery, driving the German troops back from the gates of Leningrad and, arguably, making the most significant military contribution to the ultimate Allied victory. The Second World War produced a host of spies, and the postwar period was filled with tales of international espionage, many involving atomic secrets.

The relationship between the United States and the Soviet Union turned sour soon after the end of the Second World War. The Soviets unilaterally took control of Poland and Czechoslovakia, bled them dry, restricted travel abroad, and held elections that were a caricature of the democratic process. This was the beginning of the period that came to be known as the cold war, its essence enunciated by Winston Churchill in a speech at Fulton, Missouri, in June 1946, when he coined the term "iron curtain" to express the forced separation of the Soviet republics from the Western democracies. The enmity toward the Russians also contained an element of mortal fear because the Soviet Union had developed the atomic bomb, with its monumental death-dealing potential, and this had become a major consideration in international relations. Today's generation can locate relics of this period in the yellow arrows in public buildings that point to basement bomb shelters and in the memories and pictures of schoolchildren of the period crouched under their schoolroom desks, practicing their response to possible Soviet air raids. Hundreds of thousands of American families fortified their cellars as bomb shelters and stocked them with water, canned food, and guns, preparations that now seem futile given the long-term destructive power of nuclear weapons. The cold war would not come to an end until the cataclysmic collapse of Communism.

During the cold war period, the crusade in the United States against present and past Communists was fueled by anger at Soviet expansionism, frustration over an inability to triumph over an ideological rival, and concern that the Soviet cause was and had been aided by traitors among us. To be labeled un-American was a profound insult, likely to bring ruin if it could be made to stick. The deep fear of domestic Communism seemed to be belied by the insignificant number of American Communists—an estimated 60,000 in 1948. But officials such as J. Edgar Hoover, the head of the FBI, would proclaim that the Russian revolution had been achieved by an even smaller cadre of Communists.

There was much political capital to be had in tying oneself to the campaign to root out and punish alleged Communists in our midst. The media were avid for tales of the powerful being toppled from their perches. Once the hunt became public, there often was no turning back; an accusation that collapsed could undermine the credentials of the accuser. Unmasking Communists became a hardball endeavor, often played ruthlessly.

This was the backdrop against which the highly theatrical case against Alger Hiss developed. Hiss came to symbolize all that was rotten and disloyal within the government. Those who have studied the Hiss case by and large believe that he was guilty of perjury and quite likely also guilty of espionage, that is, of passing government documents to the Soviets. The idea that Nixon, working with former Communists such as Whittaker Chambers, might have helped to frame Hiss to serve his own ends, however, seemed less farfetched after the publication of details of Nixon's orchestration of the cover-up of the Watergate break-in and the duplicity and underhand tactics preserved in Nixon's tape-recorded White House conversations.

The Protagonists: Hiss and Chambers

Alger Hiss possessed impressive credentials; he had led "a gilded life," one biographer would observe. Hiss was regarded (although not universally) as cold ("icy" was a common adjective), haughty, conceited, and off-putting; in today's vocabulary he would be called uptight. An obituary in the *New York Times* observed that he was a "slender, self-possessed patrician." Hiss had been born into an upper-middle-class family in Baltimore, the fourth of five children. The religious tradition in the family, as Hiss's son would note, was soap-swimming Presbyterianism, which meant that if you went swimming, you always took a cake of soap along so that you wouldn't waste your time.

Hiss, born November 11, 1904, was raised by his mother and aunt after his once-prosperous father, an executive in a dry-goods company, committed suicide by slitting his throat with a razor when Hiss was two and a half years old; the young boy would not learn this for another eight years. In 1929, when Hiss was twenty-five, his sister Mary Ann also killed herself, much in the manner of Violet Sharpe in the Lindbergh case, using a caustic household cleanser for the purpose. Hiss's older brother, Bosley, whom he admired greatly, died in his twenties of Bright's disease, a kidney affliction, probably aggravated by steady dissipation.

Hiss received a bachelor's degree in 1926 from Johns Hopkins University, where he was inducted into Phi Beta Kappa for his outstanding academic record, was voted the most popular student by the graduating class, and was a cadet commander in the campus ROTC unit. He then obtained a law degree in 1929 from Harvard, where he became one of the favored "hot dogs" of Professor Felix Frankfurter, later to be appointed to the U.S. Supreme Court. After Harvard, Hiss served as a law clerk for the eighty-eight-year-old Supreme Court Justice Oliver Wendell Holmes, arguably the man with the keenest intellect ever to sit on that bench. Holmes's life conveys a sense of the relatively short history of the United States: Holmes's grandmother had told him about her memories of the British coming to Boston during the Revolutionary War; as a captain during the Civil War, Holmes had met Abraham Lincoln at the front; and when Holmes retired from the Supreme Court in 1932, Franklin D. Roosevelt was about to occupy the White House. In three generations the country had gone from a colony to the beginnings of the Second World War.

After working briefly with top-of-the-line law firms first in Boston and then in New York, Hiss took up government employment in 1933 as a legal counsel in the newly created Agricultural Adjustment Administration during the Roosevelt presidency. Hiss would say that he was challenged by the prospect of being part of a team striving to lift the country out of its economic misery. He subsequently served as a staff attorney on the Senate subcommittee to investigate the munitions industry (the Nye Committee, so named after its chair), a group that sought to demonstrate the unholy profits that corporate entrepreneurs made by evading laws forbidding the sale of weapons to actual or potential war combatants. Three years later, during the summer of 1936, Hiss joined the Department of State. In 1945, he attended the Yalta conference as an adviser to President Roosevelt. It was at Yalta that Roosevelt, suffering serious health problems that soon led to his death, made concessions to the Soviet Union for which conservatives never forgave him. Hiss then served as temporary secretary-general when the United Nations was created in San Francisco that same year. After the FBI reported to the White House that Hiss might be a Soviet agent, he was covertly encouraged to move in February 1947 from his State Department job to head the Carnegie Endowment for International Peace, a nonprofit organization located in New York City.

Whittaker Chambers, Hiss's accuser before the House Un-American Activities Committee, was a distinctly different person from the elite, self-contained, self-controlled Hiss. Chambers was pudgy, unprepossessing, usually disheveled (he was commonly described as "seedy"). Before they were repaired, his teeth were appallingly rotten, his mouth containing several empty sockets and many blackened stumps. He often was out of work and out of money. Chambers generally was regarded even by his friends as obsessive and given to melodrama; he had used at least a dozen different aliases at various times in his life. But there was no question regarding Chambers's keen intelligence.

Chambers had been named Jay Vivian Chambers when he was born on April 1, 1901, in Philadelphia, making him three and a half years older than Hiss. In his autobiography, *Witness*, Chambers describes the beginning of his life in the same melodramatic fashion that he would live it: "Snow was falling and soon turned into a blizzard." Like so much else that he wrote about himself, this was untrue: the U.S. Weather Bureau records show no precipitation in Philadelphia that day and a temperature range with a low of thirty-eight degrees and a high of fifty-six.

The Chambers family moved to Lynbrook on Long Island, twenty miles east of New York City, when he was a small child. The family was poor; the father, a book and magazine illustrator, left his wife, a former stock-company actress given to melodrama, and his children to live with another man. Richard, Chambers's alcoholic younger brother, killed himself in 1926 at the age of twenty-two after two previously unsuccessful attempts at suicide. For the last try, he drank a quart of whiskey, placed his head on a pillow inside the kitchen oven, put some books on a chair on which to rest his feet, and then turned on the gas. "We were gentle people and incapable of coping with the world," said the note he left behind.

Chambers was chosen to deliver the class prophesy at his high school graduation. His first draft offended the principal; he had predicted that one of the female students was destined to become a prostitute. Chambers wrote a second version that was acceptable, but at the ceremony he delivered the original. As a student at Columbia University, he won a reputation as a brilliant writer. In 1925, still at Columbia, he joined the Communist Party, which was a permitted organization in the United States until outlawed by the Smith Act in 1940 on the ground that its aim was to overthrow the American government. Chambers was tossed out of Columbia for blasphemy (he had published in the student magazine a play humanizing Christ), and he briefly went to work as a reporter for the *Daily Worker*, the Communist Party newspaper.

After that, he got a job on the left-wing magazine *New Masses*. Chambers said that he was recruited in 1932 as a Soviet spy by Max Bedacht (who later denied the allegation), serving in the underground—the "crypts of Communism," as one writer put it—as a member of the Fourth Section of the Soviet Military Intelligence division. At the time he lived in Glen Gardner in Hunterdon County, New Jersey, the same county where the Lindbergh infant had been kidnapped. Assuming a variety of aliases, Chambers learned to photograph secret American government documents and then ship the film to Russia, often using sailors on Russian ships anchored in New York as carriers.

By the summer of 1937, Chambers was ready to leave the Communists, disenchanted by the purge trials in Moscow of out-of-favor party leaders. But he became concerned for his life when he learned of the killing in Switzerland of a Soviet agent who had denounced Stalin. He gradually began to break with the party either in late 1937 or toward the middle of 1938, taking numerous self-protective precautions and yet, at the same time, listing his number in the telephone book when he lived in Florida. As Jonathan Aitken, a Nixon biographer observes, when Chambers fought his way back into the mainstream "his conversion from Communism to anti-Communism was so sincere that it bordered on religious mysticism." He first joined the Episcopalian church and then became a Quaker, which was the religion of Priscilla Hiss, Alger's wife. William Jowitt, a British judge, would write of Chambers, "I distrust his judgment—and his evidence—just because it is so passionate," but this may represent no more than a style preference that differentiates the British upper class from Americans.

Who Said What

The matters that resulted in Hiss's imprisonment come down to a conflict between two stories, Hiss's own version of his relationship with Chambers and the statements of Chambers. Alistair Cooke, at the time a correspondent in the United States for the *Manchester Guardian* and later the host for the *Masterpiece Theater* television series, captures the essence of the Hiss case:

> The issue was very simple. Chambers, an ex-Communist, had accused Hiss, formerly in the State Department during the New Deal, of having at that time pilfered confidential State documents and passed them on to him in the service of Communism. Chambers said that Hiss had been a Communist then and was his best friend in the party. Hiss denied all of it. He said that he had never known the man as Chambers, that the man was never more than a deadbeat acquaintance. Hiss denied that he had ever been a Communist or anything like one.

It was while he was working for the Nye Committee, some time during 1934 or 1935, that Hiss claimed that he had first met Whittaker Chambers. Hiss maintained that Chambers, using the name George Crosley, sought information from him for an article he hoped to publish about the committee's work. At about that time, the Hiss family was moving to a larger apartment in Washington, D.C., and Hiss invited Chambers and his wife and their year-and-a-half-old daughter, who had no place of their own, to stay in the apartment they were vacating, since the next month's rent already had been paid. Before their few possessions arrived, the Chamberses spent a few days with the Hisses in their new place, which had an extra upstairs bedroom.

In addition to use of the vacated apartment, Hiss, having bought a new car, said that out of sympathy he gave his dilapidated 1929 black Ford Model-A roadster to Chambers. Chambers maintained that the car had been donated to the Communist Party. Hiss acknowledged that sometime in late 1935 Chambers presented him with an expensive Bokhara Oriental rug that he said some wealthy patron had given to him. Hiss said he accepted the rug because he never had been paid the money Chambers borrowed from him. Chambers, on the other hand, said that the rug was given to Hiss as a token of the Communist Party's pleasure with his services on its behalf.

Priscilla Hiss's self-evident misgivings about the Chamberses' presence in her house would be remembered by all parties. Hiss's wife remains perhaps the most enigmatic figure in the case. She was a Bryn Mawr graduate and did a year's additional work on scholarship at Yale. She had strong esthetic interests and was very self-possessed and hard-edged; many called her domineering, and few seemed to like her. As her older son, Timothy Hobson, told an interviewer years later: "Pros [her nickname] is tough. While she is answering your question politely, she might be inwardly thinking in Quaker language: 'Thee is a son-of-a-bitch.'" (Of his stepfather Hobson said, "Alger is a combination of a beatitude and an IBM machine.") Hiss had married Priscilla despite a telegram from his mother that warned: DO NOT TAKE THIS FATAL STEP. Priscilla Hiss suffered deeply over the plight of exploited humanity but was not very indulgent toward individual members of the human race. Many thought that it was she who had drawn her husband into the Communist Party and that his denials were made to protect her; if so, he was successful, since no charge was ever brought against her. Nonetheless, she seemed to be devastated by the legal proceedings, never adequately recovering a sense of tranquillity after her husband's trials.

Priscilla Hiss had been divorced before she married Alger and had a young son by her first marriage. The Hisses' own marriage would produce another son, Tony, later a writer for the *New Yorker*. Tony described his family's situation after his father's conviction as "like living in a fairy tale, with a curse that couldn't be lifted." The Hisses' marriage broke up in 1959, well after the perjury case had been judicially resolved. Alger Hiss married Isabelle Johnson after Priscilla's death in 1984.

Espionage and Perjury

Chambers would maintain that he and Hiss were very close for several years, and that Hiss passed on to him secret information that he had access to through his work for the State Department. But Hiss never came before a criminal court on a charge of espionage: the three-year statute of limitations for that offense when committed in peacetime had expired, although in 1950, as an aftermath of the Hiss case, the statute of limitations for peacetime espionage would be extended to ten years. Instead of espionage, Hiss was tried for perjury, for knowingly providing inaccurate responses to a grand jury inquiry. Hiss's conviction went a long way to legitimate the fiery hunt for real and alleged Communists in government, entertainment, and education in America over the next decade.

The Hiss case illustrates, among other matters, the ability of a congressional committee and a federal prosecutor to ensnare persons on another charge if the crime that most directly implicates them is for some reason beyond reach. Al Capone, notorious as an organized-crime killer, was convicted for income tax evasion when there was insufficient legal proof to support an indictment for the more notorious crimes that he was known—or presumed—to have committed. In our review of the trial of Bruno Richard Hauptmann we saw how a jerry-built felony-murder charge, pegged to Hauptmann's theft of a kidnap victim's sleeping garment, was employed to send him to the electric chair.

The elements of the Hiss case began to come together publicly in 1948, when Chambers, by then a senior editor at *Time* magazine, named Hiss as a onetime Communist Party member. Chambers said that he had met Hiss in 1934, not to get information for a story on the Nye Committee, but to give him orders; Hiss, he said, was already operating under Communist Party discipline.

In 1939, two days after the Soviet Union signed a nonaggression pact with Germany, Chambers had provided to Adolph A. Berle, Jr., the assistant secretary of state and President Roosevelt's intelligence liaison, a list of persons in the government who he claimed were still active Communists. Alger Hiss's name and that of his younger brother, Donald, were the last on the roster. Chambers said that the men had been cut loose from general party activities and told that their function was not to engage in espionage but to rise as high as they could in the government, to positions where they could make decisions favorable to the Soviet Union and, in Chambers's words, "mess up policy."

Later, in March 1945 and August 1948, Chambers told the FBI about Hiss, and Hiss's name also was mentioned independently by two FBI informants in 1945, neither of whom knew Chambers: one was Elizabeth Bentley, a Vassar graduate and former Communist Party courier; the other, Igor Gouzenko, was a code clerk who had worked at the Russian embassy in Ottawa. Hiss suffered little from these disclosures. It was a time in American history when a very large number of persons were being irresponsibly labeled Communists or "fellow travelers." But the whispers turned into a shout in August 1948, when Chambers appeared as a witness before the House Un-American Activities Committee. Because the proceedings were so complex, we will number the formal steps that made up the Hiss case.

1. CHAMBERS AND HUAC (AUGUST 3, 1948)

The House Un-American Activities Committee was constituted in 1938 to root out Fascists and Communists from among those holding positions of power, influence, and trust in the United States. The committee had no authority to indict, but it could refer matters to the Justice Department for further investigation. Statements before the committee were privileged; they could not be challenged as libel or slander. Many disapproved of the tactics the committee adopted, particularly its undisciplined public allegations that could ruin a person's career. Others thought it about time that traitors in their midst were being unmasked.

Chambers told HUAC members the story of his spying activities for the Soviet Union and named Alger Hiss, who he called a "very close friend," as a member of a Communist cell of eight government officials who met clandestinely in Washington. Espionage, he said, was one of the "eventual objectives" of the group, but he did not specify any such actual activity, indicating that "these people were specifically not wanted to act as sources of information." Chambers said that when he had left the party Hiss was the only person he tried to persuade to do the same. He said that he went to Hiss's house to plead with him and his wife, but the Hisses remained unconvinced and, though "he cried when we separated," Hiss refused to break with the Communist Party. Later, Chambers would say that he had failed to impute espionage to Hiss during the early stages of the case "for reasons of friendship, and because Mr. Hiss is one of the most brilliant young men in the country, [in order] not to do injury more than necessary to Mr. Hiss."

Richard Nixon, a first-term congressman and the junior member of HUAC, was particularly impressed by one of Chambers's statements, a prediction that would prove to be stunningly incorrect: "I know that I am leaving the winning side for the losing side, but it is better to die on the losing side than to live under Communism." Nixon was also impressed by the fact that while Chambers named Alger and Priscilla Hiss as well as Hiss's brother Donald as

Communists, he declared that Donald's wife was not a party member. That, for Nixon, had a ring of honesty.

2. HISS AND HUAC (AUGUST 5, 1948)

Alger Hiss was the only person named by Chambers who responded to the charge; the others, more patient or at least more wary, ultimately would fare very much better than Hiss. Six of them took the Fifth Amendment, refusing to say whether they were or had been Communists or whether they knew Alger Hiss or Whittaker Chambers.

Besieged by calls from newspaper reporters, Hiss requested to appear before the committee as soon as possible to clear his name. "I do not know Mr. Chambers and, so far as I am aware have never laid eyes on him," he telegraphed the HUAC chairman. Two days later Hiss, testifying under oath, made a very favorable appearance before the committee. Radiating confidence, he was applauded by the audience when he finished his testimony: most onlookers believed that the committee had again overreached, and that Hiss should be exonerated. Hiss's denial of Communist Party membership was categorical:

> *I am not and never have been a member of the Communist Party. I do not and never have adhered to the tenets of the Communist Party. I am not and never have been a member of any Communist-front organization. I have never followed the Communist Party line, directly or indirectly. To the best of my knowledge, none of my friends is a Communist.*

Had he left it at that, Nixon would say years later, it probably would have been the end of the matter; Hiss "would have been home free." Numerous earlier witnesses had gone their way unbothered on the basis of similar denials or even when they took the Fifth Amendment, refusing to respond to questions, usually about their possible party membership and their associates. But Hiss made two strategic blunders. First, he irritated Nixon, always thin-skinned, by treating him as a rather unsavory creature and by his suave East Coast elite manners. "He was rather insolent to me," Nixon later would tell a newspaperman. "His manner and tone were insulting to the extreme. Frankly, I didn't like it." HUAC's lead investigator, Robert Stripling, who played a major role in lining up evidence against Hiss, believed that for Nixon the case became a personal vendetta. "He was no more concerned about whether Hiss was a communist than a billy goat," Stripling would say, certainly an overstatement but one with a kernel of truth.

Second, Hiss unnecessarily and with fatal consequences denied that he even knew Chambers, albeit hedging the statement with the tendentious prose that marks a lawyer's statements: "To the best of my knowledge, I never heard of Whittaker Chambers," and "So far as I know, I have never laid eyes on him, and I should like to have the opportunity to do so." Hiss was too skilled a legal strategist by far; the equivocations characteristic of his profession conveyed the image of someone trying to hide something. Nixon correctly pegged Hiss as "much too careful a witness" and "a little too mouthy."

The remainder of the committee members preferred to take the Hiss case off their shopping list, but Nixon, in a decision crucial to his later political success, decided to pursue the matter: the flatly contradictory stories indicated to him that someone was lying. "In view of that fact," Nixon declared, "I want to proceed further." First, though, he had to determine if Chambers was telling the truth. Nixon got HUAC to appoint him chair of a three-person subcommittee specifically charged with looking into Chambers's allegations against Hiss.

Nixon's quest was considerably aided by J. Edgar Hoover's FBI, which secretly provided him with information from its extensive files. Hoover believed that if Thomas Dewey won the 1948 presidential election he was a likely choice for attorney general or for a Supreme Court appointment. The Hiss case could be used to challenge Truman during his forthcoming presidential race against Dewey. Truman already had climbed far out on a political limb when he bitingly labeled HUAC's allegations against Hiss "red herrings."[1]

3. Chambers and the Nixon Subcommittee (August 7, 1948)

The subcommittee met secretly with Chambers in a New York hotel room and grilled him relentlessly about specific, intimate details regarding his alleged relationship with Hiss and his family. Chambers said that Hiss had known him only as "Carl," his underground name, and that he never employed a last name. Much of what he told the congressmen about the Hisses was dead wrong. Hiss, for instance, was four inches taller than Chambers said he was, was not a teetotaler, and neither he nor his friends ever called Priscilla "Dilly," as Chambers testified they did. But then, he was going back more than a

---

1. The term derives from the practice of fishermen dragging a red herring across the bow of a vessel to camouflage other scents. More generally it has come to mean any diversion intended to distract attention from the real issue.

decade. For reasons unknown, Chambers, who would be blithely forthcoming during the trials about the most sordid aspects of his own life, also denied some things that obviously were correct, and used the same kind of obfuscating language that Hiss often hid behind. Thus:

> *Stripling: Did you ever go under the name of George Crosley?*
>
> *Chambers: Not to my knowledge.*

At the same time, Chambers provided very many details that seemed telling—for example, his memory that the Hisses were amateur ornithologists and had been greatly excited when they spotted a rare prothonotary warbler at a canal near the Potomac River. Chambers and later his wife also supplied numerous and specific details of the day-to-day activities of the Hisses and what their household furnishings looked like, items such as gold-stenciled Hitchcock chairs. Hiss's supporters would continuously maintain that Chambers had been fed most of this information during the three and a half months that he met almost daily with FBI agents from mid-morning until 4:00 or 4:30 in the afternoon; the FBI had taken Chambers to the various Hiss houses about which he would testify. For its part, the FBI claimed that the sessions with Chambers, and sometimes with his wife, were only to obtain as much information as could be had about the Communist conspiracy in the United States.

Yet during this phase of the investigation, Chambers continued to lie to all those who interrogated him when asked if he possessed any supporting evidence to back up his allegations about Hiss and the Communist Party. Thus:

> *Nixon: Do you have any other evidence, any factual evidence, to bear out your claim that Mr. Hiss was a member of the Communist Party?*
>
> *Chambers: Nothing beyond the fact that he submitted himself for the two or three years that I knew him as a dedicated and disciplined Communist.*

4. Hiss and HUAC (August 16, 1948)

The House Un-American Activities Committee suffered a serious image setback on August 16, the day that Hiss was to testify before it in an executive session. Harry Dexter White, a former Treasury Department official and in 1948 a faculty member at Harvard, who very likely had been a Communist agent, had appeared before HUAC three days previously. He had asked the chair in private that he be given a rest period every hour since he was recovering from a severe heart attack. The committee chair was J. Parnell Thomas, who soon would be convicted in criminal court for padding his staff payroll and receiving kickbacks from his employees. Thomas publicly embarrassed White by reading his request for rest periods into the record. Then, on August 16, White suffered a fatal heart attack, believed by many to be connected to the strain of his committee appearance. Had White lived, HUAC very possibly would have focused on him, an easier target, rather than on Hiss.

This second appearance of Hiss before the House Un-American Activities Committee was directed toward testing the information about him that Chambers had provided. Hiss was at a considerable disadvantage. Not having been given a transcript of what Chambers had said, Hiss unknowingly substantiated many of his accuser's observations about his personal habits. Had he been forewarned, Hiss might also have been able to call attention to inaccuracies in Chambers's claims.

The committee was particularly taken with an interchange in which Hiss was asked about bird-watching by one of the members who slyly suggested that he himself shared that hobby. Had Hiss ever seen a prothonotary warbler, the HUAC questioner wanted to know. Hiss's sudden excitement—"I saw one right here on the Potomac. Beautiful yellow head, a gorgeous bird!"—seemed to cinch the question of Chambers's reliability for most of the committee. Finally sensing that he was being sandbagged, Hiss wanted to know whether Nixon had been pumping Chambers for information and not allowing Hiss to see the results. Hiss said he had been told that Nixon had spent the weekend at Chambers's farm. "No," the congressman responded, "I have never spent the night with Mr. Chambers." It was not a lie, but it skipped over the point, since Nixon had thrashed over Chambers's recollections during several sessions at Chambers's farm.

Hiss also broke from his previous categoric denials that he had never met Chambers by suggesting tentatively that perhaps (after looking at newspaper photographs) Chambers was the man he had known as George Crosley, a freelance reporter and freeloading acquaintance with whom he crossed paths many years earlier when Hiss was the staff member who handled most of the public relations for the Nye Committee.

At the end of the hearing, one of the HUAC congressmen summed up the general feeling of all those who had listened to the contradictory testimony. "Whichever of you is lying," he said, "is the greatest actor America has ever produced."

5. Hiss and Chambers, HUAC (August 17, 1948)

A day later the two men were taken to confront one another in a private committee session. While Hiss now was suggesting that he might possibly have known Chambers under another name, he insisted that before he could be absolutely certain about this he wanted Chambers to read aloud. Then in a bit of low comedy he examined Chambers's teeth, much like a prospective buyer at a horse auction; it turned out that Chambers had gotten dentures since the men had first met. Finally, Hiss declared that the man known to the committee as Whittaker Chambers was someone he had known as George Crosley.

Hiss was not nearly as triumphant in this hearing as he had been in the first one. Committee members clearly were rallying behind Chambers. Hiss used the words "to the best of my recollection" 198 times. Nixon's exasperation with what he saw as evasions reached a flash point when Hiss kept qualifying his recollection about giving the Ford to Chambers. "You can certainly testify 'Yes' or 'No' as to whether you gave him a car," he asserted. "How many cars have you given away in your life, Mr. Hiss?"

The uninflected stenographic report of the hearing fails to convey the emotional pitch of some interchanges between Nixon and Hiss, but it begins to indicate the developing hostility of the men toward each other and the high stakes involved. One barbed exchange came when Chambers had been dealing with questions from Hiss about whether he might have used the name George Crosley. The record shows what was said next:

Nixon: Just one moment. Since some repartee goes on between these two people, I think Mr. Chambers should be sworn.

Hiss: That is a good idea.

One of the committee members administered the oath. Then the congressman from California spoke out in a tone of controlled anger:

Nixon: Mr. Hiss, may I say something? I suggested that he be sworn, and when I say something like that I want no interruptions from you.

Hiss retorted to Nixon that since the committee had promised that what had been said the day before would be held in confidence and, despite this, the newspapers had carried detailed stories about the session, there was "no occasion for you to use that tone of voice in speaking to me." At the conclusion of the session, the committee chair noted politely, as was the custom: "That is all. Thank you very much." Gracelessly, Hiss responded: "I don't reciprocate."

"Italicize that in the record," the chair instructed. And so that too was done, conveying the churlishness that characterized much of Hiss's behavior during the session.

6. HISS AND CHAMBERS, HUAC (AUGUST 25, 1948)

A week later, in an atmosphere well described as something between a sauna and a bullfight, the committee staged a dramatic public confrontation between Hiss and Chambers in a caucus room in Washington packed with more than five hundred people. It was the first televised congressional hearing ever, though there were but 325,000 television sets in the nation at the time. Hiss clearly was on the defensive now, and the committee treated him much less kindly than they had before Chambers had offered his barrage of details about the Hisses' lifestyle and the closeness between the two families.

Typical was an interchange in which Hiss again noted the importance of Chambers's dental work to his identification of his accuser. Nixon's response

Hiss and Chambers face each other during a confrontation before the House Un-American Activities Committee. Hiss is the man standing on the far left; Chambers, also standing, is at the far right. AP/World Wide Photos

was sarcastic: "I am just wondering," he said, "Didn't you ever see Crosley with his mouth closed?"

Toward the end of the session, in a move that by now seemed to be almost mandatory if Hiss was to have any chance to salvage his reputation, he challenged Chambers to repeat his charges outside the hearing room, where he no longer would enjoy immunity from prosecution for libel, slander, or perjury.

7. The Issue Is Joined: Hiss Files Suit against Chambers (August 27, 1948)

Chambers did what Hiss had demanded of him, appearing on *Meet the Press*, where he proclaimed: "Alger Hiss was a Communist and may be now." Hiss filed a $50,000 slander suit a month later, alleging that Chambers had made "untrue, false and defamatory" accusations against him. He later upped the amount to $75,000 because of further statements by Chambers.

The suit was a fatal mistake by Hiss: Chambers had not yet charged espionage and most certainly had not offered proof that could in any way substantiate that allegation. The only matter then at issue was whether the men had known each other. But now Hiss raised the stakes significantly, forcing Chambers to come forward with evidence that would be more compelling in defense of the defamation suit, evidence that Hiss was a Communist who had committed espionage more than a decade earlier.

8. Pretrial Depositions (November 4–5 and November 16–17, 1948)

Chambers was asked almost matter-of-factly by Hiss's attorney during the November 4 pretrial deposition hearing in Baltimore to produce "any correspondence, either typewritten or in handwriting, from any member of the Hiss family." "I would like to have those," the attorney declared, undoubtedly expecting no such documentation, "and I hope you will accept this as a notice to produce."

Chambers fooled everybody, blowing the slander case (which later was dismissed) wide open. He produced a bulky package of sixty-five pages of retyped State Department documents and four verbatim copies of international cables in Hiss's own handwriting, material that he claimed Hiss had given to him ten years earlier to pass secretly to the Soviets. The questions that the jury later would have to resolve were whether the handwritten material was generated by Hiss to brief his boss and then discarded or stolen and whether the other documents had been taken home by Hiss, copied at home on the Hiss typewriter, and the copies then given to Chambers. Why would Hiss, his attorney at the trial would ask, take so stupid a step as to provide Whittaker Chambers with memoranda obviously written by him when he might have disguised the source of the documents? Similarly, the jury had to reach some conclusion about why some of the documents had been retyped rather than photographed. The prosecution's argument was that Chambers picked up material only once every week or ten days and that Hiss could not keep sensitive documents for that long a time; he therefore typed their contents overnight and took the originals back to his office.

Chambers also said that he possessed "another bombshell." That bombshell plus the documents he had given over at the deposition had been stored for nearly a decade, he would maintain, virtually forgotten in a blocked-up second-story dumbwaiter shaft, once used for disposal of garbage. The material had been placed in an apartment occupied by Nathan Levine, Chambers's wife's nephew in Brooklyn, later occupied by the nephew's mother. At the time he hid the documents Chambers had seen them as "a life preserver" which, should the party threaten to kill him, he might stand an outside chance of using as "a dissuader." But others would point out that the nephew did not see the papers themselves when Chambers opened the package—he was elsewhere cleaning up the dust that now covered his mother's floor—and some would insist that the paper and film that were recovered could not have fit into the envelope that was said to have held them, a matter that the defense attorney later would regret not having pursued during the trial.

Chambers had doubted whether the hidden materials were still retrievable. But there they were. The contents of the envelope were given to Hiss's lawyer, who turned them over to the Department of Justice for whatever action it might take, either against Chambers for having lied when asked if he had evidence of espionage or against Hiss on the assumption that he had given the documents to Chambers. There remain skeptics who wonder how it came about that the documents recovered with only one exception were associated with Hiss, when any one of the more than a dozen persons whom Chambers identified as Communists might have filed a libel suit against him.

9. The Pumpkin Papers (December 2, 1948)

Fifteen days later, Chambers, responding to a HUAC subpoena demanding that he turn over to it any further relevant material, dramatically led committee investigators, seeking to upstage the FBI and the Department of Justice, to a patch on his farm in Maryland and reached into a hollowed-out pumpkin.

The materials secreted in the pumpkin had also been gathered from the dumbwaiter shaft and had been wrapped in waxed paper and placed in an eviscerated pumpkin for less than a day. Though only film, not documents, had been hidden, the material, in accord with what Chambers describes as "a journalistic passion for alliteration," would thereafter be known as the Pumpkin Papers. Out came fifty-eight frames of film (subsequently called microfilm, though in fact it was standard 35mm film). Each strip was a copy of a page of a State Department document. There were two cylinders of developed and three of undeveloped film. The film dealt with matters such as the Sino-Japanese war, Germany's takeover of Austria, the Spanish civil war, and American intentions in regard to the Soviet Union. There also was some puzzling trivia, such as the report that the Japanese had tried to buy a manganese mine on a Costa Rican island where no manganese was known to exist. Some of the undeveloped film was blank, having been overexposed, and some parts were concerned with matters such as life rafts and the painting of fire extinguishers and other ephemera readily available on the open shelves at the Federal Bureau of Standards library.

His original plan, Chambers said, had been to avoid hurting Hiss, who he consistently declared was "a good friend" and a man he admired deeply for his sincerity and idealism. He had only wanted to alert the government to the dangers in its midst. Others, on very slim or no evidence, used Chambers's self-admitted bisexuality to claim that he was in love with Alger Hiss and sought revenge for having been sexually spurned. Readers of this book may note the considerable physical similarity between the urbane Hiss and Richard Loeb and the unkempt and rather unattractive Whittaker Chambers and Nathan Leopold and recall the allegations of a homosexual relationship between Leopold and Loeb. To reach any conclusion beyond the physical resemblances, however, is to wander into totally uncharted territory.

Nobody disputed that some of the documents in Chambers's possession were copies of secret government material that Chambers should not have had. They all carried early 1938 dates, and it would become a matter of heated but unresolved debate whether the Woodstock typewriter on which some had been transcribed had been given away by the Hisses before or after that time. In Hiss's favor was the fact that no personal communications written on the machine by Mrs. Hiss were located with dates past May 1937. Against him was the fundamental question that neither he nor his lawyers could satisfactorily address: Who might have typed the letters on the Woodstock if not the accused or his wife, and how might that have been accomplished?

The film was sent to Eastman Kodak Company for analysis, and Nixon suffered intense anguish when an initial report came back saying that it had been manufactured in 1945, well after the period in which Chambers claimed to have obtained the documents typed on it. Nixon was on the verge of conceding defeat—he had telephoned Chambers and berated him as a liar—when a subsequent Eastman Kodak report said that a mistake had been made, that the film was of the appropriate vintage.

The FBI and the Department of Justice both sought to have HUAC turn the film over to them for use in the grand jury hearing, but Nixon would have none of that until he had exploited the cache for personal publicity. He and his lead investigator would describe the film to reporters as "hundreds" of secret papers making a pile "more than three feet tall." Inside the locked and guarded HUAC quarters, the photographed documents stacked up to little more than an inch.

10. Grand Jury Hearings (December 6–15, 1948)

Both Hiss and Chambers were summoned to testify before a federal grand jury, which chose to believe Chambers. Since Hiss could not be indicted for espionage, the grand jury charged him with two counts of perjury, one for saying that he had not stolen the documents and the other for denying that he had seen Chambers after 1935.

The grand jury members were particularly impressed with experts' testimony regarding the match between the typewriting on the documents produced by Chambers and that produced by the Woodstock typewriter, number N230099, which had first been purchased by Priscilla Hiss's father in 1927 for his insurance business. When the insurance company disbanded, the typewriter had been given to Priscilla. The Hisses then passed it along to Mike Catlett, a young man who did odd jobs for them. Catlett could not establish with any certainty when he had first received the machine, whether before or after the early March date on the Pumpkin Papers cache. After him, the Woodstock had been owned by a number of other people as it made its battered way toward a typewriter graveyard. Chambers alleged that Hiss's wife (Hiss himself was a hunt-and-peck typist) had copied the documents in the evenings; he would pick them up at one in the morning. Skeptics wondered why the Hisses, had they been engaged in spying, did not take the simpler and time-saving route of photographing the documents themselves.

The legal confrontation now had escalated well beyond Hiss's libel suit against Chambers as the players moved toward a case with much higher stakes. Equally important, the grand jury had made its choice of culprit: it equally well could have indicted Chambers for lying to HUAC when he denied having possession of specific material to tie Hiss to acts of espionage. Had Chambers been indicted, the case against Hiss would have collapsed. For Nixon, who several times was ready to abandon his pursuit of Hiss, a major setback had narrowly been avoided.

Nixon's triumph was not easily achieved. The grand jury indicted Hiss on the day its charge was to expire, and years later one of its members would reveal that the vote had been only one more than the necessary bare majority. The same juror noted: "Chambers perjured himself many times, but the final decision was 'He's our witness, we're not going to indict him.' It was a politically inspired matter."

11. The First Perjury Trial (May 31–July 8, 1949)

Hiss's trial for perjury took place in the thirty-floor federal courthouse in Foley Square in New York City. The defendant was hard-pressed for money to mount an all-out defense; he had refused to participate in any fund-raising appeals, saying he "didn't want to be another Scottsboro Boy." Hiss's attorneys were from prestigious law firms and many of them donated their services. The trial became a duel between the sophisticated and well-credentialed Hiss and the unkempt, self-declared traitor Chambers. Note, for instance, the description of Hiss by Alistair Cooke:

> There was nothing gangling or boorish about him. He had one of those bodies that without being at all imposing or foppish seem to illustrate the finesse of the human mechanism. He moved instinctively toward the economical gesture, and whatever he did had a rather charming gravity and grace: when he deferred with a dark smile to some lady in the court; when he unfolded his handkerchief and wiped his nose; when he uncrossed his legs, and his head tilted over to the left, as a lever effortlessly helping his left ankle on to his right knee. Here was a gentle certitude of behavior.

However impressive to a British onlooker, Hiss's mannerisms offended jurors who were of a different social class, despite the impressive roster of witnesses who came forward to support him, including two sitting justices of the U.S. Supreme Court. Several jurors later commented unfavorably on Hiss's habit of using his hand to grasp his calf and place one knee over the other and said that they were annoyed when he condescendingly corrected the prosecutor's grammar when he repeated the question before responding.

Hiss's principal lawyer, the flamboyant courtroom veteran Lloyd Paul

Stryker, sought unsuccessfully to have the case thrown out on the ground that it was merely a subterfuge to get around the statute of limitations for espionage. On cross-examination Stryker had an easy target in Chambers, with his numerous aliases and his self-admitted betrayal of his country. In his opening statement, Stryker called Chambers "a moral leper" and said that somebody ought to precede him into court, shouting the ancient alarm, "Unclean, unclean!"

Stryker noted that while still a Communist, Chambers had signed an oath when he applied for a government job in 1937 that he would "support and defend the Constitution of the United States against all enemies, foreign and domestic, and that I will bear truth and allegiance to the same; that I take this obligation freely, without any mental reservation or purpose of evasion . . . , so help me God."

"You took and subscribed to that oath, did you not?" Stryker asked.

"Yes," Chambers granted.

"And it was false from beginning to end, was it not, Mr. Chambers?"

"Of course," the witness said, very mildly.

"And it was perjury, wasn't it?"

"If you like."

"And you did it in order to deceive and cheat the United States Government . . . is that not true?"

"That is correct," Chambers replied in a soft and expressionless voice.

Chambers's ready admissions of deceit and the almost indifferent manner in which he granted these points conveyed the sense that such long-ago matters had nothing to do with the accuracy of what he was saying right now about Hiss and himself. Stryker nonetheless never let up in his effort to portray Chambers as totally unreliable. In his summary to the jury he scoffed at Chambers's statement that he had withheld the documentary evidence of espionage because he did not want to hurt Hiss, only to protect the country. "It reminds me," said Stryker, "of the lady who picked up a shotgun and let her husband have both barrels in the head, taking right off the top of his head. She was asked about it afterwards and she said, 'Well, I pulled the trigger sort of soft because I'd been very fond of him.'"

The trial lasted five weeks, a long time for a trial then, and ended in a hung jury after the panel had heard 803,750 words of testimony and deliberated for almost fifteen hours. Post-trial interviews with jurors published in the newspapers showed that the split was eight to four for conviction. Notable was the jurors' attempt to go beyond their charge to rule only on evidence that had been presented to them. They asked to have the Woodstock typewriter brought to the jury room and then attempted to determine experimentally whether the machine was the one on which the incriminating documents had been typed.

So outraged were some people at the failure to convict Hiss that they demanded that the judge, Samuel H. Kaufman, be impeached and that the jurors be questioned by the House Un-American Activities Committee. Nixon claimed that the jury foreman was a former left-wing activist determined to acquit Hiss regardless of the evidence.

12. The Second Perjury Trial (November 17, 1949–January 21, 1950)

The second trial began in November 1949, a time of even greater national nervousness than five months earlier, when the first trial had reached its inconclusive end. Americans now had learned that the Russians possessed an atomic bomb, and Mao's victory in China had intensified anti-Communist sentiment in the United States.

Most of the material from the initial trial was repeated and enough new testimony added so that the second hearing took three weeks longer than its predecessor. The first trial had concentrated on Chambers's character; the second focused on the Woodstock typewriter. The prosecutor was very careful not to repeat the injunction that had been part of his opening statement at the original trial: "If you don't believe Chambers's story, we have no case under federal perjury law." This trial produced a new major witness, Hede Massing, a former Soviet agent, who testified to meeting Hiss at a Communist cell gathering in 1935 and arguing with him about whether Noel Field, a Soviet spy at the State Department, would work with his group or hers. Massing had been barred by the judge from appearing at the first trial because she had no firsthand knowledge of any connection between Hiss and Chambers.

The venerable second trial judge, Henry W. Goddard, who had been appointed to the federal bench by Warren Harding, was much more lenient than Kaufman about admitting evidence. There also was a new lead defense attorney for Hiss; Hiss had not been taken with Stryker's flamboyant style and wanted a more dignified lawyer to represent him. The prosecution remained in the hands of the talented and now battle-seasoned Thomas F. Murphy.

Instead of relying on a parade of prominent witnesses who testified as to Hiss's upstanding character, the defense sought to demonstrate that Chambers was mentally unbalanced. This argument was developed at considerable length by Dr. Carl Binger, who labeled Chambers a "psychopathic personality" and a "pathological liar." Binger's testimony set a federal court precedent (though one not widely followed today); it was the first time that a psychiatrist had been allowed to attack the credibility of a witness. But his presentation was ripped to shreds by the prosecution. Murphy's cross-examination, saturated with heavy dosages of ridicule and sarcasm, continues to be used to teach law students how to deflate an expert witness. As one courtroom observer noted, "Mr. Murphy just wanted plain answers to plain questions—about the most alarming assignment anyone would wish on a psychiatrist."

Binger's testimony was based on his courtroom observation of Chambers during both trials. He declared that one symptom of Chambers's abnormality was that when he answered questions he often fixed his eyes on the ceiling. The prosecutor pointed out that Binger himself had done the same thing fifty-nine times in twenty minutes. Similarly, Chambers's equivocations, said to be a sign of personal aberration, were shown from a review of 550 pages of testimony to be considerably fewer than the 158 times Hiss had adopted the same tactic.

The second jury, eight women and four men, unanimously found Hiss guilty. They accepted that Chambers was exactly what he claimed to be, a disillusioned former Communist who had been revolted when he came to understand the tyrannical nature of Soviet rule. And they believed that he had felt it to be his patriotic duty as well as a matter of his own salvation to expose totalitarianism and its supporters in the United States. The jury concluded that Hiss had lied and that he had depended on his unsullied reputation and high social status to rebut what he portrayed as a farfetched tale by a disreputable chronic liar.

In his brief presentence statement to the court, Hiss put his finger on the most vital piece of evidence and offered a prediction that to this date remains singularly unrealized: "I am confident that in the future," he said, "the full facts of how Whittaker Chambers was able to carry out forgery by typewriter will be disclosed."

When Hiss was convicted, Dean Acheson, the secretary of state, said in a news conference that he would not turn his back on him. Joseph McCarthy, a little-known U.S. senator from Wisconsin, seized upon that comment to charge that the Department of State was "thoroughly infested" with Communists. McCarthy's remarks opened what was to become a frenzied witch-hunt that for several years ripped the country asunder. Finally, McCarthy overreached and in a famous confrontation during which he was hurling irresponsible charges, the accused's attorney asked: "Have you no shame?" Ultimately, McCarthy was censured by the Senate for his actions; the cold war by then had become somewhat less frigid.

Hiss appealed his perjury conviction, but the three-judge Second Circuit Federal Appeals Court ruled against him. Its opinion reprinted large segments of the trial transcript, focusing on, among other things, the peculiar shenanigans that Hiss adopted when he toyed with his recognition of Chambers. "The jury might well have believed," Judge Harrie B. Chase observed, "that the appellant had been less than frank in his belated recognition of Mr. Chambers as a man he had known as Crosley and had admittedly known well enough to provide for him a partly furnished apartment at cost with all utilities free, to say nothing of an automobile, old certainly, but still useful."

The U.S. Supreme Court declined to hear the case. Hiss might have won a reversal in that court if it had chosen to review his arguments, since it had recently established the principle that if there was but one witness in a perjury case, "independent proof of facts inconsistent with the innocence of the accused" also had to be established. That could have been interpreted to mean that the prosecution had to prove more conclusively that Priscilla Hiss had typed the incriminating documents on her Woodstock typewriter. But Justices Reed and Frankfurter had been character witnesses for Hiss at his first trial, and Justice Clark had been attorney general, so all three, who might have favored Hiss's claim, excused themselves from considering whether the case should be placed on the Supreme Court's calendar. Some time later, Justice Douglas would insist that in his view "no [federal] court in the nation at any time could possibly have sustained the [Hiss] conviction."

Hiss served forty-four months of his two concurrent five-year prison terms at the Lewisburg Penitentiary, one of the federal prisons contemptuously referred to as country clubs by those demanding harsher treatment of inmates. He entered the prison, predictably, wearing a natty tweed overcoat, a three-piece herringbone suit, a collar pin, and what one reporter described as "an enigmatic smile." Hiss was handcuffed to a black man, convicted of mail theft, who shamefully hid his face from the hovering photographers. Before starting his term, Hiss had sought wisdom from Austin McCormick, a prison reformer: Never talk to anybody until he talks to you first, McCormick told him, and avoid working in the infirmary (as Hiss had hoped to) because other prisoners will pressure you to steal narcotics for them. Hiss later was wont to observe wryly that his time as a federal prisoner, when he worked as a clerk in the commissary and was a model prisoner, was "a good corrective" to his three

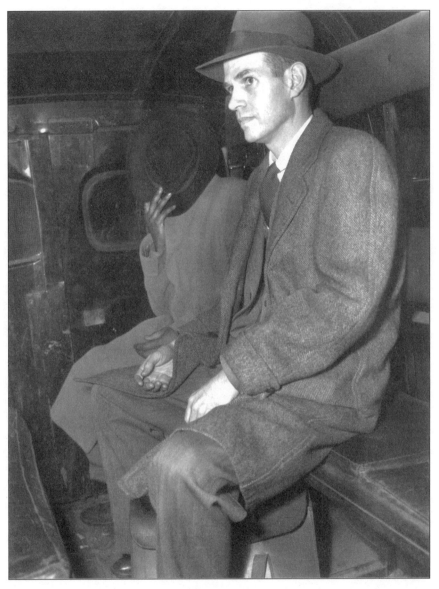

Alger Hiss sits in a prison van handcuffed to Edward Jones as he leaves New York City to serve a five-year prison sentence for perjury. AP/Wide World Photos

years as a student at Harvard Law School. He made particular friends among Sicilian organized crime potentates whom he admired for their closeness with their wives and children and their unapologetic dedication to illegal profit making. For their part, they declined to call him "Alger," saying that it wasn't a real name, and dubbed him with an Italian equivalent. It is said that when Hiss was set free from prison, inmates crowded to the prison windows to cheer him on his way.

Hiss was unable to rebuild his career following his release. For the remainder of his life he sought to establish his innocence of both espionage and perjury. In the 1950s and again in 1978, Hiss filed petitions for a writ of error, asking that his conviction be set aside; but the courts rejected the pleas. He did win some skirmishes. Congress had enacted legislation that barred him from receiving his government retirement pension—the so-called Hiss Act. The law was declared unconstitutional by the courts as it applied to Hiss, since it imposed a penalty for conduct that had occurred before the act was passed. The legislation was repealed by Congress in 1972. And in 1975, Hiss was the first lawyer ever readmitted to the Massachusetts Bar after being disbarred for a felony conviction.

Hiss worked for two years after his release from prison for a company that sold Japanese-style hair combs. In 1960 he took a job as a stationery salesman. He later said that he wasn't a great salesman, but that he could get into any door because executives wanted to see what this once-famous person was like. When Nixon became president in 1969, some interest focused on Hiss; his reputation seemed to rise as Nixon's waned and to fall when Nixon prospered politically.

Perjury *and Prejudice?*

The 1978 publication of Allen Weinstein's *Perjury* dealt a serious blow to Hiss's image. Weinstein, at the time a history professor at Smith College and now president of a Washington, D.C., think tank, the Center for Democracy, said that he had originally been convinced of Hiss's innocence but had changed his mind as he delved into the case, taking advantage of access to some 40,000 pages of documents secured from FBI files under the Freedom of Information Act. Much of Weinstein's analysis focuses on evidence relating to the Woodstock typewriter, which Hiss's supporters insist was an FBI or a Soviet forgery. Weinstein concluded that such a forgery was impossible.

Weinstein traces with meticulous care the twists and turns of the evidence;

he is, as a Nixon biographer claims, "much the closest and most careful student of the Hiss case." He pinpoints contradictions by all parties in terms of what they later claimed as contrasted to what they had said earlier. But his conclusion is unequivocal: "Although arguments will persist in the court of public opinion, the body of available evidence proves that Hiss perjured himself when describing his secret dealings with Chambers, so that the jurors in the second trial made no mistake in finding Alger Hiss guilty as charged."

Weinstein's research is mostly regarded, at least for the moment, as the last and best word on the Hiss case. George Will, writing in *Newsweek*, declared that with *Perjury* "the myth of Hiss's innocence suffers the death of a thousand cuts, delicate destruction by a scholar's scalpel" and calls the book "stunningly meticulous and a monument to the intellectual idea of truth stalked to its hiding place." Alfred Kazin, a well-regarded literary critic, observed: "After this book, it is impossible to imagine anything new in this case except an admission by Alger Hiss that he has been lying for thirty years."

But Weinstein has not escaped unscathed. Victor Navasky, a persistent thorn in Weinstein's side, quotes George Orwell that there can be subtle tactics that result in "forged history." Navasky notes that often when there are contradictory pieces of evidence, Weinstein reports only those that make Chambers's case. He illustrates his objections by reference to an important sentence in *Perjury*. It reads: "After defecting in 1938, Chambers asserted he had 'lived in hiding, sleeping by day and watching through the night with gun and revolver.'" The direct quote ("lived in . . .") is from Chambers's HUAC testimony, but the first phrase ("After defecting . . . ") is Weinstein's. It allows him to sidestep the fact that when he was discussing his fears of Communist reprisal Chambers had said—or would shortly say—on sixteen different occasions in sworn testimony that he had left the party in 1937. If Chambers had not later adjusted his story to coincide with the early 1938 dates on the documents he allegedly received from Hiss, the whole case would have collapsed. Weinstein, in essence, dances cleverly, but not forthcomingly, around that minefield. He adroitly presents as accurate that which is controversial without providing support for his adjudication of the issue of the different dates Chambers supplied.

The Navasky-Weinstein controversy was further fueled when Navasky contacted six persons quoted by Weinstein and asked them if what they had said had been accurately reported. All thought that their interviews had been distorted. Weinstein then said that he would allow Navasky to examine his original tapes and written notes, though the only occasion that his schedule "would permit such a visit over the next three weeks" was for three hours on a Sunday. Navasky showed up at Weinstein's house at the time scheduled, but was told by Weinstein's wife that he had changed his mind and would not allow access to the material. Neither has he turned it over to the Truman Library as he had promised he would.

In 1992 Jon Wiener, a history professor at the University of California, Irvine, would maintain in the American Historical Association's newsletter that he believed Weinstein was in violation of the association's Statement on Standards of Professional Conduct adopted in 1987. The standards declare that historians should "make available to others their sources, evidence, and data, including the documentation they develop through interviews." Weinstein, for his part, may well have reneged on his original position when he and his publisher were forced to pay a "substantial five-figure sum" to settle a court case with a claimant, a minor Communist Party worker he had confused with a more sinister member who used the same alias.

Later Developments

Meanwhile, President Ronald Reagan in 1984 had posthumously given Whittaker Chambers, who had died of a heart attack in 1961, the Medal of Freedom, America's highest peacetime award. Four years later the farm where the Pumpkin Papers had been hidden was declared a national historic landmark, and a reproduction of the world's best-known pumpkin is on display at the Nixon Library in California. Nixon for his part would attend an annual Halloween dinner of a group called the Pumpkin Papers Irregulars, celebrating their judicial victory over Hiss.

In 1992, with the end of the cold war, Hiss believed that he finally had found vindication when General Dmitri A. Volkogonov, in charge of the Russian military intelligence archives, announced that at the request of a Hiss loyalist he had searched the archives and that "not a single document has been found that substantiates the allegation that Mr. A. Hiss collaborated with the intelligence services of the Soviet Union. You can tell Alger Hiss that the heavy weight should be lifted from his heart." Volkogonov said that half a dozen other Russian archivists had come up with equally negative results and declared that the charges were "completely groundless." But the general backpedaled from his announcement two months later, saying that he had looked only at a limited amount of material, that many files had been destroyed when Stalin died, and that in truth he had not searched very hard.

A year later, Maria Schmidt, a historian, said that she had discovered documents in the restricted files of the Hungarian Interior Ministry that seemed to implicate Hiss as a spy. One was the transcript of a statement by Noel Field, the onetime State Department employee, alleging that Hiss had tried to recruit him for espionage. Field had fled to Prague in 1949 after Hede Massing identified him as a spy. He was imprisoned in Czechoslovakia for five years on the suspicion that he was an American agent, "an Anglo-Zionist spy." Ironically, when Field died in 1970 his ashes were placed in a special crematorium in Hungary reserved for Communist heroes.

Field had asked to be sent from Prague to Hungary after his release from prison. During his first interrogations he had said that Hiss was a "liberal without Communist attachments"; it was only later that he declared Hiss a spy. Hiss supporters insist that this subsequent statement had been coerced. They point to a note by Field found in the archives saying that "physically I am a coward," and that under torture "I do not only utter and write down the most horrible lies but partially even believe them."

Nor did the ever-changing story end there. In 1996 the National Security Agency in the United States released what became known as the Venona intercepts, captured Soviet documents sold by Finland to the United States that enabled cryptographers to decipher more than 2,000 messages sent by spies to Moscow during the Second World War. These included one dated March 30, 1945, from a high-ranking Soviet agent saying that he had been in touch with a State Department official code-named Ales who had been present at Yalta. The cable said that the agent had worked for the Soviets since 1935 and had flown to Moscow after the conference at Yalta. Four American men, including Hiss, had made that trip from Yalta. Hiss said that he traveled to Moscow from Yalta to examine the subway system. Someone at the National Security Agency had placed a notation on the document more than two decades after it was written that suggested that Ales probably was Alger Hiss. Hiss's supporters found the Venona material farfetched: one mention in several thousand communications and an identifying name that was so readily decipherable that a child would have made the connection. This scavenging of Communist archives for partisan purposes by both the left and the right keeps the Hiss affair in the limelight, but so far it has produced no certain resolution of the Hiss-Chambers controversy.

The Search for Vindication

Ever true to his fundamental character, Hiss in 1957 wrote a book, *In the Court of Public Opinion,* which reads more like a dry appellate brief than the writing of a man outraged by injustice. The book nitpicks about the accuracy of this or that piece of evidence. Hiss maintains that Chambers falsely implicated him in the network of Soviet espionage in order to keep his own tattered skirts free of the consequences of his spying activities. "The hope of leniency," Hiss writes in typical fashion, "supplies a potent motive for an accused person to implicate falsely another who, he believes, is considered by the prosecuting authorities to be a more desirable target." Hiss also observes, incorrectly as it happens, that prosecutors, given the last word in summary to a jury, enjoy an advantage because the vividness of their remarks—"inflammatory and biased"—cannot be rebutted by the defense. Contrary to this belief, social psychological research and studies concerning the order of argument in debates suggest that it is preferable to have the first word because listeners are prone to form an early judgment and become reluctant to alter it in the face of additional evidence, lest they seem to be easily led.

The Nixon Tapes (1997)

When in later life he reflected on his political career, Richard Nixon with good reason would regard the Hiss case as the first of the six major crises that he had encountered. More revealing than Nixon's carefully tailored account of the Hiss case in his book *Six Crises* are the things that he said in more informal conversations that were captured on the tape recordings that he narcissistically failed to destroy. After drawn-out litigation, the courts ruled for public release of the tapes and in 1997 Stanley Kutler served up what he saw as their most significant portions. They show Nixon often fixated on the Hiss case and using it as a guide to political strategy in his times of trouble.

Nixon's first tape-recorded reference to Hiss took place on July 1, 1971, following the publication of the Pentagon Papers, the government documents that had been acquired illegally by Daniel Ellsberg and that officials thought compromised American security or, most certainly, challenged stories being fed the public by the government about the Vietnam War.

Nixon thought steps ought to be taken to brand Ellsberg as subversive; in the Oval Office he outlined for his assistant, H. R. Haldeman, and Henry Kissinger, head of the National Security Council, the tactics that he had found valuable when he dealt with Alger Hiss. "We won the Hiss case in the papers," he told them. "We did. I had to leak stuff all over the place. Because the Justice Department would not prosecute it. [J. Edgar] Hoover didn't even cooperate. It was won in the papers. We have to develop now a program, a program for leaking out information. We're destroying these people in the papers." Nixon also noted the ensuing consequences: "I had Hiss convicted before he got to the grand jury," he said. What was needed now was someone to nail Ellsberg ("I no longer have the energy," Nixon said of himself); they needed "a son of a bitch who will work his butt off and do it dishonorably. I know how to play the game and we're going to play it."

The following day, talking with an aide on the telephone, Nixon again referred to the Hiss case, noting that in the Ellsberg matter he had plenty of allies, in contrast to his position in regard to Hiss, when "they were all against me." Six weeks later, he noted that the leaks of grand jury testimony about the accused Watergate burglars were something that had not happened in the Hiss case: "Even in the Hiss case, when we were going through that, we never got a thing out of the grand jury until they indicted." There is a note of admiration in Nixon's words; he could salute virtue, but it apparently came at too high a price to be personally practiced. One is reminded of a cartoon showing a sign on a corporate executive's desk: "Honesty Is the Best Policy," it reads, "But It Is Not Our Policy."

Nixon also had learned other lessons from the Hiss case—though some not well enough. "If you cover up, you're going to get caught," he told John Ehrlichman, another chief aide, on July 19, 1972, when the Watergate scandal was just beginning to take form. "And if you lie you're going to be guilty of perjury. Now basically that was the whole story of the Hiss case. It is not the issue that will harm you; it is the *cover-up* [Nixon's emphasis] that is damaging." Nixon returned to the Hiss case with Charles Colson, another aide, in a September 11, 1972, conversation. The Chambers-Hiss affair had taken place before the 1948 elections, he told Colson. Truman had declared that the whole business was a "red herring," and Dewey, more certain of victory than he should have been, chose not to inject the case into his campaign.

Nixon also harked back to the scenario of the Hiss case when a Senate investigative committee decided to hold hearings on Watergate. He told Kissinger in early 1973, quite correctly, that the House Un-American Activities Committee had brought hearings to an end once Hiss had been indicted for perjury and faced a criminal trial. Bitterly, Nixon asked Kissinger where his "Harvard [liberal] friends" were now, when "these assholes are saying: Oh no, the grand jury isn't enough, the court finding seven people guilty [for the Watergate break-in and cover-up] and giving them fifty years isn't enough. It's got to be now try it before a kangaroo court before the Ervin committee [in the Senate]. There's a double standard. The only thing to do is to fight it."

On the same day, Nixon reminded his secretary of state, William P. Rogers, that a committee of Congress "destroys a man's character in public and, second, if a file is turned over, you know, to the Department of Justice for prosecution, they will prosecute the poor guy. . . . We did it to Hiss."

In the midst of this there was an aside of grudging respect for Hiss. Talking with Haldeman and Colson, Nixon remarked, "You know the great thing about—I got to say for Hiss. He never ratted on anybody else. Never. He never ratted." Readers will, of course, see quickly that Nixon categorically assumes Hiss's guilt, a judgment that by the end of the century, while not universal, was dominant.

Crimes and the Times

The Hiss case highlights the temper of the time, as do the more sensational criminal justice cases. The Scottsboro defendants were almost executed in Alabama as sacrifices to the racial antagonism of the region. Hauptmann, guilty or not, was pilloried mercilessly in a trial that caricatured a fair and calm search for truth. Hiss, guilty or not, was used primarily to further the political ambitions of those who pursued him, and his situation came to symbolize the fear and hatred of the Soviet Union that ruled the judgment of large segments of the American population and the government. The Simpson case, as we shall see, reflected blacks' access to power as jury members, and also highlighted the stunning attitudinal divisions between blacks and whites about the criminal justice system. An essayist, in a piece entitled "Alger and O.J.," made an important point when noting Hiss's death: "Our best hope," Charles Krauthammer wrote, "is that in fifty years we will read Simpson's obituary as this year we did Hiss's—with puzzlement, wonder even, at a passion long exhausted."

For some, Hiss emerges as one of the great impostors before the law: his boldness takes your breath away. Hiss's stonewalling over five decades, his insistence on his innocence, might represent a masterpiece of deception, comparable and perhaps more successful than the similar behavior of Richard Nixon, his archenemy in the case, who faltered as he tried to save his skin when the Watergate scandal unfolded. In this regard, some see Hiss and Nixon as twins, high-wire dissemblers of consummate ability, both doomed in the end by their own treachery.

For others, Hiss is a victim of the temper of the time: a man who stood an excellent chance of rising to a very high position in government, defamed by a notorious liar who could not even remember which of his innumerable aliases he was living under at any one time, a twisted loser who for some reason (and that is the catch: what might the reason have been?) was determined to take this prominent man down to the depths with him.

The issue of espionage by Americans on behalf of the Soviet Union and the palpable public terror about the threat of Russia to our very existence now seems old-fashioned and farfetched—in Krauthammer's phrase, "a passion long exhausted." But the Hiss case continues to fascinate, in part because it provided detailed and intimate portraits of the lives of the Hisses and the Chamberses. The case highlighted distinctions between public images and private behaviors. Hiss appeared to be an impeccable, high-minded public servant, but the record suggested that he was a spy, a traitor to his country. Chambers was a highly successful senior editor of a national magazine, but his past was riddled with self-confessed aliases and lies and a sordid collection of bizarre personal behaviors. The story was a tragedy, a man of power in high places brought to ruin. The literary Chambers certainly saw it that way. The legal issues were intricate and complex but boiled down to a single question: Who was lying? And what was being lied about was, at least at the time, frighteningly important.

The legal system served to dispel public anxieties. The penalty for perjury was relatively minor in regard to the potential gravity of the offenses that gave rise to the prosecution. But the legal system dodged, as it often does when the spotlight is too intense, important basic issues, in this case such matters as the right of the accused to be presumed innocent and the role of a congressional committee in the prosecutorial process, an issue closely related to the constitutional separation of powers.

Cooke and Jowitt on American Justice

Two sophisticated British commentators looked for lessons in the Hiss case about the manner in which the quest for justice should be carried out, scrutinizing how the trial was conducted here and how it would have been carried out in England. Alistair Cooke noted that the Hiss trial brought out "the American inclination to substitute technique for honest argument, and a wealth of exhibits for incisive pleading," a point that with equal justification can be applied to the other cases reviewed in this book. For Cooke, a particularly pressing necessity was the establishment of rules mandating a binding code of fair practices for all congressional committees. A statement of

J. Parnell Thomas, chair of HUAC during the Hiss hearings, illustrates the root of Cooke's concern: "The rights you have are the rights given you by this committee," Thomas told a witness. "We will determine what rights you have and what rights you have not got before this committee." Lindsay Rogers, a law professor, with the tactics of HUAC in mind, declares that congressional committees "have been obscenely indifferent to the principle that every man is innocent until he is proven guilty."

An eminent sociologist, Edward Shils, sought to tie the extravagances of congressional investigations to the social origins of many of those conducting them. Politicians, he notes, have an unusually high degree of social mobility; more than most, they represent the realization of the ideal of the poor boy who takes advantage of the opportunities of an open society to rise to the top. Persons elected to Congress move from their homes to Washington, where they live away from the influence of longtime friends and associates in a world "full of pitfalls and threats to their professional success." What threatens them comes to be interpreted as a threat to America. "There is," Shils maintains, "a general suspicion among legislators of disloyalty to American standards on the part of those who challenge them and make them uneasy—most notably bureaucrats and intellectuals—and they are therewith cast outside the circle of the saved."

Conflicts continue to exist today between congressional committees whose members seek to infringe on judicial and executive prerogatives. Persons in Congress often have an eagle eye out for opportunities to enhance their reelection prospects with the help of publicity generated in high-profile committee hearings. But some reforms have been adopted. In 1955, for instance, the House established a minimum standard of conduct for its committees, adopting a rule that a committee finding evidence that might "tend to defame, degrade, or incriminate any persons" must receive evidence in secret session and allow the person involved to appear as a witness and request the appearance of supporting witnesses.

In 1950, Alistair Cooke also maintained that the media were a menace to the satisfactory operation of the American justice system and needed to be controlled. He believed that it was essential for the United States to revise its libel and slander laws. "As I see it," he wrote, there is "no good argument against forbidding the publication of anything 'alleged' to have gone on at a private [committee] hearing, or against holding newspapers responsible for airing such leaks."

The rules of evidence in American trials (in contrast to English procedures) also seemed to Cooke to produce untoward results:

. . . they allow counsel to elaborate an issue almost into oblivion; so that instead of deepening in the jury's minds the main impression you want to leave, there is a good chance that at the end of the trial the jury may be thrashing in so many cross-currents, none of which seems to lead upstream to the source of the trouble, or downstream into the broad ocean of truth, that the jury will seize at the end on any floating log that might bring them safely to shore.

The "enormous" length of time it takes for American juries to make up their minds was regarded by Cooke as support for his criticism of overly permissive rules of evidence. Veteran jury members, he added, "often say that the first few hours in the jury room are spent sloughing off the welter of counsel's rhetoric, the strangling flotsam and jetsam of introduced 'evidence.'"

It was about time, Cooke also thought, that the American press was made to follow the practice of the English media by remaining silent during pending and ongoing trials. "The indignities some papers forced on the judicial system [in the Hiss case]," Cooke observed, "seemed to strengthen the argument for the adoption of the English rule, whereby all comment, dramatization, and editorial opinion of any kind may not be printed while a case is under judgment." Such a position, Cooke maintains, "is not inconsistent with any decent definition of a free press."

In the Hiss case, not only was there the media circus that seems to come to town with such notorious court proceedings, but also the press was employed for ends that only tangentially were concerned with justice. For instance, Bert Andrews, a Pulitzer Prize–winning reporter for the *New York Herald Tribune*, was deeply involved in helping Nixon launch the case against Hiss; in return, he was given access to news scoops. In addition, the FBI leaked information to Nixon, who fed it to the media in the belief that it would advance the election prospects of Thomas Dewey, who was believed to be more sympathetic to the FBI than was Harry Truman. Roger Morris, examining Nixon's career, thinks that the Hiss case was an object lesson about "the craven ambition and ready cannibalism of the establishment, the easy disregard of secrecy and procedure on all sides, the significance of covert action and alliances and the utter politicization of every governmental act." Morris believes that Nixon's cynicism and ruthlessness were fed by his success in the prosecution of Alger Hiss and ultimately led to his own destruction by the Watergate crisis.

Another Briton, William Jowitt, who was Lord Chancellor in England under the Labour government, deplores the introduction of the psychiatric evidence by Binger in the second Hiss trial. "It is quite certain," he observes, "that under English law no such evidence would be admitted; and I sincerely hope that it never will be." "I have thought sometimes," he writes rather tartly, "that eminent doctors in this sort of case are apt to draw too generous conclusions from too slender premises."

Stephen Ambrose, in a recent perceptive and fair-minded multivolume biography of Nixon, sums up the Hiss proceedings aptly. "The case," Ambrose notes, "was filled with leaks, lies, deceptions, the deliberate use of the Justice Department for partisan political purposes, the manipulation of the press and public opinion, and brazen attempts at cover-up." But Ambrose does not deal head-on with the fundamental issue of the Hiss-Chambers business: Was justice served? That is, was a guilty man convicted? Or can justice be served only when the process by which guilt or innocence is determined is above suspicion?

For Further Reading

The most comprehensive review of the Hiss-Chambers case is Allen Weinstein, *Perjury: The Hiss-Chambers Case,* updated ed. (New York: Random House, 1997); its tilt is strongly toward Chambers. Critiques of Weinstein's material are found in Victor Navasky, "Weinstein, Hiss, and the Transformation of Historical Ambiguity into Cold War Verity," in Athan G. Theoharis, ed., *Beyond the Hiss Case: The FBI, Congress, and the Cold War* (Philadelphia: Temple University Press, 1982), pp. 215–245. See also, in the same volume, Theoharis, "Unanswered Questions: Chambers, Nixon, the FBI, and the Hiss Case," pp. 246–308, and Kenneth O'Reilly, "Liberal Values, the Cold War, and the American Intellectuals: The Trauma of the Alger Hiss Case," pp. 309–340. Jon Wiener's material on Weinstein appears in "The Alger Hiss Case, the Archives, and Allen Weinstein," *Viewpoints,* 30 (February 1992):10–12, and "Compromised Positions," *Lingua Franca* (January–February 1993): 41–48.

John Chabot Smith's comprehensive *Alger Hiss: The True Story* (New York: Holt, Rinehart, and Winston, 1976) favors Hiss. Smith covered the trial for the *New York Herald Tribune*. Ronald Seth provides an easily readable overview of the case in *The Sleeping Truth: The Hiss-Chambers Affair Reappraised* (New York: Hart, 1968). Seth insists, based on his knowledge of Russian espionage tactics, that Hiss was framed by the Soviet spymasters. Fred J. Cook's *The Unfinished Story of Alger Hiss* (New York: William Morrow, 1958) is strongly pro-Hiss, claiming that the FBI constructed the typewriter that was used to convict Hiss.

Writing in the same vein are Morton Levitt and Michael Levitt, *A Tissue of Lies: Nixon vs. Hiss* (New York: McGraw-Hill, 1979). Similar too is William A. Reuben, *The Honorable Mr. Nixon*, rev. ed. (New York: Action Books, 1958). An unequivocally pro-Chambers consideration of the case is Ralph de Toledano, *Seeds of Treason* (Belmont, Mass.: Western Islands, 1967).

On the typewriter, see the brief monograph by Beatrice Gwynn, *Whittaker Chambers: The Discrepancy in the Evidence* (London: Mazzard, 1993). Gwynn insists that the discrepancy, among others, between the capital "W" on the Woodstock used to type the government documents and the one that typed Priscilla Hiss's correspondence indicates clearly that they were different machines. She maintains that the "crude soldering of the keys" and the toolmarks on the recovered machine demonstrate that the evidence was forged. On the same subject see Herbert L. Packer, "A Tale of Two Typewriters," *Stanford Law Review*, 10 (1958):409–449.

Thomas Murphy's Cross-Examination of Dr. Carl A. Binger in U.S. v. Alger Hiss (Hiss II) (Minnetonka, Minn.: Professional Education Group, 1987) shows the derisive manner in which the prosecutor handled the psychiatrist. Another psychiatrist's rather long-winded but often intriguing appraisal of Chambers and Hiss is Meyer A. Zeligs, *Friendship and Fratricide: An Analysis of Whittaker Chambers and Alger Hiss* (New York: Viking, 1967). Zeligs's wife worked with Mrs. Hiss, and his monograph is heavily slanted in Hiss's favor. Weinstein, commenting on the book, notes meanly, but accurately, that Zeligs is "a stranger to modesty."

Two British writers produced books on the Hiss case. Both examine the events in terms of British procedures, though they are, as the English can be, extremely careful to be nothing but constructively critical of the manner in which the case was handled. The books are Alistair Cooke, *A Generation on Trial: U.S.A. v. Alger Hiss* (New York: Knopf, 1952), and William Allen Jowitt, *The Strange Case of Alger Hiss*, 2nd ed. (London: Hodder and Stoughton, 1953). Cooke was a correspondent for the *Manchester Guardian;* Jowitt was an eminent English jurist. Cooke's analysis is severely criticized in a book review by Rebecca West in the *University of Chicago Law Review*, 18 (1951):662–677. That issue of the law review offers more than a dozen articles looking at aspects of congressional investigations, often using the Hiss case for illustrative purposes.

The legal aspects of Chambers's allegations are also dissected briefly in Herbert L. Packer, *Ex-Communist Witnesses: Four Studies in Fact Finding* (Stanford, Calif.: Stanford University Press, 1962), pp. 21–51, and in Richard B. Morris, *Fair Trial: Fourteen Who Stood Accused* (New York: Knopf, 1952), pp. 426–478. On the general history of the House Un-American Activities Committee see Walter Goodman, *The Committee: The Extraordinary Career of the House Committee on Un-American Activities* (New York: Farrar, Straus and Giroux, 1968), pp. 244–267, and Robert K. Carr, *The House Committee on Un-American Activities, 1945–1950* (Ithaca, N.Y.: Cornell University Press, 1952), pp. 93–131. The experiences of one of the more reasonable members of HUAC are detailed in F. Edward Hébert and John McMillan, *"The Last of the Titans": The Life and Times of Congressman F. Edward Hébert of Louisiana* (Lafayette: University of Southwestern Louisiana, 1976); pp. 272–319 are on the Hiss case.

Written for children, Doreen Rappaport's *Be the Judge, Be the Jury: The Alger Hiss Trial* (New York: HarperCollins, 1993) presents the evidence offered at the second Hiss trial and asks young readers to decide how they would have voted if they were members of the jury.

There are some excellent recent biographies of Richard Nixon that depict his role in the Hiss case, including Roger Morris, *Richard Milhous Nixon: The Rise of an American Politician* (New York: Henry Holt, 1990), pp. 383–512; Stephen E. Ambrose, *Nixon: The Education of a Politician, 1913–1962* (New York: Simon and Schuster, 1987), pp. 166–196, 199–200, 204–205; and Jonathan Aitken, *Nixon: A Life* (Washington, D.C.: Regnery, 1993), pp. 149–158. The taped Nixon conversations are reproduced in Stanley I. Kutler, ed., *Abuse of Power: The New Nixon Tapes* (New York: Free Press, 1997). On the large part played by the Quaker affiliations of Richard Nixon, Priscilla Hiss, and Whittaker Chambers, see Chuck Fager, Book Review, *Quaker History*, 84:65–77.

Alger Hiss wrote two books seeking to put before the public his own view of the perjury case: *In the Court of Public Opinion* (New York: Knopf, 1957) was faulted as a sterile, lawyer-like brief, totally devoid of the kind of affect one might expect from a man unjustly convicted; and *Recollections of a Life* (New York: Henry Holt, 1988). In the latter, especially pp. 149–160 on the perjury case and 160–183 on his prison experience, Hiss tries to make up for the flatness of the earlier book, noting the "emotional experience of the two long and heartbreaking trials, to each of which I brought such bright hopes of vindication." An affectionate memory of his father (whom he calls "Al") is provided in Anthony Hiss, *Laughing Last: Alger Hiss by Tony Hiss* (Boston: Houghton Mifflin, 1977).

Whittaker Chambers pressed his case in *Witness* (New York: Random House, 1952), a Book-of-the-Month-Club selection, and he receives comprehensive and sympathetic treatment in Sam Tanenhaus, *Whittaker Chambers: A Biography* (New York: Random House, 1997). Willam F. Buckley, Jr., offers an intimate view of Chambers through their correspondence in *Odyssey of a Friend: Whittaker Chambers' Letters to William F. Buckley, Jr., 1954–1961*, edited by Ralph de Toledano (New York: G. P. Putnam's Sons, 1970).

Bert Andrews, the newspaper reporter who arguably breached professional ethics when he took on the role of a Nixon adviser and traded information with the congressman, tells his story, with his son Peter as coauthor, in *A Tragedy of History: A Journalist's Confidential Role in the Hiss-Chambers Case* (Washington, D.C.: Robert B. Luce, 1962). The book is breezily written and offers large verbatim chunks of hearing and trial testimony.

United States v. Hiss, 185 F2d 822 (2nd Circuit, 1950) reports the appellate decision on the Hiss case. The full transcript of the second trial can be found in *United States v. Alger Hiss*, vols. I–IX (Sayre, Pa.: Murrelle Printing Co., 1950). Hiss's later unsuccessful application for a retrial can be found in Edith Tiger, ed., *In Re Alger Hiss: Petition for a Writ of Coram Nobis* (New York: Hill and Wang, 1979–1980). A further collection of materials can be found in *The Alger Hiss Case: Basic Documents* (Wilmington, Del.: M. Glazier, 1977).

O. J. Simpson (1994): Can the Rich Buy Reasonable Doubt?

This is likely what happened:

Sometime during the hour after ten o'clock on the evening of June 12, 1994, a lone person came through the back entrance of a Spanish-style, four-bedroom condominium on Bundy Drive in the upscale Los Angeles suburb of Brentwood. In the small, almost caged area near the front gate, the intruder savagely slashed a woman, virtually severing her neck from her body, apparently after she had been rendered unconscious. The gaping wound ran from the left side of her throat to just below her ear and was so deep and so long that it exposed the victim's larynx and cervical spinal cord. In the same entryway, the killer stabbed a man to death, inflicting at least thirty wounds.

Determination of the order in which the two victims were slashed to death was based on the fact that there was no blood on the female's bare feet, while plentiful blood was present on the soles of the man's white shoes.

The woman, dressed in a black halter sundress, was thirty-five-year-old Nicole Brown Simpson, the recently divorced wife of O. J. (for Orenthal James) Simpson, a onetime football superstar and later a media notable. The couple had two children, both of whom were asleep in an upstairs bedroom in the condominium. The dead man, dressed in jeans, was twenty-five-year-old Ronald Goldman, a social acquaintance of Ms. Simpson. Goldman was a waiter at the Mezzaluna restaurant, where Ms. Simpson and her family had eaten earlier that evening. He was returning the gold-rimmed prescription sunglasses that Ms. Simpson's mother had dropped on the curb while getting into her car in front of the restaurant. A person with a mordant sense of humor later would place signs outside the Mezzaluna reading, "Don't forget your sunglasses."

At ten minutes after midnight the following morning—more than two hours after they had been slain—the bodies of Nicole Simpson and Goldman were discovered by a neighbor who had been led to the site by a howling brown-and-white Akita, a big dog that was obviously distraught. The dog, which belonged to Nicole Simpson, had blood on its belly, paws, and legs.

Few of the foregoing "facts" have gone undisputed, however. Some maintain that the killer's entry was from the front of the condominium. Others believe that Nicole Simpson, learning of the loss of the eyeglasses from her mother, requested Goldman to deliver them and was planning a sexual interlude with him—or perhaps with someone else. Her erotic invitations characteristically involved the lighting of candles in her residence, as she had done this evening. There are those who believe that there was more than one killer, and some who believe that drug dealing retaliation was central to the murders.

The savage killing of Nicole Simpson and Ronald Goldman and the subsequent arrest and trial of her former husband unleashed a cascade of events that preoccupied much of America for the following three years. Fiery disputes arose about the not-guilty verdict and the importance of the racial composition of the jury, which was made up of eight black and two white women and one black and one Latino man, though the initial pool from which it was selected was 40 percent white, 28 percent African American, 17 percent Hispanic, and 15 percent Asian. The twelve members of the jury looked like this: (1) All were Democrats. (2) Two were college graduates. (3) No one read a newspaper regularly. (4) Nine rented homes; three were purchasing houses. (5) Two had supervisory or management responsibilities at work; ten did not. (6) Eight regularly watched TV-tabloid shows such as *Hard Copy.* (7) Five said that they or a family member had a negative experience with the police. (8) Five thought it was acceptable to use force on a family member. (9) Nine thought O. J. Simpson was less likely to be the murderer because he had been a football star.

Commentators also pointed to what they saw as incompetence, perjury, and perhaps conspiratorial actions by detectives in the Los Angeles Police Department, to blatant racism in their ranks, to the considerable lawyering inadequacies of the prosecution team, and to questionable tactics by the defense lawyers. Dominick Dunne, a writer who was favored with a reserved seat at the proceedings, summarized events this way:

The Simpson case is like a great trash novel come to life, a mammoth fireworks display of interracial marriage, love, lust, lies, hate, fame, wealth, beauty, obsession, spousal abuse, stalking, broken-hearted children, the bloodiest of bloody knife-slashing homicides and all the justice money can buy.

Questions surfaced about whether television ought to be permitted in court-rooms, whether juries should be sequestered, and whether unanimous verdicts should be required in order to convict in a criminal trial.

The price of "justice" in the Simpson criminal case mounted to an estimated $6 million expenditure by the defendant and $9 million by the prosecution, of which $2.6 million went for housing, feeding, and other expenses associated with jury sequestration.

O. J. Simpson was the obvious initial suspect, and when he later was tried for the murders he became the most famous person ever prosecuted for homicide in the annals of American criminal justice, with the possible exception of Aaron Burr. As a football hero at the University of Southern California, Simpson won the Heisman trophy, awarded each year to the athlete deemed to be the outstanding football player in the nation. Subsequently, he was a running back for nine years with the Buffalo Bills and two with the San Francisco '49ers in the National Football League. His stellar athletic performances earned him a spot in the National Football Hall of Fame after his retirement. In the following years, Simpson appeared in widely seen Hertz commercials, served as a commentator on professional football games, and acted in several easily forgotten motion pictures.

Simpson's first marriage to his high school sweetheart, Marguerite Whitley, produced two children. He met Nicole, eleven years younger than he, when she was an eighteen-year-old waitress at the Daisy, a fancy Beverly Hills nightclub. They dated for a year, then lived together for six more before their marriage in 1985. The marital relationship turned tumultuous, with several raw incidents of domestic violence, usually associated with drinking, that resulted in calls to the police. Jurors heard Nicole's terrified scream, "He's going to kill me," recorded when she called a police dispatcher on New Year's Day 1989. The Simpsons would separate, then reconcile, usually on Nicole's initiative, and then split again. They were divorced in 1992; Nicole received a sizable settlement and child support payments of $10,000 a month. In April 1993 Nicole was imploring Simpson to consider reuniting the family, writing that she loved him deeply. Along with her letter she sent videos showing their marriage ceremony and the birth of their children. But three weeks before she was killed, Nicole appeared to have emotionally distanced herself from Simpson.

Along with her will, Simpson's former wife had left a picture of herself in her safe deposit box showing her face severely abraded and bruised, the result of a dispute between them. For some, the only worthwhile thing to emerge from the trial was a growing public concern with domestic violence—or "domestic discord," as the defense sought to label it in order to de-escalate the emotions engendered by terms such as "spousal abuse" and "wife battering." Defense attorneys debated introducing evidence that very few episodes of domestic violence lead to murder, but they decided that it was best to downplay the entire issue. During the year following the trial, reports to police of domestic violence increased by sixty percent in Los Angeles; the family of Simpson's slain ex-wife established the Nicole Brown Simpson Charitable Foundation for Battered Women to fight domestic violence, naming Nicole's father president and her three sisters to the board of directors.

Nicole was a self-described party animal, part of a group of fast livers who played a lot, often dancing at nightspots until the early hours of the morning. As was her husband, she was sexually promiscuous. A *New Yorker* writer suggested that oral sex with male partners, whoever they might be ("virtual strangers" it was claimed), had great appeal for Ms. Simpson and that she spent a considerable amount of time and energy indulging in that pastime. She apparently did not have a sexual relationship with Goldman, though he had been seen driving her $90,000 white Ferrari Mondiale convertible (with the personalized license plate L84AD8—late for a date). Goldman and Ms. Simpson had met casually at dances and at The Gym, a trendy Brentwood fitness center and health club. He had filed for bankruptcy in 1992, listing debts of about $12,000. In a typical tactic of slander by innuendo, defense attorney Robert Shapiro would write after the trial that "our investigation was to discover much information about Nicole that was of an intimate and possibly inflammatory nature. It was relevant to the case and we chose not to use it as part of the defense. I choose not to use it now."

The defense had learned from simulated jury tests that black women harbored a biting dislike of Nicole Simpson—a white woman they saw as milking the money of a famous black man and living an irresponsible life of luxury. The black female jurors also were hostile to prosecutor Marcia Clark, offering credence to the observation of the novelist Toni Morrison, a Nobel Prize–winner, that black women are very different from white women, but that black and white men are much the same.

During the trial, the defense dealt with Nicole's behavior and character with care, making certain that they did not too meanly blacken the reputation of a victim when nothing that she had done could possibly exculpate her murderer from legal guilt. But they pointed out that Simpson had supported her in grand scale, putting a paid-for half-million-dollar house in San Francisco in her name, and sending two of her sisters to college until each in turn dropped out. (One writer observed of the Brown sisters, "All four had breast implants, but not one had a college degree." One of the sisters, Dominique, sold pictures of her murdered sister and her children, including a snapshot of Nicole sunbathing topless in Mexico, to a newspaper for $32,500.) Simpson also had secured the Hertz franchise at the upscale Ritz-Carlton Hotel in Orange County for Nicole's father and had directed considerable business to her mother's travel agency.

Simpson had flown to Chicago for a business meeting on a late-night flight the evening that Nicole was killed. When he returned home the following day, he was interrogated at police headquarters for thirty-two minutes by homicide detectives, who primarily focused on the nasty cut that he had on his right hand. Simpson claimed at first that he did not know how he had gotten the

Marcia Clark, the lead prosecutor, presenting evidence about the white Bronco. Reed Saxon,
AP/Wide World Photos

injury, then suggested that it probably was the result of his reaching into his Bronco when he was hurriedly preparing to leave for Chicago. The wound had reopened, he maintained, when he broke a glass during the period of anguish in his hotel room after he had been told of the murder of his ex-wife. Details of the police interrogation, stunningly short and totally inept in regard to asking tough follow-up questions, would not be introduced into the trial. The prosecution presumably preferred not to have the jury hear Simpson's proclamations of innocence, and the defense wanted to avoid any focus on the inconsistent stories about the source of Simpson's cut hand.

When a warrant for Simpson's arrest was issued, his lawyer said that he would turn himself in at police headquarters. Instead, Simpson took off in the early afternoon with his close friend, A. C. (Al) Cowlings, Jr., in Cowlings's white Bronco. After the car was spotted by another motorist at 6:20 in the evening in nearby Orange County, where Nicole's family lived, it was followed by a phalanx of a dozen police cars, its every move filmed by news reporters from helicopters as it slowly wove its way along sixty miles of southern California freeways before going to Simpson's Brentwood home.

Media accounts, labeling this the most famous ride on American shores since Paul Revere's, reported that ninety-five million Americans watched the convoy. Simpson had left behind a long note, saturated with misspellings and full of self-pity and self-righteousness. He insisted on his innocence and indicated rather clearly that he intended to commit suicide. The letter ended: "Don't feel sorry for me. I've had a great life. Great friends. Please think of the real OJ and not this lost person. Thanks for making my life special. I hope I helped yours." There also were some indications that Simpson might have intended to flee the country. The destination seemed to be Mexico, until the car was spotted. In the car were his passport, $8,750 in cash and traveler's checks, and a loaded gun. There also was a disguise, a false goatee and mustache, bought two weeks before the murder at the Cinema Secrets Beauty Shop in Burbank. Neither the note nor the presumed attempted escape would be placed before the jury.

For some persons, the crucial miscalculation by the district attorney's office was made well before the first trial witness was called. It involved the decision to try the case in downtown Los Angeles rather than in Santa Monica, the court that typically assumes jurisdiction over crimes that occur in its vicinity. In Los Angeles, juries are recruited among persons who live within a twenty-mile radius of each courthouse. If the trial had been held in Santa Monica, the odds are that the jury would have had a majority of white members rather than racial and ethnic minorities. Numerous explanations would be offered for the venue change, including the central location of the downtown courthouse and its ability to more readily accommodate the media crush. There also was expressed concern about the recent earthquake damage suffered by the Santa Monica courthouse.

Some people believe that the downtown site was selected to avoid any implication that the jury might be stacked against Simpson. Earlier, a jury of white persons in suburban Simi Valley had acquitted police officers of the severe beating of a black man, Rodney King, despite a videotape that vividly showed what they had done to him. Street rioting erupted in the wake of that jury decision, an outcome the authorities wanted to avoid in the Simpson case. Others say that the choice was ruled by the arrogance of the district attorney, who was determined to be closely involved in dictating prosecution tactics and who believed that he had an open-and-shut case against Simpson. Marcia Clark, who would prosecute the case, reassured one skeptic that the state "would do equally well in L.A." and "would have a clear-cut guilty verdict regardless of where O.J. was tried." Bill Hodgman, Clark's superior until illness early in the case forced him into a background role, has offered an even simpler explanation for the case's not being tried in Santa Monica: "Nobody even thought about it at the time."

The prosecution also forfeited another strategic advantage when it decided not to seek the death penalty, though the twin killings would have permitted it to do so. This decision undoubtedly was based on the fact that Simpson did not match the stereotype of a "real" criminal, and the prosecution feared alienating jurors who might have believed a death penalty demand was too merciless. But "death-qualified" jurors, it is well known, tend to convict a defendant more readily than panels whose members may not be willing to inflict capital punishment.

The Trial

The trial of O. J. Simpson on the double-murder charge began on July 22, 1994, with the defendant answering the judge's request "How do you plead?" with "Absolutely one hundred percent not guilty, Your Honor." The trial would last until October 2, 1995, more than a year and two months later. Simpson spent 473 days in jail before the jury rendered its verdict. The prosecution called seventy-eight witnesses; the defense, with nine attorneys, summoned seventy-two witnesses. The original jury panel melted down as one after another of its members was dismissed for cause or themselves asked to be relieved. During the trial, the jury was sequestered for 266 days—housed in the Inter-Continental Hotel and permitted only weekend visits from family members. The sequestration produced an esprit de corps within the group, a climate that undoubtedly played into the rapid return of a verdict.

Two very distinct trials of O. J. Simpson were taking place. One was held in the courtroom, the other in the newspapers and, particularly, on television, with several major channels broadcasting everything that took place during the court sessions. What the cameras chose to focus on was what the viewing public saw: particular people's expressions, the judge's activities, a restless bailiff. These often were different images from those that imprinted themselves on the jurors' minds.

Besides, jurors heard only segments of what the public learned. Television showed arguments between the lawyers while the jury had been removed from the courtroom. Court intermissions and recesses were filled by a host of commentators and lawyers ("talking heads") who offered opinions about what had gone on. These people typically felt compelled to turn each day into a sporting contest, asking: "Who won?" "Who does this benefit?" "Who is ahead?" Notable was the remark by juror Marsha Rubin-Jackson when interviewed on NBC's *Dateline* after the trial. "I don't want to get this wrong," she said, "because I am standing by my verdict, but based on what I've heard since I've been out [of the courtroom], I would have to vote guilty."

THE EVIDENCE

During the afternoon before the murders, O. J. Simpson had attended a dance recital in which Sydney, his and Nicole's eight-year-old daughter, performed. There was tension between Simpson and his former wife: they did not talk, though Simpson socialized with Nicole's sister and her mother. That evening Simpson was not invited by his former wife to the family get-together at the Mezzaluna. At his home, at about nine o'clock, he and Brian (Kato) Kaelin, who roomed in the guest house on Simpson's property, took Simpson's Bentley to McDonald's and ordered take-out Big Macs and french fries.

From 9:36, when he left Kaelin, until four minutes before 11:00, when a limousine chauffeur picked Simpson up to take him to the airport, his whereabouts cannot be pinned down, though we know that he called (but did not reach) his girlfriend Paula Barbieri at 10:03, using the telephone in his Bronco. Why Simpson would use the car telephone if he was still at home, as he claimed he was, stood as one of the many incriminating bits of evidence that never was satisfactorily resolved.

Allan Park, the twenty-four-year-old part-time employee of the Town and Country Limousine Company, made a particularly good witness. Park seemed to have no ax to grind and to be relating as scrupulously as he could what he had done and seen. The limousine chauffeur arrived at the Simpson house at 10:25. Nobody answered his ring and he would testify that he did not see the Bronco parked on the property, either at the entrance where he waited or at the side of the house to which he drove in an attempt to determine if there was another entrance. At 10:56 (the driver had logged several calls to his employer, so the times were readily verified), he said that he saw Simpson go in the front entrance of the house. Lights went on in a few moments, and after a while Simpson responded to the chauffeur's ring, saying that he had been showering. His attorneys would insist that before then Simpson had been in the back of his property practicing his golf strokes.

Simpson waved Kaelin off from loading a small black bag into the limousine with the rest of his luggage, saying that he would handle it himself. Park testified that Simpson said that he felt warm, although it was a chilly night, and that he seemed nervous during the ride to the airport to catch American Airlines flight 668, the red-eye to Chicago that departed Los Angeles at 11:45. The bag apparently was no longer with Simpson's luggage at the Los Angeles airport, fueling the belief that it may have contained the murder weapon and perhaps bloody clothes, and that Simpson had gotten rid of it somewhere along the route.

Later, the only request for information from the jury during its deliberations would be for Park's testimony. After his acquittal, Simpson would say that Park had been quite accurate when he said he saw him enter the house, but the truth was that he had only momentarily stepped outside to leave his baggage on the driveway.

DNA Testimony

A large part of the trial was consumed with detailed and complicated testimony about DNA (deoxyribonucleic acid) tests on blood samples. The more than fifty DNA tests of blood showed the following five major results:

1. DNA profiles consistent with Simpson were found in five blood drops on the walkway at the Bundy Drive murder scene and in three bloodstains on the rear gate.

2. The right-hand glove found at Simpson's residence was saturated with blood. Most of it matched the victims', though three tiny samples taken from near the wrist showed DNA mixtures for Simpson and from one or both of the victims.

3. A dark, tightly woven sock recovered from Simpson's bedroom was found to have a large bloodstain at the ankle that contained Nicole Simpson's DNA profile.

4. Most of the samples taken from Simpson's Bronco were consistent with the DNA of its owner. But three small smears of blood collected six weeks after the murder from near the console contained a profile matching Simpson, his former wife, and Goldman.

5. Blood drops on Simpson's driveway and in the foyer of his house were consistent with his DNA profile, though, as the defense would stress, no blood was located on the white rug leading from the foyer to the bedroom, or elsewhere on the house furnishings.

The defense's response to the DNA on the blood-soaked sock illustrates tactics it employed to debunk the test results offered by the prosecution. The defense first highlighted the fact that the blood on the sock had not been noticed until two months after the sock was found. The prosecutor claimed that the oversight was a result of the less-than-ideal lighting conditions that made it difficult to spot the dark-brown bloodstain on the black socks. Two defense experts testified that they believed that the bloodstain had been pressed into the sock while it was lying flat, and not while on someone's leg. They said that the blood had soaked through one side of the sock and left a "wet transfer" on the opposite inner part at a point that would have been directly underneath the stain on a sock lying flat. Had Simpson been wearing the sock, such a transfer could not have occurred. The defense also argued that the blood would have dried by the time Simpson returned home and there would have been no transfer of blood to the inner segment. The prosecution retorted by insisting that the "extra" blood spot was the result of the sock being taken off inside out—the way that many people remove socks.

DNA results remain inadmissible in four American states (California, of course, is not one of them) on the ground that a high enough degree of scientific consensus does not yet exist regarding their reliability. Prosecutors declared that the DNA tests established beyond any reasonable doubt that Simpson had murdered Nicole Simpson and Goodman. The chances, they said, that the DNA droplets could have come from another person were one in several million. They also pointed out that the killer had worn size-12 Italian-made Bruno Magli shoes, which sell for $160 a pair and are carried by only forty stores in America, one of which is New York's Bloomingdale's, where Nicole Simpson often shopped. Only 299 pairs of the shoes had been distributed in the United States. The defense, however, emphasized that no record had been located that indicated that the shoes had been purchased by either Simpson.

The forensics defense, carried by two lawyers imported from New York City, insisted that the blood was contaminated, that it had been sloppily gathered and examined, and that it very well might have been planted by the detectives who sought to frame Simpson for a crime that he had not committed. The defense also claimed that Simpson could not possibly have done all the things the prosecutor said he had during the time frame proposed by the prosecution. The defense team also suggested that the murders might have been done by Colombian drug enforcers who were targeting Faye Resnick but killed Nicole Simpson and Ron Goldman by mistake. Resnick was an admitted drug user who had lived with Nicole until four days before the murder, when she checked herself into Exodus, a drug rehabilitation program. The prosecution sought to rebut this last point by noting that professional killers use guns with silencers, and that the Simpson-Goldman bloodletting was the product of rage. It also was suggested by Simpson's defenders that there had been more than one killer.

THE LAWYERS

Most postmortems of the trial concluded that the prosecution, led by Marcia Clark, forty years old and a veteran with the Los Angeles district attorney's office, had stumbled very badly. The district attorneys may not altogether have deserved the searing scorn that Vincent Bugliosi, a former lead prosecutor in their department, heaped upon them, but in the eyes of most law-trained observers Bugliosi was not far off target. "The prosecution of O. J. Simpson," he proclaimed, "was the most incompetent criminal prosecution that I have ever seen. By far." Bugliosi added: "There have undoubtedly been worse. It's just that I'm not aware of any." A newspaperman in court throughout the trial was equally biting in his appraisal: "Marcia and her troops," he wrote, "were . . . incredibly stupid, inexcusably arrogant, almost daily unprepared, and totally leaderless."

For one thing, the prosecution's jury consultant, on the basis of interviews staged with a focus group whose makeup resembled that of the actual jurors, had shown that Clark would be unpopular, disliked because her personality struck the panel members as too strident and hard-edged; to use a word they often employed, she was seen as "bitchy." The prosecution also had turned its back on reports from its jury consultant when he rated most of the jury members as twos and threes on a scale of ten, with ten indicating that they could be presumed to favor the prosecution's views. Clark believed, based on her experience, that she could form emotional ties with female jurors, through which both she and they would come to empathize with the victims and turn against the accused. She badly miscalculated the jurors' lack of fellow-feeling for Nicole, the charisma of Simpson, and the skill of his legal team. After the trial, one juror would point out that the prosecution showed "signs of stress and frustration." On many occasions, she noted, Clark "would sigh and make gestures with her hands as though she were throwing in the towel." Subtle things also probably hurt Clark. Jurors, for instance, came to resent the fact that she often arrived in court late; they were awakened at 5:30 each morning so that they could be on time. That prosecutors develop an emotional rapport with jurors is generally regarded as essential in a tough case. Clark was faulted by courtroom observers as well for what was seen as inappropriately flirtatious behavior with defense lawyers, particularly Cochran.

Clark also was severely criticized for placing Mark Fuhrman on the stand and presenting him as a choirboy when she was well aware of his racist views. Fuhrman blandly perjured himself by declaring that he had never used the word "nigger," a statement blasted to bits by the later surfacing of a tape recording he had made with an interviewer. Clark's assistant, Christopher Darden, was faulted for an experiment in which he had Simpson in open court try on the dark brown, cashmere-lined glove that was said to have been worn by the killer. Simpson struggled to get it onto his hand, allowing the defense to argue that the glove did not belong to him. Others suggested that this was one of the former motion picture actor's better performances in a career unremarkable for any display of acting talent, though several jurors would later maintain that they never doubted that the glove was Simpson's. The defense turned the episode into a slogan, which was repeatedly intoned thereafter: "If it doesn't fit, acquit." An Associated Press news report, delicately excising the offensive word for family newspapers, noted that a trial groupie outside the courtroom carried a sign that read: "If they acquit, they're full of [expletive]." The defense mocked the claim of the lead detective on the case that he had not secured a warrant before allowing Fuhrman to climb over the fence to get into Simpson's house because he feared there might be people inside who needed help. The detective said that he did not at that time suspect Simpson of the murders (which would have required him to secure a warrant), an observation that the defense and most everybody else who followed the case sensibly considered ridiculous.

THE JUDGE

In addition, the judge, Lance A. Ito, came in for almost unremitting criticism. It was claimed that Ito was awed by celebrity, a matter he demonstrated by his invitations to well-known persons who visited the courtroom to accompany him to his quarters while the trial proceedings came to a standstill. Though his rulings almost invariably favored the prosecution, Ito was hostile to Marcia Clark but rather fawning to Cochran, a man he had worked for when both were with the district attorney's office. Ito's rulings were regarded as slow and inconsistent; most particularly, possibly because of the presence of television cameras, he was said to have allowed the trial to drag on unconscionably long because he did not have the will to take a stronger stand against aimless and endless arguments and presentations of evidence. "I think he made what should have been a six-week case into a yearlong nightmare," one of his colleagues on the superior court bench said. "He gives patience a whole new meaning."

RACE

Race figured prominently in the case, though blacks on the jury would deny that it had any influence on their verdict. The defense had hired Cochran, a black attorney, and the prosecution countered by adding Darden as second in command of its courtroom contingent. Cochran later was described scathingly by a newspaper columnist as oleaginous—that is, slippery and slimy—a judgment heartily endorsed by his first wife in her book-length depiction of their roller-coaster marriage. He offended many viewers by his smooth, ingratiating manner, his moralizing and Bible quoting. David Margolick, who covered the trial for the *New York Times*, pinpointed Cochran's style, the "familiar voice—[alternately] effusive, soothing, unctuous, smoothly indignant, polysyllabically hypersincere, an amalgam of the preachers he heard as a child, the insurance salesman he once was and the disk jockey he could have been." Whites assumed that what he had to offer was something that the jury preferred to buy, but the three jurors who put their thoughts on paper faulted Cochran for "showboating" and maintained that they had not been greatly impressed by what they characterized as an overdone performance. In his summation, Cochran put on the ski cap that Simpson was alleged to have worn to disguise himself at the murder scene, trying to demonstrate that it hardly camouflaged his appearance. Commentators found this an effective tactic; the jurors later would insist that it only made Cochran look silly. Nonetheless, there was little disagreement that Cochran was extremely effective in court, and probably the most important figure producing the jury's not-guilty verdict.

Cochran's most controversial action came in his summing up, when he compared the case against Simpson to the work of the Nazis:

> *There was another man not too long ago in the world who had those same views who wanted to burn people who had racist views and ultimately had power over people in his country. People didn't care. People said he's crazy. He's just a half-baked painter. And they didn't do anything about it. This man, this scourge, became one of the worst people in the world, Adolf Hitler, because people didn't care, didn't try to stop him. He had the power over his racism and his anti-religion. Nobody wanted to stop him. . . .*
>
> *And so Fuhrman. Fuhrman wants to take all black people now and burn them or bomb them. That's genocidal racism. Is that ethnic purity? What is that? We're paying this man's salary to espouse these views. . . .*

A few moments later, Cochran told the jurors: "There's something in your background, in your character that helps you understand this is wrong. Maybe you're the right people at the right time at the right place to say, 'No more.' . . . This is wrong. What you've done to our client is wrong. . . . This man, O. J. Simpson, is entitled to an acquittal."

Cochran was accused, most vehemently by Robert Shapiro, the attorney in his own group who had hired him, not only of "playing the race card" in the case but of having "dealt it from the bottom of the deck." Some irony, of course, lay in the fact that Simpson had little connection with the bulk of the black community. He had married a white woman, lived in an all-white neighborhood, and contributed virtually none of his money and little of his effort to assist blacks. The calculated appeal to the jurors' racial identification with Simpson was particularly well illustrated when the panel members were bused to the crime scene relatively early in the case. At Simpson's house, a picture of Paula Barbieri, Simpson's girlfriend, was replaced by a Norman Rockwell print from Cochran's office showing a black girl being escorted to a southern school by federal marshals. Other pictures of Simpson with white golfing buddies and girlfriends were taken down and pictures of Simpson's mother and other black people were installed. In addition, a Bible was placed on an end table in the living room; however, the "redecorators" forgot to hoist an American flag on the pole in front of the house.

Perhaps most important to the trial outcome was the fact that the prosecution, in a term favored by attorneys, "over-tried" the case; that is, it put on altogether too much evidence that was not essential to clearly connect the accused and the deed. "Nothing was left on the cutting-room floor," one attorney noted, comparing the trial to the making of a movie. If you wanted to know what time it was, another critic noted, the prosecutors would tell you how to make a watch. Jurors, overwhelmed with this mass of material, readily were able to fix on parts of it that they quite reasonably could doubt, and they extrapolated this uncertainty to embrace the entire case. "As far as I am concerned," one juror noted after the trial, "Mr. Simpson would have been behind bars if the police work had been done well."

During his summary argument, Barry Scheck, the defense's DNA expert, specifically invited jurors to focus on the reasonable doubt of particular matters, understandably ignoring other issues that might incontrovertibly have led to a guilty verdict. Scheck revived an analogy first introduced by Henry Lee, the defense's highly regarded criminalist. If you find a cockroach squirming in your spaghetti, Scheck asked rhetorically, do you take every strand of that bowl of spaghetti to look for more cockroaches, or do you throw it away and eat no more? As an appeal to the jury's emotions, Scheck made some points; as an appeal to logic, the illustration leaves a good deal to be desired. For outsiders, the argument was but one more illustration of how lawyers will resort to any stratagem to aid a client, even if they themselves are perfectly aware that what they are saying makes little sense when it is examined dispassionately.

Another defense attorney, Gerald Uelmen, specifically detailed the defense strategy. The prosecution had offered what it called a "mountain" of incriminating evidence. Said Uelmen:

> *By going around, under, and over the "mountain" of evidence, we were suggesting that some evidence could not be trusted because those who handled it were incompetent or negligent, some evidence could not be trusted because the procedures and facilities utilized to preserve it were inadequate, and some evidence could not be trusted because it had been corruptly altered or manufactured.*

"Once you accepted these three premises," Uelmen declared, "you were left in a state of reasonable doubt about *all* of the evidence." The very considerable flaw in the argument, however, is that it too flies in the face of logic. You could readily reject many of the prosecution's premises and still find sufficient remaining unimpeachable evidence of Simpson's guilt. Put another way, the presence of a single cockroach in the spaghetti may indeed signal the likely presence of others, but it does not demonstrate that there are not other foods totally free of cockroach infestation. The lawyers' arguments, however, were not directed at logicians but at ordinary mortals who understandably saw sufficient taint in the prosecution's case to bring all of it under suspicion of failing to prove guilt "beyond a reasonable doubt." One of the jurors who originally had voted "guilty" said that she relied on just such reasoning when she quickly joined the majority: "In spite of it all," she said, "I still feel he's guilty. But the evidence just was not there and I had no other choice. He did it, they just screwed up on the evidence." This viewpoint is encapsulated in a witticism about the essence of the Simpson trial: "They framed a guilty man."

In just thirteen words prosecution attorney Christopher Darden may have come the closest to pinning down the dynamics of the case when he sought to portray Cochran's strategy: "He knew those jurors wanted to let O.J. go. They just wanted permission."

Simpson did not take the stand on his own behalf, undoubtedly because he and his legal team believed that he could be acquitted without doing so, and because they feared that if he did testify, too much evidence would be dredged up that might seem incriminating to the jury. In a mock session with Christine Arguedas, a northern California attorney playing the part of Marcia Clark, Simpson had considerable difficulty dealing with questions about domestic violence. The official explanation for his decision not to testify was that, however eager he was to tell his own story his own way, Simpson did not want to prolong the jury's services, particularly since the prosecution case obviously was "in shambles." Afterward, legal professionals distressed by the verdict suggested that American criminal jurisprudence might adopt the provision recently incorporated into British law that permits the judge and opposing attorneys to draw inferences before the jury about a defendant's failure to testify.

Virtually every commentator had expected the jury to take a week or considerably longer to reach a decision. The jurors took their first vote on October 2, 1995, less than an hour after they began their deliberations. They tore up scraps of paper, wrote their opinion, and dropped the papers into a glass jar. They stood 10–2 for acquittal. Unanimity was achieved three hours and forty minutes after deliberations began. That agreement was reached at 3:00 P.M. in Los Angeles; the judge said that the verdict would be announced the following morning at 10:00 in order to allow the attorneys to reassemble. One of the two jurors who initially voted to convict said she had changed her mind because she saw that there was no chance she would sway the others. "It doesn't make me feel very good," she said, "but on the other hand [Simpson is] not a serial killer."

Life in the United States came to a virtual standstill that next morning as Americans awaited the announcement of the jury's decision. Long-distance calls dropped dramatically during the half hour before court opened. Following the not-guilty verdict, photographers across the country took pictures of the reactions of downcast whites and jubilant, cheering blacks. The pictures provided a vivid demonstration of the stunningly sharp splintering of opinion by race that had marked the Simpson case since its inception.

O. J. Simpson reacting to the jury's unanimous not-guilty verdict. Reports said he had been told about the outcome by court personnel hours before it was officially announced. Myung J. Chun, AP/Wide World Photos

THE RACIAL DIVIDE

Innumerable polls at various points before and during the trial indicated the striking split between whites and blacks. The judge, commenting on racial issues that arose during the trial, noted: "This is the last great challenge to us as a nation. And for those of us who grew up in the sixties and had hoped this would go away, it's a big disappointment. How we evolve and solve this problem will be our memorial in history."

In July 1994, near the start of the trial, a USA Today–CNN–Gallup Poll found that about 60 percent of the black population thought that the charges against Simpson were untrue, a view with which only 15 percent of whites concurred. Sixty-four percent of the black respondents compared to 41 percent of the whites believed that Simpson would not receive a fair trial. Seventy-seven percent of the blacks against 42 percent of the whites said that they were sympathetic to Simpson.

These figures did not change significantly either during or after the trial, though we do not know the depth of feelings associated with the shorthand answers. Black respondents may have felt a need to be loyal to one of theirs, and what they said may not necessarily have been what they truly believed. An attitude that was said to be operative during the Anita Hill–Clarence Thomas hearings, when Hill accused the Supreme Court nominee of sexual harassment, may also have been at work. "You never go against your men," black women were reported as saying. Others believe that the long burden of oppression that blacks have endured in the United States led them to excuse or at least to favor Simpson. One black man offered this observation: "I think he did it. But I don't think he's guilty." Finally, it was pointed out that the black press, in contrast to the larger-circulation dailies, insistently portrayed Simpson as an innocent man wrongfully charged.

On a more personal level, blacks to a strikingly higher degree than whites have experienced or know people who have experienced discourteous and sometimes brutal police behavior. The City of Los Angeles pays out millions of dollars each year in judgments and settlements in lawsuits brought by minorities who charge law enforcement officers with excessive use of force. Nobody could deny the rotten image the police in Los Angeles often deservedly hold in the city's minority communities.

What the prosecution could have done (but did not) in the Simpson trial was to acknowledge the shame of the brutality but to insist that the jury differentiate such acts from the framing of innocent suspects, a behavior rarely documented and one making little sense in the Simpson case, where evidence against the defendant would have had to be planted well before the police even knew whether he might have an airtight alibi.

What the Jurors Said

It is an axiom of social-science research that if the motive for various kinds of human behavior is not apparent, it will do little good to ask those who engaged in the behavior why they did what they did. They are not likely to tell you, and, more important, they are not likely to truly understand what prompted their action. People almost invariably try to present themselves to others and to themselves as reasonable and sensible. It is a rare criminal, for instance, who will say, "I committed that crime because it gives me considerable pleasure to hit little old ladies over the head and steal their purses."

So the reasons the Simpson jurors claimed were behind their verdict have to be seen as explanations about what satisfied their desire to make sense, and not necessarily as accurate or complete insights. Nonetheless, what they said is important because it reflects what they think will persuade others of the integrity of their verdict.

Three of the jurors, including its forewoman, a fifty-one-year-old black woman whose dignity and dedication drew universal admiration, put into print their reflections about what led them to their decision. A good deal of what they reported, including the fact that they thought Cochran was showboating and that they were unimpressed by the glove experiment, contradicted analyses by trial onlookers. An observation by one of the jurors about the flowery closing arguments gives a taste of their views.

> *The whole thing with those closing arguments was I felt it was all a script. Everybody had his or her little script. I hated it because at that point you're supposed to be tying in all the evidence and tying in everything. So you're sitting there and trying to just focus on the issues and here they are, Marcia Clark, the woe-is-me and blah, blah, blah, trying to get the tear thing. And Johnnie Cochran is going on about Proverbs and this, that, and the other, and the hat routine and "if it doesn't fit, you must acquit." You don't need all of that. . . . We hated it. When we brought up the subject everybody [on the jury] said, "God, wasn't that the most miserable thing you ever had to deal with in your life?"*

The jurors did, however, put considerable credence in the testimony of the expert witnesses, though they resented being condescended to by some of them. They found Henry Lee's discussion for the defense of the forensic evidence particularly impressive. Self-presentation at least in part came to overrule content. Jurors remarked how much they appreciated it when Lee walked toward them and smiled genially before he took the stand.

Lee may well have been a pivotal person in the defense's case. Amanda Cooley, the jury forewoman, noted: "Dr. Henry Lee was a very impressive gentleman. Highly intelligent, *world-renowned*. I had a lot of respect for Dr. Lee." Another juror told a newspaper reporter after the trial that the jury viewed Lee as "the most credible witness. . . . Dr. Lee had a lot of impact on a lot of people." Even the judge, counseling a prosecutor, told him that with Lee he should "accentuate the positive in a friendly and professional manner, given his reputation, and then get out." One of Lee's well-rehearsed observations, variously reported in vernacular Chinese-English as "something wrong" or in grammatical English as "something is wrong," made a powerful impression on the jury. So effective was Lee that the prosecutor who cross-examined him felt compelled (out of frustration) to later label Lee's notably shrewd remarks "one of the most ambiguous, unclear, utterly meaningless statements that I have ever heard any forensic scientist offer in a court of law." Perhaps the prosecution would have preferred the language Lee reportedly employed when he first reviewed his findings with the defense team: "Something is fucked up here," he allegedly told his "breathless audience."

Vincent Bugliosi, in a careful analysis of Lee's testimony, insists that much of it was misleading and misinformed, and that jurors were overpersuaded by Lee's reputation and style (he always looked the jurors in the eye, for instance). Lee testified that he found three important "imprints" on the terra cotta walkway at the crime scene when he visited it. One was a size-12 print introduced by the prosecution; the other two, Lee said, also "could be" shoe prints, thus suggesting that there might have been a second assailant. In fact, however, blown-up photographs demonstrated that one mark identified by Lee had been made by a trowel when workers laid the cement years earlier and that the other was a worker's shoe print that was permanently embedded in the concrete. The jury, insists Bugliosi, "should have been skeptical of every single one of his conclusions once the imprint testimony proved to be claptrap."

The Civil Suit

Simpson's legal troubles did not end with the not-guilty verdict in the criminal case. A year later, he was back in court to defend against three wrongful-death civil suits, one brought by Goldman's father and sister, the other by his mother, divorced from the father, and the third by the Browns on behalf of Nicole Simpson's estate. The suits, which later were consolidated into one case, had been filed by the survivors of the murder victims during the early part of the criminal proceedings in order to be on record before the one-year deadline. By law, the civil case had to be delayed until the conclusion of the criminal trial.

The civil trial, held in Santa Monica, took just three months; the standard for the verdict was the preponderance of evidence, not the criminal trial's criterion of "beyond a reasonable doubt." The unanimous jury verdict, reached after seventeen hours of deliberation, declared that Simpson was financially liable for the deaths of his former wife and her ill-starred friend. The Browns and the Goldmans were to divide compensatory damages of $8.5 million and punitive damages of $25 million, though there was doubt that either party would see much of the money, given Simpson's depleted finances and his considerably weakened future earning power. The civil jury, in contrast to the jury that heard the criminal trial, was made up of nine whites, one Asian American, one Latino, and one person of mixed black and Asian descent.

Besides its more rapid pace, there were striking differences between the criminal and the civil trials. The judge, Hiroshi Fujisaki, ruled with a no-nonsense hand. He would not allow the defense to introduce what he regarded as fanciful explanations of what might have happened—the "shotgun approach" Fujisaki labeled it—unless they could cite "chapter and verse" of some reasonable basis for their theory. There were no courtroom cameras; neither were artists permitted to sketch participants during courtroom sessions. Interviews with the media outside the courtroom by lawyers or relatives were also banned; so was transmission of the day's proceedings over the Internet.

The testimony that the civil jury heard differed from what the criminal trial jury had listened to, particularly since Simpson by law had to take the witness stand. This time he was confronted with photographic evidence that he had owned size-12 Bruno Magli shoes: Simpson granted that the shirt and jacket in a picture of him were his but maintained that the picture must have been doctored to include the shoes. That brought forth many more pictures of Simpson wearing the inculpating shoes, including one that had been published in a newspaper years ago. On the witness stand, though he held up reasonably well, Simpson often had to fall back on "I don't know" and "I have no idea" responses when confronted with tough questions, such as how his blood had come to be found in the bathroom of his house. He continued to deny categorically that he had ever beaten Nicole, a position contradicted by unimpeachable evidence. Civil jurors also heard about a call that a female named Nicole had made to a battered woman's shelter days before the murder, about Simpson's poor performance on a lie detector test (though the jury later was told to ignore this evidence), and about his freeway flight. The last included his car telephone statement during the chase to one of the detectives, in which Simpson declared that "the only person who deserves to be hurt is me."

In addition, this jury learned that Simpson had owned a blue-black sweatshirt similar to what the killer was presumed to have worn and that not long before the murder he had received a telephone message from Paula Barbieri breaking off their relationship. Mark Fuhrman did not testify; the judge had decided that his racial opinions had no bearing on the case.

There were, despite it all, a few positive gleamings for Simpson. He had to sell his house in the face of the verdict against him, but he can rely on a $25,000-a-month income from a judgment-proof $4.1-million pension fund that he had established earlier. In addition, another judge, just prior to the civil suit verdict, awarded custody of his children to Simpson, removing them from Nicole's parents. California law heavily favors keeping custody with a biological parent; besides, a psychologist's report to the court had said that though he was "impulsive," Simpson's capacity for empathy was higher than either of Nicole's parents'. And, the report added, "The children love him."

Should We Change the System?

None of the postmortems on the Simpson criminal trial gave it a clean bill of juridical health. Critics found fault with many aspects of the proceedings. Alan Dershowitz, for instance, looking at things from the defense perspective, offered this laundry list:

> The trial took too long. Much of the expert testimony was incomprehensible to me—and I have been teaching law and science for a quarter of a century. There were too many attempts, by both sides, to manipulate the jury pool. Judge Ito permitted far too much argument—and paid attention to far too little. There was far too much bickering over trivialities. Too many lawyers placed their own agendas before that of their client. Too many prospective jurors managed to avoid jury service. And the judge treated the jury in too patronizing a manner.

These are some of the major issues that came to the fore in the wake of the Simpson trial:

MONEY AND JUSTICE

Questions about what had gone awry inevitably arose in the minds of those who believed that Simpson was flagrantly guilty of the twin murders of his former wife and Ronald Goldman. Many agreed with the judgment of William Julius Wilson, who thought that the Simpson trial had demonstrated that "[t]here's something wrong with a system where it's better to be guilty and rich and have good lawyers than to be innocent and poor and have bad ones." Honoré de Balzac, the French novelist, had long before put the same matter another way, characterizing a jury as "twelve men [for then only men could serve on juries] chosen to decide who has the better lawyer."

Some say that the Simpson case represents an example of jury nullification, a situation in which the panel rejects the law on the books and that enunciated by the judge and imposes a personal opinion about what ought to be done with the accused. Others believe that the case merely provided a much-publicized illustration of an obvious theme, that money trumps justice. Simpson had purchased attorneys who were more skillful than the prosecution team, even though the county's lawyers could draw on the very considerable funds and resources of the government to help them in their case.

Dershowitz grants that Simpson likely would have gone to prison had he been a defendant with less money. But, Dershowitz argues, if you need a difficult and very serious operation and have a great deal of money, wouldn't you hire the very best surgeon that money could buy? Gerald Uelmen, another defense attorney, offers the argument that "we accept without question the reality that the wealthy among us live in nicer houses, drive nicer cars, eat better food, and get better medical care." The underlying premise of both statements is arguable. There are some people who do not "accept without question" such conditions. Perhaps a bit more persuasive is the view that especially talented defense attorneys, in those rare cases where they appear, can so shake up law enforcement agencies that the police will straighten up their act and no longer slumber comfortably with an assurance that they can get away with all kinds of shabby, even illegal operations.

Is there anything that can be done to make "justice" more equitable, less of a commodity the results of which can be purchased by those with sufficient wherewithal? Few people would limit the outlay that the wealthy defendant might make to defend against a criminal charge; but the playing field on which the contest that is criminal justice is waged might be made somewhat more level by encouraging outstanding lawyers, as the British do, to both prosecute and defend in different cases, so that they acquire a sense of both sides and use their talents to secure convictions as well as acquittals.

JURY ISSUES

The Simpson jury had been selected after each person summoned filled out a 264-item questionnaire. Critics maintain that the process is not a search for an impartial jury, but rather the opposite, a quest for a panel that will be biased in favor of your side. Jo-Ellan Dimitrius, the defense's jury consultant, was the first person thanked by Cochran after the verdict was announced. She did not truly "select" the jury, Dimitrius said; instead, she "deselected" persons who seemed to be "foreclosed from hearing the defense's side of the case."

The Supreme Court ruling in *Batson v. Kentucky* (476 U.S. 79, 1986) disallowed "deselecting" jurors on the basis of race or gender. In *Batson* a prosecutor in a burglary case against a black man had used his peremptory challenges to strike all four blacks from the venire. Despite the ruling, attorneys often are accorded considerable leeway to make exclusions that are rationalized on other grounds, though fundamentally based on race and gender. In the Simpson trial the defense used its peremptories to exclude from the jury five whites and just one African American, while the prosecution eliminated eight blacks and just two whites.

Critics maintain that the process would be fairer if the judge was given a stronger role in jury selection and if peremptory challenges without cause were more limited and the reasons that allow potential jurors to be excused were more restricted. In England jury selection is an expeditious process. Lawyers are not allowed to question potential jurors and they cannot dismiss anyone from the panel without a specific legal ground. There also have been calls for restrictions or even the elimination of jury consultants who analyze the traits and views of prospective panel members.

Jury sequestration also has been attacked, though it is pointed out that of some 150,000 civil and criminal cases tried each year in the federal and state courts only about 100 involve sequestration. In the Simpson case, the long isolation of the jury seems to have led to a bonding that may have inhibited jury room confrontations. Besides, "pillow talk," that is, conversations with spouses during weekends, undoubtedly offered a conduit through which information and viewpoints that jurors were not supposed to hear were conveyed to them.

Other remedial approaches advocated include allowing jurors to discuss the case among themselves as it unfolds and to submit questions to the judge that might be asked witnesses. The argument is that through discussions jurors can clarify things that concern them and that they therefore will find their job more rewarding. The argument on the other side is that once people express an opinion to others, they tend to hold on to that view even when strong evidence against it emerges, because they do not want to appear to be swayed easily.

Anecdotal evidence of the possible value of allowing juror questions is reported by Stephen Adler from a 1990 Chicago case against Johnson & Johnson that involved liability for merchandising a tampon that was blamed for a toxic shock syndrome death. The judge solicited juror questions following the testimony of each witness. More than forty questions, some with multiple parts, were forthcoming, and the judge asked the witnesses to respond to twenty-seven of them. "They were good, sensible questions," he later said. Adler notes that the process had the additional value of providing lawyers with ongoing information about which parts of the testimony might be confusing the jurors.

There also have been recommendations that there be a significant increase in jurors' pay, from current rates such as the $5 a day paid in Los Angeles to $40 or $50 daily. Some companies and most government agencies compensate employees who do jury duty for the difference between their salary and what they receive from the county, but this tends to tilt panels toward those with such reimbursement prospects or persons who are retired and for whom jury stipends represent extra income. Reducing the number of exemptions from jury duty and suspending the driver's licenses of those who fail to show up when called are other proposals to strengthen the representativeness of jury panels.

Calls for an end to unanimous jury verdicts have been heard as well, particularly in terms of allowing an 11–1 majority to carry the day, so that a single holdout cannot cost the taxpayer or the defendant the expense of another trial. This agenda item, however, lost a great deal of its power when the Simpson jury, contrary to most expectations, was not hung, but returned a unanimous verdict. Unanimity is the outcome of 87 percent of California jury trials and 95 percent of those throughout the nation. Only two states, Oregon and Louisiana, sanction nonunanimous verdicts in criminal cases, respectively allowing 10–2 and 9–3 outcomes to prevail. Both states still report hung juries, but at a rate slightly under the national average. In six states felonies can be decided by juries with fewer than twelve members: six jurors will do in Connecticut, Florida, Louisiana, and Oregon, and eight in Arizona and Utah. But these lower numbers are not allowed in cases in which there may be a death penalty.

Opponents of the elimination of the need for jury consensus say that it is as true today as it was when the principle was adopted centuries ago that in a free country it is preferable that one hundred guilty persons go free than that one innocent person be convicted. They also insist that when a 10–2 verdict is sufficient, the majority listens much less carefully to the minority, and thus avoids the possibility of being swayed by a convincing argument that may initially lack numerical support. In England, where less-than-unanimous verdicts are permitted, the jurors are required to deliberate for at least two hours before they may return a 10–2 or 11–1 verdict.

POLICE PERJURY: "TESTILYING"

Johnnie Cochran's assignment when he was a district attorney was to deal with complaints against the police. When he entered private practice, Cochran's law firm specialized in civil cases seeking damages for police misconduct: during the year before the Simpson trial the firm had won judgments of more than $43 million. Cochran therefore was thoroughly conversant with rogue policing. Dershowitz, a criminal law professor at Harvard, has used the term "testilying" to denote police perjury in order to obtain a conviction in "their" cases. Together, Cochran and Dershowitz were able to mount a formidable assault on the integrity and the ability of the police officers involved in what the judge constantly referred to as "the Simpson matter."

Tacit understandings govern most of the work of our criminal courts. Defense attorneys, usually public defenders on the county payroll, soon learn that they pretty much must go along in order to get along. They may fight tenaciously for a client, but only to a point. If they too often take up too much court time, quarrel too strenuously, or otherwise disrupt the routinized workings of the court, judges will turn on them and prosecutors will no longer enter into plea-bargaining deals that make everybody's life (except perhaps defendants') a good deal calmer and more predictable.

Police perjury is a common ingredient of this cozy arrangement. The police often cannot make legal arrests, though they are aware (or think they know for certain) that a crime has been committed and that they have identified who did it. They develop an understandable interest in "winning" against what they come to define as "the enemy." They do not like to work diligently to solve a case only to have the evidence they illegally acquired thrown out of court because it is tainted.

In the Simpson case, detective Philip Vannatter very likely lied when he said that he did not suspect that Simpson was the murderer and therefore had not deemed it necessary to obtain a search warrant before he entered Simpson's house by having Furhman climb over a wall. He presumably lied on the witness stand again when he said that he thought that Simpson might have fled the jurisdiction, since he had been clearly told by Simpson's daughter by his first marriage, who was in the house, that her father was in Chicago on a business trip. More dramatically, detective Mark Fuhrman brazenly lied when he said that he never had used the word "nigger" during the previous ten years. A taped record of an interview with Furhman by a would-be script-writer had him employing the term forty-two times, and others would testify to chilling stories that he told about how he hated blacks and other minorities and concocted evidence to send them to jail. In September 1996, Fuhrman, who had retired from the police, pleaded no contest to a single count of perjury for lying under oath about his use of racial slurs. He was given a $200 fine and three years' probation.

The impetus for "testilying" inheres in the exclusionary rule that declares that evidence obtained through searches and seizures in violation of the Fourth Amendment shall not be admitted in court against the accused. Federal criminal justice came under the exclusionary rule in 1914 as a result of the decision in *Weeks v. United States,* which declared that the police and the courts should not be aided "by the sacrifice of those great principles established by years of endeavor and suffering." The Supreme Court also would reverse state convictions if it felt that they had been obtained under conditions that violated "the sense of justice" of the people. The roster of such cases included in-stances of protracted questioning of terrified, retarded, or befuddled suspects, flagrant brutality, and the holding of suspects incommunicado. These rever-sals have included *Rochin v. California* (1952), where the police unlawfully en-tered the defendant's home and, after he allegedly had swallowed evidence, took him to the hospital and had his stomach pumped.

California adopted an exclusionary rule for its trial courts in *People v. Cahan* (1955) after concluding that "other remedies have completely failed to secure compliance [by the police] with constitutional provisions." Operating without an exclusionary rule, California trial courts (its supreme court declared) "had been required to participate in and, in effect condone the lawless activities of law enforcement officials." Then, in 1962, in *Mapp v. Ohio* the U.S. Supreme Court imposed the exclusionary rule on all American courts.

Before the *Mapp* decision, police officers could testify that they stopped a person because he "looked suspicious" and that when they searched him they found narcotics. In the wake of the *Mapp* ruling, police began to invent more or less (often less) plausible tales about how they had found items such as drugs on a suspect. A New York criminal court judge, quoted by Dershowitz, comments on a case in which a law enforcement officer testified that a drug suspect just happened to drop a small plastic envelope that contained marijuana:

> *Were this the first time a policeman had testified that a defendant had dropped a packet of drugs to the ground, the matter would be unremarkable. The extraordinary thing is that each year in our criminal courts policemen give such testimony in hundreds, perhaps thousands of cases—and that is the problem of "dropsy" testimony.*

Like Lance Ito in the Simpson case, judges often arrive at their position by way of the district attorney's office, and by the time they join the judiciary they have become insensitive to the charade that permits acceptance of such testimony. Most often they justify their unwillingness to suppress the evidence on the ground that, were they to do so, a criminal would be turned loose and very possibly would prey upon others. In addition, it typically is the officer's word against the suspect's, and judges believe that, absent adequate proof of police wrongdoing, they are obligated to accept the version provided them by the officer.

In his taped interview, Fuhrman offered examples of how he would tamper with evidence and make the grounds for arrest more compelling:

> *You find a mark [on a drug user's arm] that looks like three days ago, squeeze it. Looks like serum's coming out, as if it were hours old. . . . That's not falsifying a report. That's putting a criminal in jail. That's being a policeman.*

One solution to the testilying problem would be to eliminate the exclusionary rule. But the rule came into being only because an angry and aggrieved Supreme Court thought it had been driven to find a way to put an end to unconscionable violations of constitutional law. Some people who believe that illegally obtained evidence should be allowed to be introduced into the trial say that, if deemed necessary, there could be a separate proceeding—either in the regular courts or within the police department—to decide whether to penalize an officer who gathered such evidence. Objections to this procedure rest on the pragmatic ground that officers rarely would be disciplined, and the practice of violating the law would flourish.

Others take a much tougher stand against the exclusionary rule. They point out that crime is not a sport that is engaged in by gentlemen and gentlewomen and played under delicate rules that demand good sportsmanship. It is a cruel exploitation of innocent people. Tactics that contribute to the control of crime ought to be permitted if they are reasonably tolerable. Thus, they declare, the only defense against evidence that is obtained illegally should be that the evidence is false; that is, for instance, that the narcotics found by the police actually were not the accused's. If the police are shown to have fabricated the evidence, then very stringent measures, including tough criminal penalties, should be taken against them.

LAWYERS AND THE PRESS

The Simpson trial involved continuous feeds and leaks to the media, as each side sought to put its best foot forward. In England, cases that are *sub judice* (pretrial or in trial) cannot be discussed by the attorneys outside the court, a provision that many believe ought to be implemented in the United States. During the Simpson trial, the California State Bar Association adopted a rule, later approved by the state supreme court, that prohibits trial participants from making extrajudicial statements to the press that they know to be prejudicial. A complementary legislative enactment (informally called the "cash for trash" law) that would have kept jurors and witnesses from accepting more than $50 for information about a trial until ninety days after its conclusion was overturned as unconstitutional by a federal court.

CAMERAS IN THE COURTROOM

The seeing-eye lens of the television camera was blamed by many persons for what they deemed to be the unholy fanfare surrounding the Simpson trial. Cameras were located behind the jury box, so that pictures of jurors would not be shown, and were operated by a remote control system; the judge had a panel on his desk that allowed him to shut down the cameras if he believed it necessary. Participants in the trial, most notably the attorneys and the judge, were said to posture and preen for the cameras, and the depiction of courtroom scenarios that unfolded beyond the jury's eyes was regarded as providing a distorted picture against which to evaluate its verdict.

Today, all but three states (Indiana, Mississippi, and South Dakota) allow cameras into courtrooms at the discretion of the judge. There are, however, limitations in many states on such coverage, so that only about twenty-six states routinely permit televising. Following the Simpson trial, judges were more likely to ban cameras from their courtrooms. The major argument against the use of cameras lies in the contention that they make a serious event into entertainment. President Clinton, voicing opposition to televising court trials, used the Simpson case to support his view, saying that it was conducted in a "circus atmosphere."

The most prominent argument in favor of televised trials is that they allow citizens to take advantage of the provision of the Sixth Amendment that provides a constitutional right to a public trial. Televised trials, some maintain, provide viewers with a better understanding of how the criminal justice system really operates, thus forming a sound basis for reform if it is deemed necessary. Supporters of courtroom television declare that the cameras do not cause the behavior they transmit; they only expose it.

It has been argued that the television cameras added some dignity in the Simpson case to what otherwise would have been even more unseemly proceedings. Had the cameras not been in court, it is said, the only footage available to the public would have shown lawyers scrambling to get their sound bites on the air. "The case would have been tried in the press, but without the benefit of rules of evidence," Dershowitz insists. "Television in the courtroom," he claims, "helps to keep everyone more honest."

Others were less taken with the show business aura that came to envelop the Simpson trial. A Los Angeles newspaper reported that the lead defense attorney had purchased two new suits, that the judge's wife carefully checked his hair gel each morning, and that the court clerk made an effort to keep her pen out of her mouth. Noting this, one commentator asks, "Is it unreasonable to suggest that if people alter their physical appearance because of the camera, they might alter their words?" Such a critique, however, presumes, with no evidence, that the changes are necessarily for the worse. Knowing that they are being scrutinized closely, might not persons behave with more care than otherwise?

After a comprehensive review of the positive and negative consequences of televised trials, a legal scholar concluded that the disadvantages outweighed the benefits and that cameras ought to be banned. The primary objection was that irrelevant considerations stalked into the courtroom along with the television cameras:

> *[A] fair trial depends on detached neutrality. The remote public, by virtue of television, corrupts detached neutrality. The bias of television may coalesce around politics, culture, and the like. However, the biggest bias is self-interest, political and financial, but mainly commercial. The media is business. Big business. The one final question to ask is, whose story is it anyway? The humiliation of parading an alleged rape victim's undergarments in the courtroom as occurred in the William Kennedy Smith trial is a*

necessary part of the judicial process. Further humiliation by making such evidence the fare of national television may make for fair commercial television, but does it make for a fair trial?

The undergarment example may for some seem a weak point in what may be a strong argument: humiliation and a fair trial do not seem to be necessary correlates, though both may be considerations to be argued on their own merits. The author concluded, "though there is much potential good from in-court cameras, there is too much actual bad." That position may be impeccable, but it shows a lawyer-like skill in advocacy more than an attention to detail. After all, why not measure actual good against actual bad effects rather than the potential of one kind and the actuality of the other?

The ongoing role of television in courtrooms is for the moment uncertain. Particularly intriguing is the prediction of Don Hewitt, producer of the show *60 Minutes,* that in the future judges will approve network coverage of trials only if no commercials are sold and that cities will begin auctioning off the rights to trial television coverage as a means of recouping their expenses.

INQUISITORIAL JUSTICE?

A more radical position on the need for reform and the way to achieve it has been adopted by those who view the Simpson trial as highlighting inherent and irremediable flaws in the American criminal justice system. Opinion polls demonstrate a startling absence of confidence among Americans in their criminal justice system. A 1993 poll, for instance, found 67 percent of the public expressing confidence in the military and 53 percent in the church. Congress got only 19 percent support, but even that exceeded the 17 percent favorable rating accorded the criminal justice system.

The belief has been growing that American criminal courts are combat zones, attorney driven, and that they are overdependent on the skill of lawyers to the neglect of a fair-minded search for truth. Some people argue that it is unfortunate that the administration of criminal law in continental European countries has been dubbed "inquisitorial" and suggest that this judge-directed method may in fact be superior to the traditional Anglo-American system.

Conclusion

Jeffrey Toobin, a lawyer who covered the Simpson trial for the *New Yorker,* thought that "the reason anyone will care about this case five years, ten years from now is because of what it illuminates about race in America." Others believe that it was not race but money that carried the day in the Los Angeles courtroom. They note that nothing has changed since 1884, when William Howard Taft, then an assistant prosecutor, later a Supreme Court chief justice and president of the United States, said: "It is well-nigh impossible to convict a man who has money in this country under our present system of prosecution." For many, the fact that Simpson walks about freely, debating at Oxford University, attending a fund-raiser to support efforts against domestic violence, seeming to be having a jolly time, and, above all, trying to hustle money, seems shameless and unconscionable. For cynics, this indicates that in the end, whether justice was or was not achieved makes very little difference. The survivors of the victims may feel terrible, but Simpson's freedom poses little or no threat to anybody else. It is hardly likely to encourage others to kill, believing they will be exculpated, nor is Simpson (presuming that he is guilty), likely to harm another human being, given the almost two decades that it presumably took him to accumulate the rage manifest in the murders of Nicole Brown Simpson and Ronald Goldman.

For Further Reading

There has been an outpouring of book-length commentaries on the trial of O. J. Simpson, with no end in sight. Except for the judge, for whom it would have been unseemly, the major criminal justice personnel signed lucrative contracts with publishers to convey their spin on what had taken place.

Several volumes offer a straightforward chronology of the case, extracts from the testimony, and other information regarding what happened. Among them are Frank Schmalleger, *Trial of the Century: People of the State of California vs. Orenthal James Simpson* (Upper Saddle River, N.J.: Prentice-Hall, 1996); Robert J. Walton and LaGard Smith, *Trial of the Century: You Be the Juror* (Colorado Springs: Marcon Limited, 1994); *In Pursuit of Justice* (Los Angeles: Los Angeles Times, 1995); Linda Deutsch and Michael Fleeman, *Verdict: The Chronicle of the O. J. Simpson Trial* (Kansas City, Mo.: Andrews and McMeel, 1995); and Clifford Linedecker, *OJ A to Z: The Complete Handbook of the Trial of the Century* (New York: St. Martin's Griffin, 1995).

A collection of articles of varying sophistication appears in Jeffrey Abramson, ed., *Postmortem: The O. J. Simpson Case* (New York: Basic Books, 1996), and in Gregg Barak, ed., *Representing O.J.: Murder, Criminal Justice and Mass Culture* (Guilderland, N.Y.: Harrow and Heston, 1996). Symposiums on the trial appear in the *Southern California Law Review*, 69 (1996):1233–1678; and in the

Journal of Social Distress and the Homeless, 5 (1996):273–334. A second-guessing review of eight of the major books is found in George Fisher, "The O. J. Simpson Corpus," *Stanford Law Review*, 49 (1997):971–1019. Also of value is Devon W. Carbado, "The Construction of O. J. Simpson as a Racial Victim," *Harvard Civil Rights–Civil Liberties Law Review*, 32 (1997):49–103.

After the trial, from the prosecution side came *In Contempt* (New York: Regan Books, 1996) by Christopher A. Darden and Jess Walter, a best-seller largely because of its appealing personal revelations; and Hank M. Goldberg, *The Prosecution Responds: An O. J. Trial Prosecutor Reveals What Really Happened* (Secaucus, N.J.: Birch Lane Press, 1996), a book marred by the fact that, as a continuing employee, Goldberg felt compelled to whitewash all prosecutor flaws and miscalculations. Later, Marcia Clark and Teresa Carpenter checked in with *Without a Doubt* (New York: Viking, 1997). A reviewer for the *New York Times*, echoing others, found the book suffused with self-pity and noted that "as her title suggests, self-reflection and an appreciation of ambiguity are not Marcia Clark's strong points." Ms. Clark received a $4.2 million advance for the book. An idealized appraisal of one of the victims that also corrects some erroneous information is found in The Family of Ron Goldman, with William and Marilyn Hoffer, *His Name Is Ron* (New York: William Morrow, 1997).

The defense contributions include Johnnie L. Cochran, Jr., and Tim Rutten, *Journey to Justice* (New York: Ballantine, 1996); Robert L. Shapiro and Larkin Warren, *The Search for Justice: A Defense Attorney's Brief on the O. J. Simpson Case* (New York: Warner Books, 1996); Gerald F. Uelmen, *Lessons from the Trial: The People v. O. J. Simpson* (Kansas City, Mo.: Andrews and McMeel, 1996); and Alan M. Dershowitz, *Reasonable Doubts: The O. J. Simpson Case and the Criminal Justice System* (New York: Simon & Schuster, 1996).

Three books were written by jurors. A particularly important contribution is the combined thoughts of three panel members: Amanda Cooley, Carrie Bess, and Marsha Rubin-Jackson, *Madam Foreman: A Rush to Judgment?* (New York: Dove Books, 1996). Michael Knox and Mike Walker, *The Private Diary of an OJ Juror: Behind the Scenes of the Trial of the Century* (New York: Dove Books, 1995), is the report of a man who was removed from the jury about midway during the trial. Tracy Kennedy, who also had been taken off the jury, wrote *Mistrial of the Century* (New York: Dove Books, 1995) in collaboration with Alan Abramson.

Detectives on the case sought to defend their performances too; see Tom Lange, Philip Vannatter, and Dan E. Moldes, *Evidence Dismissed: The Inside Story of the Police Investigation of O. J. Simpson* (New York: Pocket Books, 1997), and Mark Fuhrman, *Murder in Brentwood* (Washington, D.C.: Regnery, 1997).

The civil case is reviewed in Daniel Petrocelli and Peter Knobler, *Triumph of Justice: The Final Judgment on the Simpson Saga* (New York: Crown, 1998). Some writers and newspaper folk who covered the trial have added their insights to the verbal flood. These include Jeffrey Toobin, *The Run of His Life: The People v. O. J. Simpson* (New York: Random House, 1996), well written but questionably accurate on some key points of fact and interpretation. Joseph Bosco's *A Problem of Evidence: How the Prosecution Freed O. J. Simpson* (New York: William Morrow, 1996) provides the most comprehensive roster of unanswered questions and rumors that could, if accurate, exculpate Simpson. Tom Elias and Dennis Schatzman, *The Simpson Trial in Black and White* (Los Angeles: General Publishing Group, 1996), features alternating chapters by a white and a black journalist. Lawrence Schiller and James Willwerth's *American Tragedy: The Uncensored Story of the Simpson Defense* (New York: Random House, 1996) provides some inside information, largely secured from Robert Kadashian, a close friend of Simpson, but the book is outrageously overwritten.

Jewell Taylor Gibbs, *Race and Justice: Rodney King and O. J. Simpson in a House Divided* (San Francisco: Jossey-Bass, 1996), and Toni Morrison and Claudia Brodsky Lacour, eds., *Birth of a Nation'hood: Gaze, Script and Spectacle in the O. J. Simpson Case* (New York: Pantheon, 1997), focus on the racial aspects of the case. The authors see deep-rooted white racism as driving public interest and the angry reaction to the jury's not-guilty verdict. Bitterness is the overpowering emotion in most of the essays in the Morrison-Lacour volume. Several are powerful and poignant expressions of African American sensitivity about hostile white attitudes toward blacks as demonstrated in overt and covert responses to the murders and the trial.

Also joining in are Simpson's niece, Terri Baker (with Kenneth Ross and Mary Jane Ross), *I'm Not Dancing Any More* (New York: Kensington, 1997), and his onetime girlfriend Paula Barbieri, *The Other Woman—My Years with O. J. Simpson: A Story of Love, Trust, and Betrayal* (Boston: Little, Brown, 1997). Ms. Barbieri's book reads like a Harlequin romance. It offers insight into the narcissistic worlds of modeling and acting and a story of newfound religious belief. The author's most perceptive observation is: "I have been many things in my life, but a great judge of human behavior isn't one of them."

The major "non-book" was not written by Joe McGinnis, who had a reserved front-row seat at the trial and a $1.75 million advance for his anticipated report on it. Returning the advance to his publisher, McGinnis labeled the trial "an utter farce," and declared that the judge suffered "total loss of control over the proceedings." Those proceedings, McGinnis said, involved "ludicrous witnesses" and "that nauseating group of cretins" who made up the jury. Dominick Dunne would have been well advised to follow McGinnis's lead. His *Another City, Not My Own: A Novel in the Form of a Memoir* (New York: Crown, 1997) is the least worthwhile Simpson trial book. Dunne's effort is (in our opinion) a thoroughly self-indulgent, name-dropping, sophomoric production. We agree with Gary Indiana, a reviewer who described Dunne's work as "a gurgling mess of repetitious and numbingly banal opinions."

There was a rash of quickie books, including Marc Cerasini, *O. J. Simpson: American Hero, American Tragedy* (New York: Windsor, 1994); Don Davis, *Fallen Hero* (New York: St. Martin's, 1994); and Sheila Weller, *Raging Heart: The Intimate Story of the Tragic Marriage of O. J. and Nicole Brown Simpson* (New York: Pocket Books, 1995). Faye D. Resnick, who shortly before the murder had lived with Nicole Simpson, wrote two books, one with Mike Walker, *Nicole Brown Simpson: The Private Diary of a Life Interrupted* (New York: Dove Books, 1994), the other with Jeanne V. Belle, *Shattered: In the Eye of the Storm* (New York: Dove Books, 1996). The first is saturated with scandalmongering tales about the victim, whom Resnick called her best friend and portrays as a brainless, self-obsessed creature. One reader, understandably, said that he felt like taking a long, cleansing shower after reading it.

Books about trial participants include Clifford L. Linedecker, *Marcia Clark: Her Private Trials and Public Triumphs* (New York: Pinnacle Books, 1995), and Marc Eliot, *Kato Kaelin: The Whole Truth* (New York: Harper Paperbacks, 1995). There also is O. J. Simpson, *I Want to Tell You: My Responses to Your Letters, Your Messages, Your Questions* (Boston: Little, Brown, 1995).

The most provocative book of the lot was something of a sleeper. Written by Vincent Bugliosi, the former star of the Los Angeles County district attorney's office, the man who had prosecuted Charles Manson, among others, *Outrage: The Five Reasons Why O. J. Simpson Got Away with Murder* (New York: Norton, 1996) is, as the *New York Times* reviewer described it, a "well-informed analysis in welcome contrast to much of the insipid or pointless commentary about the Simpson trial." Bugliosi has stinging contempt for the way the prosecution handled the case and not much kinder words for the defense attorneys or the judge.

In *O.J.: The Last Word* (New York: St. Martin's Press, 1997), the prominent Wyoming lawyer Gerry Spence, an early candidate to defend Simpson, finds much to fault about the trial, including the language abilities of the television commentators (many of them, he writes, "thought syntax was a mouthwash"). Spence believes that the state should have sought the death penalty against

Simpson, noting that 39 percent of murderers executed do not have a previous conviction. He also advocates selecting judges not by election or political appointment but by putting the names of all practicing criminal lawyers with a certain level of experience into a hat and drawing names out. Those selected would then serve for a limited period of time.

An interesting if inconclusive attempt to scrutinize all possible murder scenarios in terms of the time lines proposed at the trial and material unearthed by the writers is offered in Donald Freed and Raymond P. Briggs, *Killing Time: The First Full Investigation of the Unsolved Murders of Nicole Brown Simpson and Ronald Goldman* (New York: Macmillan, 1996).

The jury system is discussed in three recent books: Jeffrey Abramson, ed., *We the Jury: The Jury System and the Ideal of Democracy* (New York: Basic Books, 1994); Stephen J. Adler, *The Jury: Trial and Error in the American Courtroom* (New York: Random House, 1994); and James P. Levine, *Juries and Politics* (Pacific Grove, Calif.: Brooks/Cole, 1992). The classic early research on jury behavior, still invaluable as a resource, is Harry Kalven, Jr., and Hans Zeisel, *The American Jury* (Boston: Little, Brown, 1966).

Regarding the televising of criminal trials, see Marjorie Cohn and David Dow, *Cameras in the Courtroom: Television and the Pursuit of Justice* (Jefferson, N.C.: McFarland, 1998). See also Paul Thaler, *The Spectacle: Media and the Making of the O. J. Simpson Story* (New York: Praeger, 1997).

The court decisions discussed here that enunciate the exclusionary rule are *Weeks v. United States*, 232 U.S. 383 (1914); *Rochin v. California*, 341 U.S. 165 (1952); *People v. Cahan*, 282 P2d 905 (Calif. 1955); and *Mapp v. Ohio*, 367 U.S. 643 (1961).

On the DNA testimony see Harlan Levy, *And the Blood Cried Out* (New York: Basic Books, 1996), especially pp. 157–188, and William C. Thompson, "DNA Evidence in the O. J. Simpson Trial," *University of Colorado Law Review,* 67 (1996):827–857.

Chapter Seven

Conclusion

Five celebrated criminal cases:

- In the Leopold and Loeb case the defendants, both under twenty, for no apparent reason killed a fourteen-year-old boy they casually knew. They offered highly intellectualized explanations for their behavior. The crime was gratuitous, despite the melodramatic attempt to secure a ransom.

- At Scottsboro, nine illiterate black hoboes, two under the age of sixteen, all called "boys," were pulled out of a railroad car and dragged into custody by hastily deputized lawmen. They were sentenced to be executed in several successive trials. None was killed by the state but they served sentences upwards of nineteen years for an offense they did not commit. The Scottsboro men became symbols of Jim Crow racism in the southern states, a byword for how the criminal justice system could be used by whites to maintain political, economic, and social control. The blatant triumph of racial prejudice over legal norms brought the case to the attention of the world.

- Without Charles Lindbergh's sensational solo flight to Paris there would not have been the kind of trial that ended in the execution of Bruno Richard Hauptmann. The public idolization of Lindbergh allowed him to control the criminal investigation in the Hauptmann case until the baby's body was found. Despite evidence that appeared much more suspect after the FBI files were obtained years later by a Freedom of Information action, Hauptmann, an illegal immigrant from a despised country, went to the electric chair in large measure to appease the public's thirst for someone's blood to atone for the murder of the child of a celebrated couple.

- The trials of Alger Hiss offered a volatile combination of Richard Nixon's political ambition and strategic acumen (mixed with a good dosage of pure luck) and the ill-kempt and melodramatic Whittaker Chambers. Arrogant and obdurate denials by Alger Hiss of the most self-evident of Chambers's allegations created a fascinating drama. Chambers told all. Hiss denied everything. To the day of his death, Hiss insisted that sooner or later he would be vindicated.

- In the O. J. Simpson case, the defendant was a very wealthy and very famous black man accused of murdering his glamorous blonde ex-wife. The interracial marriage, the searing episodes of domestic violence, and the Mark Fuhrman tapes showing blatant perjury by a law enforcement officer elevated a family slaying into an absorbing television drama.

The five famous cases produced five different outcomes. Leopold and Loeb were sentenced to life imprisonment, but spared the death penalty. The Scottsboro defendants, excepting the two juveniles, were sentenced to death several times, but none was executed. In a ceremony dripping with irony, the last of the Scottsboro defendants would be pardoned in 1984 for the offense he had not committed. The pardon was granted in person by Alabama Governor George Wallace, one of the staunchest opponents of racial integration during the early days of the civil rights movement. Wallace wanted to make a run for the presidency and he needed to clean up his image if he was to have any prospect of making a decent showing.

Bruno Richard Hauptmann went to his death proclaiming his innocence, Alger Hiss served a forty-four-month sentence when he was convicted of perjury in his second trial, and O. J. Simpson walked out of the Los Angeles courtroom a free man.

What lessons might be drawn from these epic moments in the annals of the administration of criminal justice in the United States during the twentieth century?

We know that the outcomes bore no relationship to the sensational nature of the cases: all episodes were famous before their outcomes were known. But was justice served? Did the trials have an impact on the criminal law and its administration that was equivalent to the impact they had on the public consciousness? Would the same results have come about had the earlier cases been tried in more recent times?

The answers to such questions are as varied as the details of the cases themselves. The simplest overall response will come as a surprise to very few, if any: It pays to have a great deal of money when you are up against it in a criminal court because money buys good attorneys and diligent, clever investigators. The criminal justice system is sufficiently malleable to provide openings for skilled lawyers if the evidence is—or can be made to appear to be—somewhat ambivalent and ambiguous. But it takes a very large defense fund to overcome the enormous initial advantage in resources enjoyed by the prosecution. As in war, imagination, intelligence, and courage can be very important, but materiel advantages—the airplanes and the ammunition—are what in the end pretty much dictate how things will go.

For us, probably the most unexpected aspect of the cases was the importance of the man (for it always was a man) who sat on the bench. Judges in American jurisprudence tend to be regarded as umpires in a few-holds-barred fray between combative opposing lawyers. They are stereotyped as wise, sober, and above the battle. But in the trials that we have looked at, the judges very often played a crucial role. It was Judge James Edwin Horton, Jr., in the Scottsboro case who almost brought the charade to an end with his courageous refusal to endorse the verdict after the first Decatur trial, and it was Judge William Washington Callahan in the subsequent Decatur trials who peremptorily shut down any attempt at an effective defense by his rulings and his insistence that he could not contemplate any white woman, however degraded, having a sexual relationship with a black man.

Both Callahan and Judge Thomas W. Trenchard in the Lindbergh case demonstrated the way in which an adroit judge can convey his personal views forcefully to jury members by his tone of voice and facial expression, matters that never find their way into the official trial transcript. The decision to spare Nathan Leopold and Richard Loeb from death was made by Judge John R. Caverly. The striking difference in the manner in which the two Hiss trials played out was in considerable measure a function of the rulings of the judges. In the first Hiss trial, Judge Samuel Kaufman was pilloried by Nixon for what he said were Kaufman's leanings toward the defense. Kaufman refused to allow Hede Massing, attempting to corroborate Chambers's story, and Carl Binger, the psychoanalyst trying to document what he saw as Chambers's mentally ill personality, to testify in the first trial. Judge Henry W. Goddard, in the second trial, was much less stringent about testimony than Kaufman and he permitted both Massing and Binger to offer evidence, perhaps significantly affecting the outcome of the trial.

In the Simpson trial, the presiding officer again figured prominently. Judge Lance Ito invariably is chastised as having run the case poorly, unwilling to take a firm stand against showboating and to cut off long-winded speeches and irrelevant examination of witnesses by both sides. He also uniformly is regarded as having been submissive to the enticements of the defense attorneys and blinded from doing his job in a professional manner by his own fascination with being in the media limelight. Another judge might well have meant a different verdict in the Simpson criminal case.

The qualities of the attorneys also were of overwhelming importance in virtually all of the cases. Second-guessing the manner in which the Alger Hiss case was tried, a law professor, Richard Morris, in *Fair Trial* illustrates the small but significant ways in which an attorney's talent can score points or fall short:

> *Stryker had shown Chambers to have been a liar in the past, but that was not the issue. The question was whether he was a liar now. Stryker's questioning betrayed a failure on his part to come to grips with the crucial issue. Confronting Chambers with his denial before the grand jury that he had any "direct knowledge" of espionage, Stryker asked the witness: "Was that answer true or false?" "That answer was false." "Then you admit that you testified falsely and committed perjury before the grand jury in this building, is that right?" "That is right." Stryker's phrasing was psychologically inept. The implication of Chambers's answer seemed obvious: he was lying then, but he is telling the truth now. Profiting by this lapse, Claude B. Cross, at the second trial, phrased the question differently: "You lied either then before the grand jury or before this jury?" he asked Chambers. "That is right," the witness was compelled to answer. Again: "And you lied then or you are lying now?" "That is right."*

Leopold and Loeb might well have been hanged without the superb pleading of Clarence Darrow. The Scottsboro defendants were on the verge of being executed after they were so ineptly defended in their first trial, but the strikingly competent work of Samuel Leibowitz kept them alive until local public outrage abated with the passage of time. The newspaper that hired Hauptmann's attorney (this would not be allowed today) expected exclusives because of the money it laid out. The ill-prepared attorney took the case to publicize himself, not to work for his client's cause—and Hauptmann went to the chair. Lloyd Paul Stryker thought he could easily obtain at least a hung jury in the Hiss perjury trials, but Hiss wanted a more dignified defense and so obtained a much less dramatic (however more erudite) attorney—and lost. And whatever one might think of his tactics and his choice of themes, Johnnie Cochran did for his client exactly what was needed for an acquittal—and did it extremely well.

The prosecutors proved to be in general a less colorful lot; they often played partisan roles designed not to separate the guilty from the innocent but to gain glory. John Mason Brown in *Through These Men* has offered what remains one of the best delineations of the kind of abilities that it takes to be a successful prosecutor—and, for that matter, a good defense attorney:

> *The prosecutor's by obligation a special mind, mongoose quick, bullying, devious, unrelenting, forever baited to ensnare. It is almost duty bound to mislead, and by instinct dotes on confusing and flourishes on weakness. Its search is for blemishes it can present as scars, its obligation to raise doubts or sour with suspicion. It asks questions not to learn but to convict, and can read guilt into the most innocent answers. To natural lapses of memory it gives the appearance either of stratagems for hiding misdeeds or, worse still, of lies, dark and deliberate. Feigned and wheedling politeness, sarcasm that scalds, intimidation, surprise and besmirchment by innuendo, association, or suggestion—all these methods and devices are such staples in the prosecutor's repertoire that his mind turns to them by rote.*

Note, in the same vein, the advice supplied attorneys in a book called *How to Win Lawsuits before Juries:*

> *When you have forced the witness into giving you a direct answer to your question you really have him under control: he is off balance, usually scared. This advantage should be followed up with a few simple questions such as, "You did not want to answer that question, did you?" If the witness says that he wanted to answer it, ask him in a resounding voice, "Well, why did you not answer it when I first asked you?" Whatever his answer is you then ask him, "Did you think you were smart enough to evade answering the question?" This battering and legal-style "kicking the witness around" not only humiliates but subdues him.*

In the annals of criminal trials, a classic illustration of the quickness of mind that can make a courtroom gladiator successful is the story about Edward Carson, a distinguished Irish barrister, who asked a witness, "Are you a drinking man?"

"That's my business" was the man's response.

"And have you any other?" Carson shot back.

There were numerous illustrations in the five celebrated cases of the kind of tactics scathingly inventoried by Brown. One of the worst was a minor early moment in the Simpson trial when Carl Douglas, a junior member of the defense team, excoriated Ron Shipp, a policeman testifying against the defendant. The tactic seemed to backfire, with the jury and the audience viewing it as overkill, and Douglas was restricted to a lesser role throughout the remainder of the trial. Perhaps—though perhaps not—this indicates that people today are more alert to and less taken in by bullying tactics that have served criminal court attorneys so well in the past.

Overall, the performances of the prosecutors seemed a mixed bag compared to those of the attorneys who faced them for the defense. Robert Crowe was no match for Darrow in the Leopold-Loeb case; neither was Edward Reilly in the same league as David Wilentz. Thomas Murphy, on the other hand, did a yeoman's job in both Hiss trials, aided by some very sophisticated work by his investigators. The Simpson prosecutors were never really in contention with the defense. They badly underestimated what they had to do, in part because they had never come up against so strong a defense team, and they made very poor tactical decisions. Probably most important, putting aside the issue of legal acumen, the jurors did not like the prosecutors, particularly Marcia Clark, and that made her job extraordinarily more difficult, perhaps almost hopeless.

That winning was of considerable importance in advancing the careers of the attorneys involved is well illustrated by our cases. Knight went on to become lieutenant governor of Alabama, Wilentz to become the most powerful personage in the New Jersey Democratic Party for many decades. Murphy became New York's police commissioner before being appointed to a judgeship. Leibowitz became a judge known for his tough stance toward criminal offenders, but he got that job in New York, not in Alabama. Others who lost their cases fared less well. Most faded into obscurity, at least in terms of public renown, but at least there was solace for the Simpson district attorneys in the stunning book advances—$4.2 million for Marcia Clark—that they received for spinning stories about how they lost the case but shouldn't have, and besides, it was someone else's fault.

All the world's a stage," William Shakespeare has one of the characters in *As You Like It* proclaim. "And all the men and women merely players/They have their exits and their entrances/And one man in his time plays many parts." Social psychologists agree. We all acts in ways that we presume—and hope—will bring about those things we desire. Of course, we have to anticipate how others will respond to the roles we play, a complex task that often fails to work out the way we believed it would. One of the reasons adolescents can be difficult for their elders to deal with is that they are trying on various behavioral costumes, seeking to locate the one that is comfortable, comforting, and rewarding.

The criminal trials that we have scrutinized provide in encapsulated form the drama of life, and they are structured by formal rules. Much is omitted in the trials, leaving room for our imagination; we see in the courtroom only a suggestive slice of the relevant reality. Witnesses being cross-examined cannot explain in a complicated way a complicated issue or choose the questions they will answer. The struggle for control of the discourse is ongoing. A criminal trial often is very good theater, especially since the stakes are real, not simulated.

The space-bound and time-bound aspect of criminal trials also provides an excellent setting for the expression and reflection of attitudes toward matters such as authority and political power. Trials have a beginning, a middle, and (usually) a dramatic end. Then the audience can go home and the listeners and viewers can turn off their radios or television sets.

Trials also often demand consummate acting skills from those who desperately try to persuade jury members of the truth of their version of what went on. If they were guilty as charged, imagine the talent demonstrated by Richard Hauptmann, Alger Hiss, and O. J. Simpson to blatantly lie throughout a grueling process, never certain when they might be entrapped by an irreconcilable contradiction. In the Hiss case, the dramaturgy of the event was specifically entered into the record. "Whichever of you is lying is the greatest actor that America has ever produced," said F. Edward Hébert, the Congressman from Louisiana and member of the House Un-American Activities Committee. Similarly, psychoanalyst Meyer Zeligs noted that Hiss paid such extraordinary attention to the state of Chambers's teeth that "it was thought that he was play-acting." Certainly Chambers seemed to think so and he makes an explicit reference to the theatricality of the trial in *Witness*, his autobiography:

> *Not its least horrifying aspect was that it was great theater, too; not only because of the inherent drama, but in part because, I am convinced, Alger Hiss was acting from start to finish, never more so than when he pretended to be about to attack me physically. His performance was all but flawless, but what made it shocking, even in its moments of unintended comedy, was the fact that the terrible spur of Hiss's acting was fear.*

Criminal trials reduce complex external events to words and exhibits. The alleged rapes featured in the Scottsboro case are not seen but described by words that never can recreate with total adequacy what went on or was supposed to have gone on. Alger Hiss was tied to incriminating documents by circumstantial evidence, but there was no videotaped evidence of his opening his house door, receiving documents from Chambers, and giving them to Priscilla Hiss to type on the Woodstock. It takes imagination—and imagination can be faulty and can be manipulated—to make the leap from its verbal reproduction to an actual event.

At the same time, it becomes exceedingly difficult to recreate the highly significant moods of the times that played so prominent a part in the way the cases went: the racism in Alabama, the public worship of the Lindberghs, the ravages of the Great Depression, the fear of Communism and the terrors of atomic bombing at the time of the Hiss trial, and the impact of the Rodney King case on the verdict of the Simpson jurors. In the King case white police officers had been videotaped savagely beating a black motorist who had committed no crime. They had been found not guilty by a white jury; the memory of that episode and its aftermath permeated the Simpson courtroom.

How much has changed from the time of the earlier trials to today? Is Scottsboro so far out of tune with present conditions that its ingredients are difficult to believe? Any answer has to be qualified: certain matters would never be tolerated, but other kinds of mischief, sometimes equally reprehensible, now prevail. The vituperation of Wilentz's summation, lacerating Hauptmann as an alien fiend, would not be permissible today, though it obviously was accepted without a flutter six decades ago.

Trials as theater also provide tableaux that remain vivid. The rotund chameleon Whittaker Chambers staring at the staight-backed Alger Hiss as Hiss is taunted from the dais by Richard Nixon. In the Leopold and Loeb hearing the exhausted but soft-spoken Clarence Darrow making an overmatched and ambitious prosecutor appear flat-footed. The Scottsboro trials might never have taken place without the vivid persona of Victoria Price, shrewd and earthy, or the dogged determination of the prosecutor to make the capital charges stick. In the Hauptmann case there is the memorable moment in which Wilentz shakes his fist at the defendant on the witness stand, calling him a liar, a liar, before a transfixed audience.

In the Simpson trial a boomerang came back to figuratively decapitate Marcia Clark after she had treated police officer Mark Fuhrman as a choirboy, only to discover that he had been flatly lying. Then there were the defense attorneys at the Simpson trial, each pushing his way into the spotlight: the smooth and confident Johnnie Cochran; F. Lee Bailey, an old bull putting his head down and shaking it when his territory was threatened; Alan Dershowitz, the academic gadfly with credibility problems of his own; and Robert Shapiro, the member of the team being nudged nearer to the sidelines each day.

Trials, like theater, can enthrall a prurient audience as they reveal details of the intimate lives of real people, lives that can vary dramatically from those of the ordinary citizen. The very wealthy Leopold and Loeb families with their strange nursemaids corrupting the young children turned over to their care; the wretched condition of unemployed black hoboes in the South and the brutality of the white-controlled legal system; the dreamlike lives of Charles and Anne Lindbergh at a time when most people just scraped by without social security, welfare benefits, or unemployment insurance. Then there was the bizarre and mesmerizing life of Whittaker Chambers, with multiple identities and strange underground espionage activities; and the sudden transformation of the same man to a God-fearing, intensely patriotic martyr, intent on saving his country from the Communist scourge. The Hisses for their part testified about life in the Washington and New York legal and social communities and that of left-wing intellectuals, in addition to the internal activities and bickering in the upper and lower echelons of the federal government. In the Simpson case the defendant had been a spectacular football player. By then a multimillionaire, he and the murdered woman to whom he had been married were living their lives amid rumors of drug use, hot-tub parties, promiscuity, and stories of domestic violence. And in the background hovered a cast of colorful characters, each absorbing in terms of the way they had chosen to live their lives, often in a manner so strikingly different from the humdrum existence of most of the rest of us.

Subtler matters that may (or may not) have been of utmost significance in the cases never surfaced in the courtrooms. We never heard what happened to the casts made of the footprints left at the Lindbergh estate and in the cemetery by the alleged kidnapper. Many witnesses were not called, certain evidence was mothballed. Neither the dramatic chase of Simpson's Bronco along the southern California freeways, the apparent suicide note, nor the police interrogation was brought before the jury.

Both Bruno Richard Hauptmann and Alger Hiss, some observers believe, protested their innocence in the face of strong contrary evidence because of their close attachment to their wives. Hauptmann, it was claimed, could not tolerate shattering the trust and love that Anna Hauptmann so thoroughly gave him by implicating himself in the kidnapping-murder. Life, it seemed to him, would have been meaningless if her support was withdrawn and her good opinion of him destroyed. Alger Hiss, some said, was protecting his wife, a woman who had been involved in the espionage as deeply as or more deeply than he had. Priscilla Hiss, of course, despite the evidence accepted by the jury that she had typed the incriminating documents, was never indicted.

Nixon later said that his excitement at Alger Hiss's revelations had so stimulated him that he got no sleep the night before he was to interrogate Priscilla Hiss. He was unprepared and failed to follow up on the inconsistencies and gaps in her testimony or to take advantage of her extreme nervousness. For all practical purposes that chapter of the story concluded then, Nixon believes, and only because of his fatigue.

More generally, the five cases exposed sharp divisions in American society along race, class, and ethnic lines. Yet there was surprisingly little gender tension. No case directly involved women challenging the control of men over the social and legal order, although the role of Marcia Clark as the Simpson prosecutor sometimes was seen in terms of gender politics. Nor did any of the cases involve women as defendants, a likely reflection of the considerably lower rate of serious offenses committed by women in contrast to men.

How did these trials affect crime and criminal justice? Some changes that owe their origin to them are easily chronicled; others are far too subtle to pin down with any confidence. In the Simpson trial, for instance, millions of Americans who had never before heard the terms "voir dire" or "sequestration" developed firm views about how juries should be selected and treated. Judges in cases that followed the Simpson trial showed that they had absorbed some lessons from it, at least for a while: television cameras found it much more difficult to gain entrance to proceedings and lawyers came under stringent bans to refrain from trying their cases in the press.

Justice Oliver Wendell Holmes, Jr., the eminent jurist for whom Alger Hiss and his brother both served as law clerks, contributed what is probably the best-known aphorism that can be applied to the cases that we have looked at. In his 1904 dissenting opinion in *Northern Securities Company v. United States* (193 U.S. 197), Holmes noted first that "although I think it is useless and undesirable, as a rule, to express dissent," he nonetheless felt bound in this instance to do so, presumably because of the importance of the case. He then declared:

> *Great cases, like hard cases, make bad law. For great cases are called great, not by reason of their real importance in shaping the law of the future, but because of some accident of immediate overwhelming interest which appeals to the feelings and distorts the judgments.*

"These immediate interests," Holmes went on to say, "exercise a kind of hydraulic pressure which makes what previously was clear doubtful, and before which even well settled principles of law will bend."

At issue in *Northern Securities* was a caper in which James J. Hill, the controlling force in the Great Northern Railroad, and J. P. Morgan, who dominated the Northern Pacific Railroad, had established the Northern Securities Company, into which they placed most of the shares of the two railroads, which were direct competitors along many of their routes. The action was alleged by the government to violate antitrust law. The 5–4 majority decision found that the Morgan-Hill tactic had the tendency to reduce competition and the almost certain outcome of operating against the public interest. Holmes, in a carefully crafted dissent, took issue with the majority view that what had been done, whether beneficent or malevolent, was prohibited by the antitrust law. The law, he claimed, did not say anything about competition. Would the Justice Department have punished two grocers who decided to combine their businesses? Holmes believed that the financial magnitude of the case and the power of its protagonists had unacceptably swayed the court into issuing an unsatisfactory ruling.

Can the same be said of the celebrated criminal cases that we have reviewed? Are they "hard" cases that produced "bad" law?

Holmes's terms—"great," "hard," and "bad"—have a considerable element of subjectivity. The cases that we have considered were "great" but not necessarily "hard" ones. They were sensational and celebrated episodes that became complicated only because of the positions adopted by the participants and, at times, the skills of the attorneys.

What, then, can be said about the law they produced?

Only the Scottsboro case impelled Supreme Court rulings, but it produced landmark decisions that basically realigned the power of the states and that of the federal courts when in *Powell v. Alabama* it extended constitutional protections to state proceedings based on Justice Sutherland's declaration that the Scottsboro defendants had not received adequate legal representation. The case also saw the U.S. Supreme Court push strongly for fair representation of blacks on grand and petit juries. But if we desire to look only at cases that had a stunning impact on the administration of criminal justice, we would be well advised to examine not the ones that we have chosen but those of Ernesto Miranda and Clarence Gideon, and the appeals of a little black girl named Brown who sought admission to a white public school then off limits to her, and a pregnant woman given the name of Roe who wanted a legal abortion. Sensational cases apparently rarely make path-breaking law. That they may occasionally produce "bad" law is reflected in the Hiss Act, which disallowed federal pensions for persons convicted of certain crimes, but they also can impel "good" law, such as the Supreme Court decisions following the Scottsboro trials, and the Lindbergh kidnapping statute, bringing the crime under federal jurisdiction.

There are, however, subtle eddies that run from our celebrated trials, though these are not readily pinned down. To take the Simpson case as the most recent example, whites have had to face the reality of deep racial divisions in our society from which they previously were more likely to be shielded. Jury selection and sequestration, television cameras in courtrooms, defense and prosecution tactics, and proper performance of the judicial and attorney roles all came in for criticism and produced suggestions for change. Most of these changes, it needs noting, seemed more spur-of-the-moment products of annoyance rather than the result of careful thought. Such suggestions for change seem to flow more often from the freeing of those deemed guilty than from the conviction of those found responsible for the offense with which they are charged. When such changes occur they often reflect the temper of the time as much as the details of the cases. In the United States today public opinion leans heavily toward uneasiness about crime, and people seek to redress what they perceive as a procedural tilt toward those charged with criminal behavior.

The so-called crimes of the century with which we have dealt represent fascinating commentaries about human and criminal justice activity at moments of high tension and great stress. There is no single or simple way to tie together the lessons that they might convey, though we have sought to indicate ingredients that they share as well as their individual characteristics. Their drama and their mystery, the details of the crimes themselves, and the nature of the people involved are what elevated these cases into the category of crimes of the century. They are cases with the power to tell us about their times and about our history. In some ways too—most particularly in how we react to each of them—they also tell us something about ourselves.

Index

Acknowledgments

We are grateful to the many people who have provided us with information and insights, as well as practical kinds of support services, as we have sought to gather and analyze materials dealing with the five criminal cases that make up the core of this book. Our largest debt is to the array of authors before us who have described and interpreted the events. We have drawn on what they have written and have tried to reconcile and revise their ideas in terms of our own understanding of what took place. The sources we relied on are listed in the For Further Reading pages at the end of each case discussion. We want to acknowledge especially that it was in the front matter in Allen Weinstein's *Perjury* that we first came across the E. L. Doctorow quotation with which we conclude the Introduction.

At the University of California, Irvine, Judy Omiya and Teri Denman, both superb departmental administrative assistants, provided invaluable help with a wide variety of chores. Carol Wyatt, as always, efficiently and intelligently handled the word processing, assisted by Dianne Christianson and Mirella Marinelli. Also contributing mightily to our work was Julia Gelfand, an indefatigable and highly knowledgeable librarian, and Patricia Staump, Pam LaZarr, and Mimi Upton, who handled interlibrary loan requests. Thanks are also due Joseph Wells, Dennis and Lori Suzucki, Steve Reynard, Marco Turk, Don Menaguale, Brian Newberg, John Cahill, and Mary Josephine Dodge.

Thanks as well to Natasha Sankovitch for her marvelous research assistance and friendship, to Marcia Lehr, Pegeen Bassett, and others at the Northwestern University School of Law Library for their inspired assistance. Thanks also to David Van Zandt, dean of the Northwestern Law School, and to the Law School for summer research support in 1996 and 1997. The Northwestern Library was able to supply transcripts of both the Hiss and the Hauptmann trials as well as material concerning Leopold and Loeb. Fred E.

Inbau, Robert P. Burns, Kathryn Watterson, and Susan Hahn stand out among the many people who provided assistance, listened patiently, and read parts of the manuscript. Gratitude also goes to the staff at the National Archives on Varick Street for their patience, and all the librarians, researchers, and friends for their time and thoughtful comments, which were greatly appreciated.

It has been a delight to work with the group at Northeastern University Press. Bill Frohlich, the Press director, first suggested the topic, brought us together as co-authors, and has been enormously supportive of our work as it developed. Tara Mantel, like Bill, read early drafts of chapters and made many valuable suggestions. We also want to express our appreciation for the skilled copy editing by Carol Beckwith and the fine indexing by Laura Moss Gottlieb, for Ann Twombly's work as production director, and for Jill Bahcall's handling of the marketing of our book.

We want to express our deepest gratitude to all of these people and organizations for their help and to make it known that whatever deficiencies exist in this work are the result of our own shortcomings.